# IPT's HANDBOOKS AND TRAINING MANUALS

**For Pricing And Ordering Information Contact:**

**IPT PUBLISHING AND TRAINING LTD.**
BOX 9590, EDMONTON, ALBERTA CANADA T6E 5X2
www.iptbooks.com
Email: iptpub@compusmart.ab.ca

Phone (780) 962-4548, Fax (780) 962-4819
Toll Free (888) 808-6763

Accepted Ordering and P
 – Personal Cheq
 – Money Orders
 – Company Purch
 – Visa
 – Mastercard

P9-APO-570

# BOOKS PUBLISHED BY IPT

IPT's METAL TRADES
HANDBOOK

IPT's INDUSTRIAL TRADES
HANDBOOK

IPT's INDUSTRIAL FASTENERS
HANDBOOK

IPT's CRANE AND RIGGING
HANDBOOK

IPT's PIPE TRADES
HANDBOOK

IPT's ELECTRICAL
HANDBOOK

IPT's ROTATING EQUIPMENT
HANDBOOK

IPT's SAFETY FIRST
HANDBOOK

IPT's METAL TRADES
TRAINING MANUAL

IPT's INDUSTRIAL TRADES
TRAINING MANUAL

IPT's INDUSTRIAL FASTENERS
TRAINING MANUAL

IPT's CRANE AND RIGGING
TRAINING MANUAL

IPT's PIPE TRADES
TRAINING MANUAL

IPT's ELECTRICAL
TRAINING MANUAL

IPT's ROTATING EQUIPMENT
TRAINING MANUAL

IPT's SAFETY FIRST
TRAINING MANUAL

# IPT's
# SAFETY FIRST HANDBOOK

by BRUCE M. BASARABA
(B.Ed., M.A., Journeyman Millwright)

Published by
IPT PUBLISHING AND TRAINING LTD.
BOX 9590, EDMONTON, ALBERTA, CANADA T6E 5X2
www.iptbooks.com
Email: iptpub@compusmart.ab.ca

Phone (780) 962-4548, Fax (780) 962-4819
Toll Free 1-888-808-6763

Printed by
Quebecor Jasper Printing, Edmonton, Alberta, Canada

The material presented in this publication has been prepared in accordance with recognized safe working practices and codes, and is for general information only. In areas of critical importance the user should secure competent advice from an engineer or safety consultant with respect to the suitability of the material contained herein, and comply with the various codes, standards, regulations, or other pertinent legal obligation. Anyone utilizing this information assumes all responsibility and liability arising from such use.

First Printing, March 1999

ISBN #0-920855-34-2

# ACKNOWLEDGEMENTS

The author and publisher wish to thank the following for their assistance in developing this publication:

Jasper Printing, Inc.

Illustrations:    Ken Jurina  and Cindy Joly - Top Draw
                    Cassandra Strumecki - CAS Consulting Services Inc.

Layout and coordination of illustrations:  Sincere thanks to Cassandra Strumecki and Ian Holmes for their work organizing this book into its present format.

Proofreading - A special thank you is extended to the following for their many hours spent proofreading this book:

Len Luce: (Holiday, Florida) Len Luce & Associates.  Safety Specialist, OSHA (retired). Member of American Society of Safety Engineers (ASSE). Member of Construction Safety Association. Member of World Safety Organization. Member of Who's Who in Safety. Expert Witness.

Neil Thompson:  Extensive background in open pit and surface mining and heavy equipment operation and has held numerous positions in management, training and workplace safety

# TABLE OF CONTENTS

## TABLE OF CONTENTS

# SAFETY IS AN ATTITUDE

Safety is an attitude, a frame of mind.

It is the awareness of one's environment and actions, all day, every day.

Safety is knowing what is going on;

knowing what can injure anyone or damage anything; knowing how to prevent that injury or damage

and then acting to prevent it.

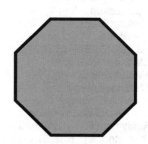

## PLEASE MAKE SAFETY **YOUR** ATTITUDE

# SECTION ONE

## FUNDAMENTALS OF SAFETY MANAGEMENT

## Introduction

Safety and occupational health management is fundamental to all business and industry where there is worker involvement. Leadership in these areas is a daily requirement and continues to be an ongoing challenge. All workers, supervisors, managers and business owners must consider worker safety and occupational health as part of the long term business plan and operating strategies. In recent years there have been many notable advances in the integration of safety and occupational health into management systems. For instance:

- Safety is equally important to the success of the business, just as is quality, production, customer relations, and cost control.
- Effective safety management, along with occupational health must be fully integrated into the total management system of the organization.

- Safety management is a fundamental responsibility of the workers, frontline supervisors, managers and the company's senior executives and business owners.
- Safety accomplishments result from the consistent application of sound management principles and practices.
- The daily responsibility for the safety and health of workers is the most important responsibility of all workers, supervisors and business owners.
- The fundamentals of safety management include the need for effective "due diligence". This means that the organization and its leadership have taken every reasonable precaution to avoid personal injury, harm or death in the workplace.

Integrating preventive safety and health measures into all aspects of the business operation must be one of the key strategies for reducing workplace injuries and illnesses.

Designing and developing formal safety and health systems into the various workplace processes is not an easy task. In order to do this effectively requires commitment from the business owners, managers, supervisors and workers. Another key element to improving safety and health performance in the workplace is to formulate a strategy for promoting an awareness campaign in these areas. Methods for establishing employee awareness vary, but no matter what methods are used, the key is to have all employees become involved with supporting and participating in safety initiatives. The organization must keep the awareness level visible and work hard to continue to encourage and reinforce all employees to be safety conscious and self-motivated when it comes to working safely.

*Note: Integrating preventive safety and health measures into every aspect of the industrial or business workplace is probably the most important strategy for reducing incidents, injuries and illnesses. The full integration of safety and health into the various management processes is not a one time activity.*

*In order to be effective, there must be a conscious effort to maintain employee awareness and to constantly plan for employee involvement. There should be periodic reviews to determine how effective the programs within the management system are, and changes must be made to accommodate any deficiencies in the program policies, standards, procedures or practices.*

Many industries now include environment in their systems for managing safety and occupational health.

Over the past several years, environmental awareness and the need for improved management efforts for protecting the environment have heightened to a point where now environmental management is integral to the business activities. This is no different than what many organizations are experiencing today with the strong emphasis on quality.

## Safety Management Process

Many traditional approaches to managing safety and health have developed a reputation for being merely a "program of the month". However, many industry and labor leaders have recognized that safety management is more than a series of programs put together to react to some mishap or accident.

Instead, they are approaching it as a process where there is a long term strategy for continuous improvement.

The focus should be "process" based, eliminating the need to install quick fix programs to try and correct a situation that has usually already occurred. An ongoing process for managing safety builds more credibility than just having a series of misaligned programs which have been quickly thrown together more as a "reaction" tactic which says to employees, "look, we are doing something about this now." An on-going process for managing safety has to be part of the whole organizational systems, which really is implying, "this is the way we do things around here." It is not just "double talk", or paying "lip service" to safety.

Establishing a process for safety management within an existing workplace requires a focused team effort.

While some safety programs produce quick results, and when the program ends or slowly loses its enthusiasm, the positive impact of the program diminishes. The real results come if an effective process for safety grows and matures.

One should begin to see behaviors and attitudes in the workplace change from the past feelings of negativism, lack of concern and non-compliance. Long term results for good management of safety come from improvements to the system which work at sustaining the right behaviors and feelings for safety. Effective safety performance is clearly linked to the employee and management attitude and morale, and to the leadership which helps to shape behaviors.

It is imperative that the organization identify the shortcomings immediately and work at making the necessary corrections before it is too late. Once negative behaviors settle into the workplace, it will be even more difficult to correct the negative situation.

Employee involvement is essential in sustaining long-term safety results. Without employee involvement there is usually minimal commitment. Employees tend to support what they create.

Allow people to help develop the process for managing safety in the workplace. The ownership felt by the employees will improve the overall success of the management system for a longer period of time, even throughout those periods of organizational change, economic challenge, and labor and management issues and differences.

## Safety Leadership

Safety leadership is best described as being "motivational" leadership. People at the top of organizations, including both management and labor, can greatly influence and motivate the people within the organization in many areas, including safety.

Leadership is commonly defined as "the person's ability to influence someone to do something." Therefore, safety leadership is explained as the ability to influence positive views and practices towards safety responsibilities.

Motivation to be responsible must begin with the leader's words and actions, and the workers must be self-motivated to do what is required of them to manage accordingly.

There are several effective ways leadership can influence people to see for themselves how safety is part of their working day.

In every workplace one usually finds "the way things are supposed to happen", and then there is "the way things really get done." If workers and leaders are serious about reducing job risks which cause accidents, illnesses and incidents, they must help to make safety management more than just another extra job to do in an already full workday. Safety must be seen and accepted as part of every employee's daily work plans and responsibilities. People within the organization must "buy in" to the concepts for working safely. It is not only important to each individual, but it is also important to the worker's family, the community and to the long-term success of the organization.

To be truly effective, the leadership must clearly demonstrate its belief that safety excellence is just as achievable and important as production, quality, costs and profits.

If the leadership demonstrates the commitment to maintaining a consistent message on the importance of safety, then there is a better chance for long-term "buy in" and acceptance from all employees.

## Safety Defined

The word safety is an adjective used to describe a condition which reflects the total absence of hazards. Or paraphrasing the Occupational Health and Safety Act , it could be stated that a safe workplace is one where the "employer furnishes employment and a place of employment which is free from recognized hazards that are causing or likely to cause death or serious physical harm to them".

Change is the order of the day in the field of safety and occupational health protection.

These positive changes in many instances have been a long time coming, but the changing attitudes and improved management systems for safety are becoming more evident each day. There is a more proactive stance being taken by workers and employers. Workers in particular have been dissatisfied with "after-the-fact", post-injury illness measures of program success (examples: number of fatalities, disabling injuries and illnesses, worker's compensation costs and various incidence rates). Now more managers and safety professionals speak of "non-injury" measures of safety and occupational health program effectiveness (examples: numbers and types of critical incidents observed, the results of behavioral interviews from workers on the job, how many workers were removed from risk as a result of specific actions taken at the work site, and other measures that reflect a safety attitude of "continuous improvement").

Perhaps, business and industry has moved from an environment where the worker was the "culprit" who was blamed for incidents to one where employee input is aggressively sought on how to prevent workplace mishaps.

## Safety Attitude

It is important that a positive attitude towards safety be established early in any workplace. It must foster and promote a working atmosphere where safety is valued by every employee. It begins with a show of commitment from senior management and labor leaders. From this top-down approach, a climate that promotes safety cascades downward to all levels of employees. Ultimately, the goal is to have a shared commitment from all employees.

Organizations having continued success with their safety performance see safety as an integral part of their business strategies.

There are several principles which serve as the foundation for safety. These include:
- A belief that all accidents, incidents, injuries and occupational illnesses can be prevented.
- A belief that safety is everyone's responsibility.
- Safety is a condition of employment.
- Training is essential for helping to improve workplace safety.
- Safe work practices will be reinforced and all unsafe acts, conditions and practices will be reported and corrective actions will be taken.
- Occupational incidents, injuries and illnesses will be investigated, causes determined, and appropriate corrective actions taken.
- Off the job safety is an important element of the overall safety effort.

- Management and workers are directly responsible and accountable for preventing injuries, incidents and illnesses.
- Prevention of incidents, injuries and illnesses makes good business sense.
- People are the most critical element in the continued success of safety excellence.

A good safety record can be measured in direct cost savings, such as in worker's compensation expenses, insurance premiums and health care costs. There are also indirect benefits associated with safety performance. These include: productivity, quality, delivery, customer confidence, employee relations, labor and management relationships, and company image.

Establishing a safety attitude and environment is seen as a long term process which requires time and patience on everyone's part.

The process includes the following key elements:
- Having a well publicized vision and mission for safety in the organization.
- Setting specific safety goals and objectives.
- Developing realistic safety policies, standards and procedures.
- Informing, educating and training employees in workplace safety.
- Inspecting, investigating and auditing safety systems for compliance and improvements.
- Following up on employee safety concerns, ideas and improvement suggestions.
- Having methods in place for implementing corrective actions and demonstrating control.
- Allocating sufficient resources for managing the safety system.

## OHS Laws and Rights (Canada)

The Canadian federal government, in cooperation with the provinces, has established comprehensive regulations for workplace safety. Occupational health and safety legislation in all jurisdictions imposes minimum standards on employers, including protection for worker rights, which are:

- The right to know.
- The right to participate.
- The right to refuse.

**The Right to Know:** The right of workers to know information about specific hazards in their workplace is a legally enforceable right for workers in Canada. It requires that the employer provide vital information and specifications on hazardous materials in the workplace. This information must be made readily available and accessible by the employer to all employees.

In 1988 the joint federal-provincial Workplace Hazardous Materials Information System (WHMIS) was established (see Section Six). The system continues to provide a nationally legislated information transfer system from suppliers to employers to employees regarding the various hazards posed by controlled products, including chemicals and dangerous materials in the workplace, and how to handle or avoid such hazards. The procedure requires caution labels, Material Safety Data Sheets (MSDS) and worker education programs for the various hazardous materials found in workplaces which are considered hazardous.

**The Right to Participate:** In Canada, the right to participate ensures the involvement of workers in management decision making with concerns to work related matters.

These include the scheduling of work, safety regulations and standards, work methods and practices, and the training of new employees.

Traditionally, workers had little influence on issues concerning safety and their work environment. Occupational health and safety legislation in most Canadian jurisdictions now provide for the establishment of Joint Occupational Health and Safety Committees (JOHSC) equally comprised of employee and employer representatives in all workplaces having more than a certain number of employees in the company's workforce. Generally, the JOHSC has the position and power to receive, consider, and dispose of employee complaints and concerns regarding health and safety at the worksite.

It may also recommend educational and training programs for worker protection, to participate in health and safety related inquires, inspections or investigations, to access government and employer reports regarding health and safety issues of the employees it represents and to request from an employer whatever information it considers necessary to identify existing or potential health and safety hazards at the place of work. In Canada's provinces, where the regulation for right to participate is reasonable, a JOHSC can be very useful, productive and provide an excellent way to further improve health and safety in the workplace.

**The Right to Refuse:** The right of a worker to refuse unsafe work for which the worker feels he or she has a risk of injury is regulated federally and in each of the provinces.

Every jurisdiction in Canada gives employees a right to refuse unsafe work under certain specified conditions.

All workers must be informed of this right when they are newly employed in any Canadian business or industry.

*Note: The right to refuse unsafe work is a necessary right that will continue to exist and will be protected by legislation, but in each jurisdiction there must be clear guidelines for ensuring reasonable application of this worker right. The right to refuse unsafe work is restricted to serious health and safety concerns. It must not be used as a bargaining tool for those issues between employees and employers which, more often than not, have little to do with "unsafe work."*

As a very minimum, the requirement should be based on objective concerns and the criteria for the objection has to be considered serious, as there may be an imminent safety or health concern.

## OSHA Laws and Rights (USA)

The Occupational Health and Safety Act in the United States encompasses the workplace conditions of almost all private sector employers.

The Act requires employers to provide their employees with safe and healthy working conditions and assigns the Occupational Health and Safety Administration (OSHA) the responsibility for developing workplace health and safety standards. The United States has developed numerous regulations aimed at improving the general safety of workplace conditions and protecting the health of workers exposed to toxic or other hazardous substances. The regulations and standards tend to be quite detailed and typically contain extensive specifications.

In the United States, employees have the right to request information from their employer on specific health and safety hazards in the workplace.

Also, workers have the right to information on what precautions must be taken and procedures to be followed if the employee is involved in an accident, incident or is exposed to a toxic material or hazardous substance. The employer has the legal obligation to inform the employee of OSHA safety and health standards which are applicable to their workplace. In addition, employers must establish a comprehensive hazard communication program which includes provisions for container labeling, material safety data sheets, and an employee training program for handling hazardous materials (see Section Seven).

Currently, the United States does not have mandatory worker participation rights similar to Canada, but OSHA strongly encourages employers and employees to work together, jointly, to help reduce workplace hazards and minimize risks.

In the United States, employees do have the right to seek personal safety and health protection on the job without fear of punishment. The law states that the employer "shall not" punish or discriminate against employees for exercising such rights as complaining to the employer, union, OSHA, or any other government agency about job safety and health hazards.

Although there is nothing in OSHA law in the United States which specifically gives a worker the right to refuse to perform unsafe or unhealthy work, the regulations have been upheld by the U.S. Supreme Court, to provide that a worker may refuse to perform work when faced with an imminent danger which could lead to serious injury or death. The conditions necessary to justify a refusal to work are very stringent.

Any worker in the United States who feels that they have been unfairly punished or reprimanded as a result of exercising their rights can contact the nearest OSHA office within 30 days of the time they learn of the alleged discrimination and unfair treatment.

Depending on whether there is sufficient evidence to support that the employee was unfairly treated or reprimanded for exercising safety and health rights in the workplace, OSHA may ask the employer to restore the worker's job, earnings, and benefits.

In the United States, each state can develop their own specific occupational health and safety programs under state plans which must be approved and monitored by OSHA. Those states which assume responsibility for their own occupational health and safety programs must have provisions which are equal to or greater than those of OSHA, and this must include the protection of employee rights.

## Why Do Accidents Occur?

What causes accidents? Some people think it's just the luck of the draw. Safety never can be taken for granted. No organization attains a good safety record through luck or chance. Behind every fine safety record that an organization achieves you will usually find much planning, promotion, and a great deal of hard work.

Mostly, accidents in workplaces occur as a result of risks in the work place with people, machinery, tools and equipment and materials. The more risks present in any one or more of these areas, the greater the likelihood of an accident. A good start to reducing the possibility of accidents occurring is to take some time and proactively control the risks.

## Why Do Employees Perform "At Risk" Behaviors?

There are many reasons why employees perform "at risk" behaviors, and typically these behaviors are the result of several common factors in the workplace that either encourage employees to work in a manner that is at risk, or prevent employees from working safely.

Some of the more common reasons as to why employees work at risk include:

- The employee is poorly prepared/trained for the job.
- The management system encourages/promotes at risk behavior.
- Employees may be rewarded or recognized for their at risk behaviors.
- The equipment and facilities are in less than adequate working condition.
- Disagreements as to what a safe work practice or method is.

- Previous work experiences where at risk behavior was the norm.
- The work environment and organizational culture condone at risk practices.
- It's simply the employee's choice to take risks.
- Strong push for production, therefore there is less emphasis on safe work practices.

## Proactive Safety

Proactive safety is defined as the "aggressive pursuit of zero accidents in the workplace". In order to achieve this goal there has to be a knowledge of safe operating procedures and principles by all workers and each worker must also have the "right attitude" towards safety. Proactive safety means that the workers take full responsibility to act safely before being told to do so, or whenever the situation demands safe behavior. Practicing proactive safety means practicing prevention and protection.

One of the best ways to prevent something from happening is always to be on the look-out for hazards and act before they become accidents. It takes both the employer and the employee to make proactive safety work. When used together, prevention and protection provide the best defense against accidents. When employers and employees both prepare themselves for zero accidents mentally, it is possible to stop having accidents.

**Prevention:** Pay attention to hazardous situations, and do something about it. Eliminate incidents and hazards. An incident is defined as a deviation from some acceptable standard. A hazard is an incident without adequate controls applied or the potential to result in damage or injury. When an incident does result in damage it is called an accident, but accidents are preventable.

Any person faced with the circumstances of an incident or a hazard, who has the opportunity to intervene but fails to act on that opportunity, has become a contributor to any damage or injury that might result. Safety responsibility belongs to both the employer and the employee. All accidents result from incidents, but not all incidents result in accidents. Anyone who can intervene to prevent an incident will be at least partially responsible if an accident occurs because of failure to act. If you see a hazard and don't do anything to correct it you are responsible for the damages or injury.

**Protection:** Use the right equipment and standard procedures that are designed to protect you from injury if an accident does happen. By using the right safety protection equipment the employee is practicing proactive safety.

**Leadership:** One of the most effective ways to foster the right attitude to total accident prevention is through influential leadership. Leadership is quite different from management. All employees in the work place, at all levels, can become proactive safety leaders. Rather than just concentrating on rules, procedures and practices as management does, leadership is the ability to motivate employees toward a certain behavior and attitude through positive influencing techniques.

One of the main qualities required of any leader is having a vision. The vision for achieving zero accidents means that the leader sees this as a realistic goal which can be reached and it also means taking the initiative for helping making the goal a reality. Positive steps must be taken to help reach this goal. Leaders also can help inspire others to reach for this goal by providing optimism, enthusiasm and support.

The leader must focus on the possibilities and how to make it work, explain what they see and want, make it clear that the goal can be reached, and work hard to excite others when progress is made so that they can share the vision.

Leaders create expectations. Expectations are what people believe will take place, either because something has happened before, or because it is possible under the existing circumstances. Leaders can create the expectation that zero accidents is possible. Because this may be a new or seemingly far-reaching goal, the leader must make the vision believable by explaining it carefully, in familiar terms. Once the group can see that this goal has been reached elsewhere, or that achieving it is possible based on their experience, they can then move forward with the expectation of success.

Expectations not only encourage people to reach for zero accidents, they can also create the behavior necessary to make that goal a reality. If people believe that a goal will or should be achieved, they will begin to change their behavior, creating and maintaining an environment that makes it possible.

Most employees have a hard time following a leader they don't trust, therefore, leaders must build the trust of those they lead. They maintain that trust by giving the employees confidence that their goal can be reached, and by reaffirming that confidence as they move toward the goal together.

As well, when a leader trusts the judgement and ability of others, each member of the group gains confidence to move forward and to envision the leader's goal as his or her own.

Being consistent is also important in maintaining trust. Leaders must make their words and their actions consistent to show that they are willing to stand by their own ideas.

Employees are much more likely to follow leaders whose actions and words match their own beliefs and words because such leaders prove that they believe what they are saying by demonstrating consistency.

Leaders must also keep the vision alive for the employees. Doubts or uncertainty caused by difficulties or setbacks can dampen enthusiasm, so the leader must reinforce the idea that the goal of zero accidents is achievable. A leader whose vision waivers will soon lose the confidence of the employees. It is important that the leader be persistent in believing the value and the achievability of the goal.

There are at least four main elements necessary for maintaining leadership:
- The leader must have a strong sense of purpose.
- The leader must demonstrate to his/her employees a positive attitude.
- The leader must use positive persuasive and influential techniques.
- The leader, in order to see success, must be persistent.

Leadership for proactive safety is determined more by confidence and experience than by knowledge of rules and practices. When workers, as those shown in illustration #1, at all levels learn to use these proactive safety leadership characteristics in their workplace safety systems, they will be rewarded with enthusiastic participation and innovation in developing effective safety procedures and protection methods.

These employees will be rewarded with success in achieving their goal of zero accidents in the workplace.

Illustration #1 - Zero Accidents

# SECTION TWO

## PERSONAL PROTECTIVE EQUIPMENT (PPE)

## Introduction

Workers often face unsafe working conditions and practices, and during every work day many are involved in serious job-related injuries, and unfortunately there are fatalities as well. Employers and employees should try to minimize the hazards as much as possible at the source. The use and wearing of personal protective equipment (PPE) is one further measure workers can take to minimize the risk of injury and illness from on-the-job hazards.

Personal protective equipment (PPE) is designed to protect the worker from health and safety hazards that cannot practically be removed from the work environment. Generally, personal protective equipment is designed to protect many parts of the body, including: head, face, eyes, ears, hands, arms, and feet.

### Personal Protective Equipment Regulations and Standards

In the United States OSHA has issued regulations governing the use of PPE in general industrial applications. These regulations for PPE are:

- General Requirements:
  29 CFR 1910.132
- Eye and Face Protection:
  29 CFR 1910.133
- Respiratory Protection:
  29 CFR 1910.134
- Occupational Head Protection:
  29 CFR 1910.135
- Occupational Foot Protection:
  29 CFR 1910.136
- Electrical Protective Devices:
  29 CFR 1910.137
- Occupational Noise Exposure:
  29 CFR 1910.95

The OSHA sources for these various PPE regulations are shown in table #1.

## SOURCES OF OSHA PERSONAL PROTECTIVE EQUIPMENT (PPE) STANDARDS

| OSHA Section | Sources |
| --- | --- |
| General Requirements: 1910.132 | 41 CFR 50-204.7. |
| Eye and Face Protection: 1910.133 | ANSI Z87.1-1968, Eye and Face Protection. |
| Respiratory Protection: 1910.134 | ANSI Z88.2-1969, Standard Practice for Respiratory Protection. ANSI K13.1-1967. Identification of Gas Mask Canisters. |
| Occupational Head Protection: 1910.135 | ANSI Z89.1-1969, Safety Requirements for Industrial Head Protection. |
| Occupational Foot Protection: 1910.136 | ANSI Z41.PT91, Men's Safety-Toe Footwear. |
| Occupational Noise Exposure: 1910.95 | ANSI S1.4-1971(1976), Specifications for Sound Level Meters. ANSI S3.6-1969, Specifications for Audiometers. |
| Electrical Protective Devices: 1910.137 | ANSI Z9.4-1968, Ventilation and Safe Practices of Abrasive Blasting Operations. |

Table #1 - Sources of Standards

The following list of PPE CSA Standards and ANSI Standards are common for industry and business in Canada:

- Industrial Protective Headwear: CSA Standard Z94.1-M1977.
- Safety Requirements for Industrial Head Protection: ANSI Z89.1-1986.
- Protective Footwear: CSA Standard Z195-M1984.
- Men's Safety-Toe Footwear: ANSI Z41.PT91.
- Industrial Eye and Face Protection: CSA Standard Z94.3-M1982.
- Eye and Face Protection: ANSI Z87.1-1968.
- Selection, Care and Use of Respirators: CSA Standard Z94.4-M1982.
- Compressed Breathing Air and Systems: CSA Standard CAN3-Z180.1-M85.
- Standard Practice for Respiratory Protection: ANSI Z88.2-1969.
- Identification of Gas Mask Canisters: ANSI K13.1-1967.
- Listing of Respiratory Protective Devices: NIOSH Certified Equipment List, 1994

- Procedures for the Measurement of Occupational Noise Exposure: CSA Standard CAN/CSA-Z107.56-M86.
- Hearing Protectors: CSA Standard Z94.2-M1984.
- Specifications for Sound Level Meters: ANSI SI.4-1971 (R1976).
- Specifications for Audiometers: ANSI S3.6-1969.
- Canadian Electrical Code, Part 1: CSA Standard C22.1-1990.
- Electrical Overhead Systems and Underground Systems: CSA Standard C22.3 No.1-M1979.

## Hazard Assessment

It is the employer's responsibility to establish, administer and support an effective Personal Protective Equipment Program in the workplace. The following sections will identify specific types and uses of PPE.

Before an employer can begin to develop an effective system for PPE it is recommended that they conduct a "Hazard Assessment" to determine what hazards are present, or likely to be present, which necessitates the use of particular personal protective equipment. Nobody suggests that an employer should only rely on PPE to protect against workplace hazards, but rather to use PPE along with adequate engineering controls, sound manufacturing practices, reliable maintenance systems, and effective communication and safety awareness campaigns.

Employers must survey the workplace periodically to ensure that it is free of unnecessary hazardous conditions. From these periodic surveys, the employer will note situations where PPE is used and can determine if there should be additional measures taken. Common workplace hazards that the employer should include in the survey are:

*Sources of Movement:* Machinery or processes where any moving parts or rotating equipment exists; workers must be protected from these various sources of movement.

*Heat Sources:* Situations where high or low temperatures exist. Any brief or lengthy contact or exposure may be harmful to workers.

*Chemical Exposure:* Situations where harmful exposure to chemicals will result in serious injury or illness. Exposure to chemicals may be from handling, storage, shipping, spills, leaks, or process during production.

*Harmful Dust and Particles:* This is a work environment with exposure to harmful dust and particles produced from manufacturing processes, cutting and grinding operations, spraying systems, and any other operation or process which produce fines, dust or airborne particles.

***Sources of Light Radiation:*** Emissions of harmful light may come from sources such as welding, brazing, oxy-acetylene cutting, heat treating, furnaces, arcing, and high intensity lights.

***Falling Objects***: There are many sources in a workplace where falling objects or potential for falling and dropping objects exist. Particular attention must be given in areas such as: warehouse shelving, stacked pallets, overhead cranes and hoists, shipping and receiving, work benches and work stations, and overhead conveyor and material moving systems.

***Rotating Equipment:*** Sources where there are rotating parts, rolling elements, twisting and turning motions, spinning processes and oscillating parts will have the potential for serious injury to the workers.

***Sharp Objects***: Sources of sharp objects on machinery and equipment where hands and feet in particular can be seriously pinched, pierced, torn or ripped.

***Electrical Hazards***: There are many common electric hazards where workers can be seriously injured. Electrical hazards common to the workplace include: overloads, shocks, shorts, and arcing. Any of these can cause severe burns from explosions or electrocutions.

***Co-worker Conduct:*** Fellow workers, through acts of misappropriate conduct, such as horse play, fighting, and workplace violence can lead to serious injuries and illnesses.

Upon performing a hazard assessment, where the employer surveys the hazardous areas just identified, the employer then is responsible for selecting and supplying the most appropriate personal protective equipment.

All workers should be trained in PPE, in particular, training must be provided in the following areas:

- Requirements for which types of PPE to be worn.
- Requirements for when PPE is to be worn.
- Recognized practices for wearing PPE.
- Methods for proper sizing and adjusting PPE.
- Specific limitations of PPE.
- Requirements for maintaining, storing and disposing of PPE.

*Note: It is always recommended that the employer have complete verification that each employee has received PPE training. Periodic refresher training in PPE is helpful as this keeps the level of awareness up and can identify any changes to either hazardous conditions or to the PPE applications.*

## Types and Uses of Personal Protective Equipment

Six types of personal protective equipment will be discussed in this section of the handbook:

A. Occupational Protective Headwear.
B. Occupational Foot Protection.
C. Occupational Eye and Face Protection.
D. Occupational Respiratory Protection.
E. Occupational Hand Protection.
F. Occupational Hearing Protection.

## Protective Headwear

Where there is a hazard, or potential hazard for a head injury in the work place, protective headwear that meets the standards set out by CSA Standard Z94.1-M1977 or OSHA - 29 CFR 1910.135 must be provided. Specifications for headwear must meet ANSI Z89.1-1986, Industrial Head Protection Requirements.

Head protection is required if the worker is exposed to risks from injuries sustained from impact and penetration from falling and flying objects and from limited electric shock and burns. In most industrial type workplaces it is mandatory that all workers wear approved head protection. This requirement became law because of the many unnecessary head injuries recorded over the years.

Head protection is generally required and must be worn by all workers and contractors in most areas of the workplace, with the exception of the following in most cases:

- Lunchrooms
- Washrooms
- Offices, meeting and training rooms
- Workplace vehicles and equipment if equipped with seat belts and/or roll over protection

Head protection used in the workplace is commonly referred to as "hard hats." Hard hats are designed to protect from impact and penetration caused from falling objects hitting a person's head and bumps sustained from side blows. There are many types of designs for hard hats, but each design must have special features which include:

- The shell of the hat is designed to absorb some of the impact.
- The suspension of the hat, which consists of the headband and strapping, is critical as it must be comfortable and able to absorb and control impact from above the head blows as well as from sideblows to the head.
- There must be suitable adjustment to fit the wearer and to keep the shell at a minimum distance from the top and side of the wearer's head.

- Hard hats are tested to withstand the impact of an eight pound (3.6 kg) weight dropped five feet (1.5 metres).
- All hard hats must meet other requirements including weight, flammability, and electrical insulation.

Illustration #2 identifies the various parts and features of a typical hard hat worn by industrial workers. It is important to select the correct hard hat for the job.

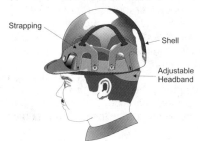

Strapping

Shell

Adjustable Headband

**Illustration #2 - Hard Hat Features**

Illustrations #3A, B and C identify three classes of hard hats. These three classes are:

*Class A Hard Hats:* This hard hat is made from insulating (non-conductive) material which protects the wearer from falling objects and electrical hazards up to 2,200 volts. Many industries would consider this class of hard hat as too lightweight and therefore not suitable for most work environments.

*Class B Hard Hats:* This hard hat is made from insulating (non-conductive) material and protects the wearer from falling objects and electrical hazards up to 20,000 volts. Class B hard hats are very common throughout many typical industrial workplaces. They offer suitable protection and are well accepted by the workforce.

*Class C Hard Hats:* This hard hat is designed to protect the wearer from falling objects only.

This Class C hard hat is unsuitable for use in and around electrical hazards or in environments where corrosive materials are present.

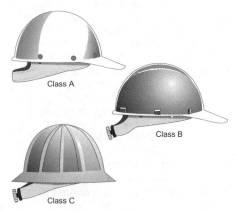

Class A

Class B

Class C

**Illustration #3A, B, C - Hard Hat Classes**

## Foot Protection

Where there is any hazard of foot injury, or electric shock through the foot in the workplace, approved protective footwear must be worn. Also, wherever there is a hazard or potential hazard of slippage in a work area, nonslip footwear is required to be worn. The standards for occupational footwear include CSA Standard Z195-M1984 and OSHA - 29 CFR 1910.136. Specifications for occupational footwear must meet ANSI Z41. PT91, Men's Safety - Toe Footwear. Protective footwear is designed to guard the worker's feet from impact, compression, hot and cold temperatures and dangerous liquids and chemicals. Like other personal protective equipment, the type of protective footwear the worker needs depends upon the job they are performing or on the working conditions.

### Foot Injuries

Typical foot injuries are most likely to occur:

- When heavy or sharp objects fall on the foot. See illustration #4.

Illustration #4 - Heavy/Sharp Objects

- When some heavy or sharp object rolls over on the foot. See illustration #5.

Illustration #5 - Rolls On Foot

- When some sharp or pointed object pierces through the sole or side of the worker's footwear. See illustration #6.

Illustration #6 - Step on Sharp Object

- When there is a chance of slipping and falling due to slippery surfaces. See illustration #7.

**Illustration #8 - Getting Caught**

**Illustration #7 - Slippery Surfaces**

- When there is a chance that the worker's feet can get caught in machinery. See illustration #8.

- When there is a chance that the feet can be in contact with electrical hazards. See illustration #9.

**Illustration #9 - Electrical Hazards**

- When high or low temperature extremes exist and/or dangerous liquids or chemicals contact the foot. See illustration #10.

**Illustration #10 - Spills**

*Falling Objects:* Injury statistics in North America indicate that six of every ten foot injuries in the workplace are caused by a heavy object falling on the foot. What should be of interest is that in most of these foot injuries, the object that causes the injury falls from heights of four feet or less (1.2 m). Even though this is not a great distance, the potential for serious pain and injury is high.

Nor does the falling object have to weigh very much to cause injury.

In most foot injuries caused by falling objects, the cause for the fall usually involves those objects which were improperly stacked or stored on shelving or work benches, or objects placed too close to the edge of a table or shelf.

If workers are exposed to risks of falling packages, objects, parts or heavy tools, they must wear sturdy, protective footwear that has a steel-reinforced toe area. See illustration #11.

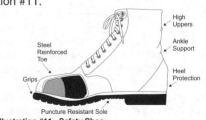

**Illustration #11 - Safety Shoe**

This type of safety shoe is made with a steel-reinforced boxed-in toe to protect the foot from being crushed or pierced. Most types of safety footwear have puncture resistant soles and are designed with grips for walking on wet and slippery surfaces. This type of safety footwear also provides good ankle and heel protection, as well as a high upper section for further foot and ankle protection.

*Puncture Injuries:* Accidentally stepping on sharp or pointed objects is another common cause of foot injury in the workplace. It is always important to be careful where stepping and to try and keep the work area free of hazards. It is very easy to have regular shoes punctured by nails or screws. Safety footwear, with puncture resistant soles will provide the necessary protection from this type of foot injury.

*Slips and Falls*: Another common way workers injure their feet is by slipping, sliding and falling on slick or wet surfaces in the workplace. It is very easy to break, bruise, sprain or severely twist a foot or ankle in a hard fall because the walking surface was slippery. One of the best ways to prevent this type of injury from happening is to ensure that any spills or leaks on the floor are immediately cleaned up and to have safety boots with slip-resistant soles for good grip.

*Dangerous Liquids and Chemicals:* Those workers exposed to dangerous liquids and chemicals may easily suffer a foot injury because of spills and leaks. It is important to wear approved footwear which is capable of protecting feet from these types of materials. Rubber or synthetic safety footwear may be needed when working around certain liquids and chemicals. Avoid wearing leather safety boots when working with caustic chemicals because these substances can quickly eat through the leather to the feet and be harmful to exposed skin.

Illustration #12 identifies a type of high top rubber boot which is approved foot protection for wearing when working around dangerous liquids and chemicals.

Foot guards, several of which are shown in illustration #13A, B and C are available for almost every part of the foot, including the toe, instep, ankle, shin and metatarsal areas of the foot.

**Illustration #12 - High Top Rubber Boot**

### Safety Footwear Features

There are various types of attachments which can be easily added to either safety boots or regular shoes to offer further foot protection.

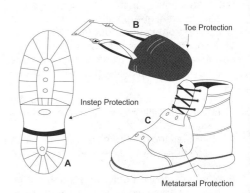

**Illustration #13A, B, C - Various Foot Guards**

Safety boots made out of rubber or plastic can provide protection against water, chemicals, flammable liquids, oils, and grease. Slip-resistant soles are available to prevent falls on wet or slippery surfaces.

Steel-toe caps, puncture resistant insoles and metatarsal guards offer a wide range of protection from various foot hazards.

There are three types of safety boot footwear designed to protect workers from various electrical and explosive hazards. These include:

- Conductive footwear which prevents the buildup of static electricity in the worker's body.
- Non-sparking boots which prevent sparks in any area where explosive mixtures are located.
- Non-conductive boots are required to be worn by those workers who are exposed to any type of electrical hazard on the job.

### Preventing Workplace Foot Injuries

The vast majority of on-the-job foot injuries are easily avoidable. They are not caused so much by unsafe conditions as they are by unsafe acts. Workers can reduce foot injuries from occurring by following three basic rules:

*Rule #1:* Always think ahead. This is the first rule in preventing foot injuries, because what you really are doing is attempting to anticipate dangerous conditions. If you are thinking ahead, you will:

a. Avoid complacency, because when you become complacent your guard is down and the unexpected is going to occur, and this is usually when serious injuries happen.

b. Learn to anticipate danger, give some thought as to where your feet are going to be, and make sure that your foot stance and placement is level and steady. There should be nothing which makes you trip, slip or slide, causing a stumble and fall.

c. Take the time to do things correctly, as everyone knows, there is a right way and a wrong way to do every job. Make sure you follow the right way and avoid unnecessary risks which could cause severe foot injuries.

d. Never be in such a hurry to get jobs finished that personal safety is forgotten. Often when one is in a hurry to do something, that is the time when an unexpected incident occurs which can lead to serious injury to not only the feet, but to other parts of the body.

**Rule #2**: Always make sure that the work area is neat and orderly. Periodically take a good look at the work area and look for ways to minimize and eliminate any potential foot hazard. For example:

a. Look for ways the work area can be rearranged or cleaned up to reduce the risk for foot injuries.

b. Clean up any spills or leaks from oils, greases, water, ice or other substances.

c. Look for loose objects on shelves or bench edges and either reposition them or do something to block them in order to prevent them from falling.

d. Look for sharp or pointed objects on walking surfaces and either remove or cover the hazard so others will not sustain a foot injury.

e. Look for loose wires and other tripping hazards which can cause stumbles or falls.

f. Restack barrels, boxes and cartons which are placed in precarious positions with potential for falling.

g. Return tools and equipment which have been left laying around instead of being put away in their proper storage areas.

h. Check for obvious electrical hazards which can lead to serious foot injuries.

**Rule #3:** Cover your feet with protective footwear: Wearing an approved safety boot or shoe is the best way to avoid unnecessary foot injuries.

With so many types of safety footwear available to workers, there is no excuse for not having adequate foot protection. Whatever the need is, or what your preference for approved safety protection footwear may be, such as: dress shoes, casual shoes, lady's footwear, cowboy boots, heavy work boots, or even safety sneakers and running shoes, there is a good chance that these are available.

### Personal Foot Care

*Tip #1:* Wear socks that are 100% cotton, as cotton is one of the best materials for absorbing sweat. Cotton will keep feet cooler and help prevent skin rashes or other skin problems. It is always a good idea to change socks frequently, depending upon how much one's feet perspire. Clean and dry socks will help prevent harmful foot infections and reduce the chances for skin diseases in the foot area.

*Tip #2:* Many working conditions are damp and wet and there is a good chance that footwear will become wet.

Always attempt to completely dry out footwear before wearing them again the next day. Some people will have two sets of footwear, allowing the wet pair to have a complete day to dry, while the other pair is worn. Damp and wet safety boots may become stretched or distorted and this can quickly cause foot injuries, such as blistering and swelling. There are many good over-the-counter foot powders and sprays for preventing rashes and infections.

*Note: Take care of your feet. Don't take your feet for granted and if you see particular areas of danger and foot hazards in the workplace, don't hesitate to take action, whether you can take care of the situation yourself or if it requires the attention of a supervisor.*

## Eye & Face Protection

Where there is a potential for injury to the eyes, face, ears or front of the neck of an employee in the workplace, the worker must be provided with and wear approved eye or face protection. The standards for occupational eye and face protection include CSA Z94.3-M1982, Industrial Eye and Face Protectors and OSHA 29 CFR 1910.133. Specifications for occupational eye and face protection must meet ANSI Z87.1-1968, Eye and Face Protection.

### Common Workplace Eye and Face Hazards

Workers must always wear approved eye and face protection in those environments where the risk for injury is high. Eye injuries continue to be very common in the workplace. Eye injury can result in permanent disfigurement or loss of sight. Severe eye and face injuries can be caused by:

***Airborne Particles:*** Flying or airborne dust and particles, such as metal fragments from drilling and grinding, sawdust, airborne fibers, wood chips, fibrous particles, sand and dirt. Any of these can easily cause irritation, penetrate and/or cut the eye. See illustration #14.

Illustration #14 - Flying Airborne Particles

***Dangerous Substances***: Dangerous substances include: chemicals and dangerous liquid fumes and vapors, smoke from fires, and caustic chemical liquids and solids. Any of these can easily enter the eye and cause irritation, burning, scarring or loss of vision. As well, many of these dangerous substances will be a hazard to exposed facial skin. See illustration #15.

***Contact:*** Contact with objects, such as pieces of metal, piping, equipment components and parts, tree branches, and hanging objects, Any of these can easily cause severe internal and external damage to the eye, as well as damage to the facial region.

***Sharp Objects:*** Pointed or sharp tools and equipment, such as screw drivers, awls, nail guns, prybars, punches, and welding rods can easily penetrate, poke, scratch or puncture the eye and facial region. Caution must always be taken when around pointed or sharp tools and equipment. See illustration #16.

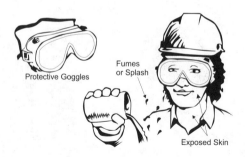

Protective Goggles

Fumes or Splash

Exposed Skin

**Illustration #15 - Dangerous Substances**

Sharp Object at Eye Height

**Illustration #16 - Sharp Objects - Eye Contact**

***Intense Light:*** Radiant and intense light, glare, electric arcing, as well as thermal energy sources, such as sun light, bright artificial lighting, welding flashes, metal cutting, furnace tending, and laser light can easily cause irreparable damage to the eyes. Extreme caution and mandatory eye protection must be worn at all times if there is risk for eye injury from these common workplace sources.

***Caution: When working with high-powered lasers, the eyes are exposed to non-iodizing radiation that can severely burn the retina and cornea. Certain classes of lasers are so intense that even looking at a reflection of the laser's intense light beam can cause an eye injury. See illustration #17.***

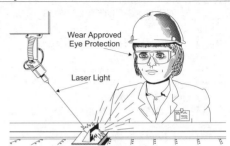

Illustration #17 - Intense Light

***Welding Hazards:*** During the arc welding process workers must protect their eyes and face from visible light rays, ultraviolet light rays, infrared rays, flying pieces of metal particles, hot sparks and slag. Approved lenses must be worn to prevent eye or facial injuries and burns. Table #2 should be used to select the recommended welding filter lenses for various types of welding processes.

| WELDING FILTER LENSES ||
| Lens # | Uses |
| --- | --- |
| Shade 4 | Light oxy-acetylene welding and cutting |
| Shade 5 | Optional to above |
| Shade 6 | General oxy-acetylene welding |
| Shade 8 | Sheet metal arc welding |
| Shade 9 | Light arc welding |
| Shade 10 | Medium arc welding |
| Shade 11 | Heavy arc welding |
| Shade 12 | Used with heavy electrodes |

Table #2 - Welder Filter Lenses

Illustration #18 identifies one of the more common welding lens and shield designs available to welders. To protect the welding filter lens from sparks, the filter lens should have two clear glass cover lenses, one positioned in front and one behind. These two glass cover lenses are in addition to the one replaceable plastic lens in the fixed position in the shield.

Arc flash is the term used to describe an injury to the eyes caused by ultraviolet rays. These rays burn the eyeballs and they become covered with tiny water blisters. This condition is often described as "having sand" in the eyes, as it feels gritty and very sensitive. The eyelids flutter uncontrollably and tears are usually profuse. It is very important that the welder wear the appropriate filter lens to ensure protection from ultraviolet rays and the affects of arc flash.

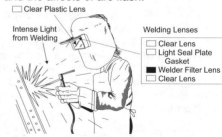

Illustration #18 - Intense Light From Welding

**First Aid For Eye Injuries**

If an eye injury occurs, quick action may reduce the extent of the injury and may ultimately save your sight. The following list offers several basic first aid steps to be taken at home or work:

- Don't rub the eye if it is irritated or injured. Pull your eyelid out and down over your lower lid and let your natural tears wash out the irritable particles. Do this only once. If it does not work, seek immediate medical help.

- If particles are in the eye, flush the eye with water until the particles are rinsed out. If they don't rinse free, bandage the eye loosely and get immediate medical care.

- Don't try to remove embedded objects or particles from the eye. Close the eye and loosely bandage the injured eye to keep it still. Then get immediate medical help.

- For chemical splashes, remove contacts if wearing them, and immediately flush the eyes and face with water for at least fifteen minutes. Then get immediate medical help. Always try to look directly into the stream of water, using your fingers to hold the eyes open. If only one eye is involved, ensure that the water runs well away from the uninjured eye. Don't contaminate it. Never use an eye cup to flush the eye, or attempt to bandage it. This can cause the chemical to become trapped in your eye.

- For flash or radiation burns, you may not feel any real discomfort or pain for several hours. If your eyes feel "gritty" or are sensitive to light, swollen and red, keep them closed and seek immediate medical help.

- Cuts and punctures to the eye must be treated with extreme care and caution so as to not further injure the eye.

- Lightly bandage the cuts and punctures in and around the eye. Never flush the eye with water or attempt to remove the object if it remains stuck in the eye. Seek immediate medical help.
- If a worker receives a blow to the eye apply a cold compress to the eye for at least fifteen minutes. Reapply the cold compress hourly to reduce swelling and to relieve discomfort and pain. Seek medical attention immediately if the eye becomes black or discolored.

*Note: Anyone who has suffered an eye injury should follow up with regular eye examinations. Simple eye injuries have the potential for future serious eye problems, such as glaucoma and cataracts.*

### Emergency Eyewash Facilities

It is important to have emergency eyewash facilities strategically located in the workplace. All employees should be familiar with the location and operation of these facilities.

There are several types, including eyewash fountains, combination eye and face wash fountains, drench showers, hand-held drench showers, portable eyewash stations and eyewash bottles. No matter the design, each is designed to supply large amounts of flushing water to wash and rinse away eye contaminants. Illustration #19 identifies a combination eyewash and drench shower unit which is commonly installed in many industrial workplace settings. It is easily activated by either hand or foot control.

The location of eyewash facilities is important because eyes can become increasingly more damaged if flushing and cleaning is not immediate. Probably the first fifteen to twenty five seconds of the injury is the most critical time period. ANSI Z358,1-1990 recommends that eyewash facilities be located within 100 feet (30 m), or a ten second walk of the immediate work area.

Eyewashes should not be installed where workers would have to pass through doorways, go up or down stairs, or to zig-zag between equipment and machinery to get help.

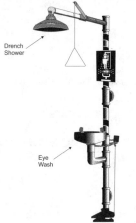

Drench Shower

Eye Wash

**Illustration #19 - Combination Eyewash and Drench Shower**

*Note: It is a good idea to practice using the eyewash and to become comfortable with how it works. It is a natural human reaction to squeeze the eyes closed tightly when something such as a stream of water is hitting them.*
*This reaction might prevent you from thoroughly rinsing and flushing out your eyes quickly in case of an emergency.*

### Types of Protective Eyewear

In North America hundreds of eye injuries occur every year in the workplace. Generally, 90% of these injuries could have been prevented or have reduced severity if proper eye and face protection was worn. All industrial types of eye protection must meet the standards and requirements of CSA, OSHA and ANSI. The following types of occupational eye and face protectors will be discussed:

a. Safety Glasses
b. Impact and Splash Goggles
c. Face Shields

## Safety Glasses

Safety glasses are the most basic type of eye protection. Illustration #20 represents two of the most common types of safety glasses. Special features of safety glasses include:

- Full protection to the eyes must be provided in the front and the sides of the glasses. Side shields, as shown in illustration #20 can offer good side protection.
- Side shields which are designed to be attachable/detachable are acceptable.
- Safety glasses should be worn under face shields and welding helmets for added protection.
- The glasses should be lightweight and durable, capable of providing reliable impact resistance.
- Some safety glasses are specially supplied with "anti-fog" and "anti-scratch" protective coatings.

- Safety glasses should fit well, and provide some adjustment features to make for a comfortable fit.

Side Shield

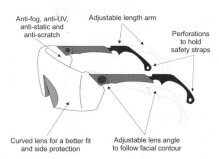

Anti-fog, anti-UV, anti-static and anti-scratch

Adjustable length arm

Perforations to hold safety straps

Curved lens for a better fit and side protection

Adjustable lens angle to follow facial contour

**Illustration #20 - Types of Safety Glasses**

- Safety glasses may be tinted or shaded to protect from glare, sunlight and other intense light sources. Use caution though, as some tinted glasses could limit vision when moving from a brightly lit to a dim area.
- Make sure that proper filtering lens are selected for offering maximum protection when working in and around any welding operation or other radiant energy sources.
- Safety glass lenses can be made of glass, which can be quite heavy when worn for long periods of time, and plastic, which is usually quite lightweight and durable.
- If prescription glasses are worn, specially approved and ground lens materials which serve as approved safety glass lenses can be obtained.
- If contact lenses are worn, always remember to put safety glasses on to protect your eyes and to keep dust and particles out of your contacts, as this can be painful and cause abrasions. Some chemicals can react with certain contact lens materials and can also cause injuries. Remember, contact lenses are not considered eye protective devices. If eye hazards are present, you must wear approved eye protection in addition to or instead of contact lenses.
- Use a headstrap if safety glasses are difficult to keep on.
- Remember to protect your eyes by wearing safety glasses when working on home jobs and activities.
- Inspect safety glasses each time before wearing them. Look for scratches, pits and broken, bent or cracked parts.
- Keep safety glasses clean, store them in a clean dry, protected place, and replace the glasses if they are damaged or fail to fit properly anymore. Damaged eyewear prevents clear vision.

## Impact and Splash Goggles

Impact and splash goggles are similar to safety glasses but fit closer to the face and eyes. Good fitting goggles offer protection for hazards involving liquid splashes, fumes, smoke, vapors, dust, splatter, flying particles and larger pieces. Goggles are designed to fit the face snugly and are very effective in sealing the entire eye area. Some models of goggles can be worn over safety glasses or prescription glasses. All goggles come with a flexible type of headstrap.

Illustration #21A identifies a typical design of goggle which offers good protection to the workers eyes from hazards such as flying particles and liquid splashes. This type of goggle may be purchased with specially coated lens and with ventilation holes to prevent fogging.

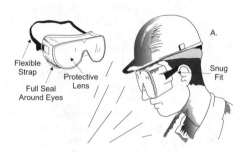

**Illustration #21A - Protective Goggles**

B.
Cup Design

Filter Lens

C.

Soft Sides

Flip-up
Filter Lens

**Illustration #21B, C - Cutting and Welding Goggles**

Illustration #21B identifies a cup type of goggle which is suitable for most types of oxy-acetylene cutting and welding work and illustration #21C identifies a type of goggle used by welders. It has soft sides, probably more comfortable than the cup style of goggle, and has a flip up filter lens for welding, and a clear "chippers" lens for protection against chips, slag and dust.

## Face Shields

Full face shields, as shown in illustrations #22A and B, offer complete eye and face protection from hazards such as flying particles and objects, liquid splashes and splatters. There are many varieties of face shields. Some will fit over a hard hat while other designs are worn directly on the head. A face shield must always be used with other eye protection, such as safety glasses or goggles.

The visor part of the face shield, as in the type shown in illustration #22B, offers excellent protection to not only the face, but to the chin and neck areas. Usually, the visor can be replaced if it becomes scratched or cracked. The face shield must fit comfortably and not leave too large a space between the face and the inside region of the visor. Just as in safety glasses and goggles, visors can be shaded or tinted and offer anti-glare protection as well.

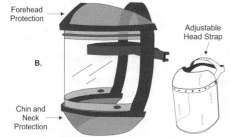

**A.**

Attaches to Hard Hat

Safety Glasses Worn in Addition to the Face Shield

Forehead Protection

Adjustable Head Strap

**B.**

Chin and Neck Protection

Illustration #22A, B - Full Face Shield

### Safety Eyewear Tips

- Even if only passing through a work area, or visiting or observing, if eye hazards are present, you must wear approved eye protection, as you could accidentally be hit with some airborne object or flying particles and debris.

- When removing your safety glasses or goggles after working around dust or fine debris, tilt your head forward and remove the eye protection from the back of the head, as this prevents any loose materials from falling into your eyes.

To prevent moisture build up on the eye protection, use types which are vented. Also there are several good anti-fogging products available which may help to minimize this problem. Fogging is often the reason or excuse workers use for not wearing their eye protection.

Something has to be done to reduce the problem, even if it means periodically wiping the lens area off with a cloth.

- Eye specialists and safety equipment suppliers should be consulted when workers seem to be having difficulty with their eye protection or are having problems adjusting to a certain type of eye protection.
- To prevent safety glasses from slipping off, attach either an adjustable headband or a stretch type elastic handband to them.
- To keep plastic lenses scratch free, clean them under running water and air dry.

*Note: Protecting your eyes from workplace hazards is probably one of the easiest things you can do for yourself and your family while performing daily work tasks. This simple practice can easily prevent a serious eye injury. Always follow the company policy and standards for wearing eye protection. Take the time to identify the potential eye hazards in the work area. Prevent accidents from happening to you and others by using tools, equipment and machinery safely. Remember, it takes only a single act of carelessness to damage your eyes forever. That is far too much of a risk to take with something as precious as your eyesight.*

## Respiratory Protection
### Respiratory Protection Devices

Where there is a risk of hazardous airborne substances or oxygen deficient atmosphere in the workplace, approved respiratory protective devices must be worn. Standard respiratory protective devices are listed in the NIOSH Certified Equipment List, published by the National Institute for Occupational Health and Safety. Respiratory protective devices referred to by the NIOSH Listing shall be selected, fitted, cared for, used and maintained in accordance with the standards set out in CSA Standard Z94.4-M1982. Where air is provided for the purpose of a respiratory protective device, the air shall meet the standards set out in clauses 5.5.2 to 5.5.11 of CSA Standard CAN3-Z180.1-M85, Compressed Breathing Air Systems. The OSHA standard for respiratory protection is 29 CFR 1910.134.

Specifications under ANSI include ANSI Z88.2-1969, Standard Practice for Respiratory Protection, and ANSI K13.1-1967, Identification of Gas Mask Canisters.

### Respiratory Protection Program

Respirators are probably among the most important types of personal protective equipment available to workers who are exposed to hazardous conditions and atmospheres. Hazardous atmospheres fall into two basic categories:

***Oxygen Deficiency:*** Air is normally 21% oxygen. When the atmosphere contains less than 19.5% oxygen by volume at sea level, it is considered "oxygen deficient." The likelihood for oxygen deficiency is high for confined spaces such as tanks, process towers, silos, sewer mains, cylinders, ship holds, truck tankers, boilers and heat exchangers. In any oxygen deficient area, an atmospheric air supply respirator must be used.

***Airborne Contamination***: Inhalation is the fastest way for airborne contaminants to enter the worker's bloodstream. It is very important that workers protect their respiratory system if they are exposed to airborne contaminants.

There are three groups of airborne contaminants:

a. Particles: Small, invisible particles do the most damage as they can easily cause tissue damage to the lungs and other parts of the body. Some particles are larger, therefore more visible, like dust, dirt, chips, grindings, fumes, smoke, mists and sprays.

b. Gases: There are many effects of gases, and none are good for the respiratory system. Many gases can be quite acidic or alkaline in nature, and can damage the breathing system and other body parts. Toxic gases are extremely hazardous and dangerous, as they can cause irreparable damage to the lungs or other vital organs.

c. Combination of Particles and Gases: In working atmospheres there can be many situations where both dangerous airborne particles and hazardous gases pose extremely dangerous conditions for the workers. Approved respiratory protection devices must be worn.

***Note: Any breathing and respiratory hazards at your worksite should be checked immediately by knowledgeable professionals using reliable air sampling equipment. Workers must first know what type of hazard is present in order to select the proper respirator.***

Under existing regulations, employers must establish and administer an effective respiratory protection program. Such employer initiated and lead programs should include:

- Written standard operating and process standards and procedures.
- Method for assessment of workplace hazards.

- Selection of respiratory protection devices to suit the various hazards present.
- Only approved and certified respiratory protection equipment supplied and used.
- Complete training and instructions for proper respirator use.
- Complete awareness and knowledge of respirator equipment limitations, maintenance and proper fitting tests of user.
- Regular schedule for cleaning, inspecting and disinfecting respiratory devices.
- System and place for properly storing in convenient, clean location(s).
- Schedule for performing routine maintenance.
- Periodic inspections and surveys of work area conditions and employee exposure.
- Regular evaluation to ensure the program is practical and effective.
- Regular scheduled medical checks for respiratory condition of workers.

The decision whether workers wear respiratory protection devices is typically based on three clear factors:

1. Exposure limits allowed for particular contaminants.

2. Accurate scientific measurement to determine the hazard level in the work area.

3. Amount of oxygen measured in the work area.

## How Do Lungs Work?

Without oxygen, a person will die within a few minutes. Lungs are designed to take in oxygen from the air that is breathed in. The lungs work best when they are free of contaminants and gases, as blockages will prevent them from functioning properly. When you breathe, your lungs pull air in through the nose and mouth, down through the trachea and into the bronchi, as shown in illustration #23.

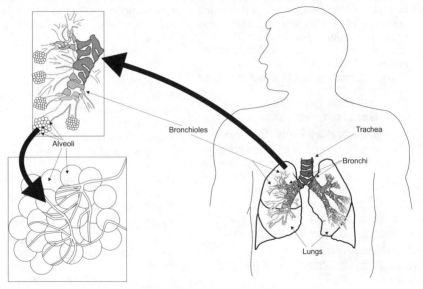

**Illustration #23 - How The Lungs Work**

- In the lungs, the bronchi divide into many smaller and smaller airways, commonly called bronchioles and alveoli.
- In the alveoli, oxygen molecules pass into the bloodstream.
- Carbon dioxide is exhaled out the nose and mouth.
- The red blood cells carry the oxygen molecules to the other cells of the body.

## Types of Respiratory Protection Devices

There are three groups of approved respiratory protection devices commonly used for various atmosphere conditions in the workplace. These are:

1. Air-purifying Respirators
2. Air-line or Supplied-air Respirators
3. Self-contained Breathing Apparatus

### Air-purifying Respirators

There are three categories of air-purifying respirators.

Each category refers to the respiratory protection offered. The three categories include:

a. Particulate Removal
b. Vapor and Gas Removal
c. Combination of the Two

*Note: Air-purifying respirators are approved for use only when:*

*a. The atmosphere contains sufficient oxygen to sustain life.*

*b. Contaminant concentration levels are known.*

*c. Contaminant levels do not exceed the limitations of the air-purifying respirator facepiece or cartridge.*

### Types of Air-purifying Respirators

Air-purifying respirators attempt to cleanse or filter the air before it is breathed into the lungs.

There are three types of air-purifying respirators and none of these should be used in operations or processes where there is a chance that the air will be oxygen-deficient, such as in firefighting and confined space entry work.

***Dust/Mist Masks:*** These masks are made of paper or soft non-woven fibers which simply fit over the mouth and nose, as shown in illustration #24, and generally offer respiratory protection against nuisance dusts and fine mists only.

Illustration #25 identifies a type of dust/mist mask which uses an exhalation valve for improved worker comfort. These respirators are quite popular with the welding trade, especially when welding on aluminum, galvanized or stainless steel. This design provides some "fume fever" relief.

Illustration #25 - Dust/Mist Mask With Exhalation Valve

Illustration #24 - Dust/Mist Mask

***Cartridge Type Respirators:*** Cartridge type respirators are commonly used in conditions where low concentrations of organic gases, pesticides and paint vapors exist. Illustration #26 shows a typical "half-mask".

Illustration #27 shows "full facepiece" cartridge respirator. Either of these designs can come with one or two cartridges. The cartridge selected must contain the suitable chemical for the specific contaminant the workers will be exposed to. These respirators should only be used for contaminants which give off a warning odor or irritation if the cartridge fails to work. Do not use cartridge type respirators against gases that are highly toxic.

**Illustration #26 - Cartridge Type Respirator**

Eye and Face Protector

**Illustration #27 - Full Facepiece Respirator**

*Powered Air-purifying Respirators:* Illustration #28 identifies a battery powered air-purifying respirator which has a small motor driving a fan which draws the contaminated air through filters and supplies filtered air to the worker. The intent is to have the powered motor and fan assembly make breathing more comfortable and improve the fit of the mask for the worker. This design is ideally suited for welding in areas where the welder may require the extra protection of a positive pressure respirator.

## Air-line or Supplied-air Respirators

Air-line or supplied-air respirators can be used in working conditions where there is oxygen deficiencies or when contaminants are in concentration levels that are not immediately harmful to life or health. The air for this type of respirator usually is supplied from either a bank of pressurized compressed air cylinders or a compressor. The compressed air is directed to the respirator through a high pressure hose. The respirator mask is available in three designs: half mask, full facepiece, or hood type.

Full Hood

Air Supply Line

**Illustration #28 - Battery Powered Air Purifying Respirator**

Illustration #29 shows one type of air-line respirator where a "continuous flow" of air is supplied which keeps the facepiece under positive pressure. With this type, any leakage will be from the inside outward, therefore, no contaminants should enter the facepiece.

Another type of air-line respirator is the "demand air flow" type, as shown in illustration #30, which supplies air only when the user inhales (breathes in). A similar type is the "pressure-demand" type which keeps the mask under positive pressure during both inhalation and exhalation.

Continuous Flow

Demand Air Flow

**Illustration #29 - Continuous Flow Air-Line Respirator**

**Illustration #30 - Demand Air Flow Air-Line Respirator**

Illustration #31 identifies a supplied-air system where the user wears a full hood. The air is supplied directly to the hood by a long length of trailing air hose.

Full Hood

Trailing Air Hose

**Illustration #31 - Supplied Air System**

*Note: Air-line or supplied-air respirators provide virtually unlimited air supply for*

*work in many types of hazardous conditions. One must always remember that a length of hose accompanies you wherever you go, and this could be a major drawback, as hose length may limit the safe working area and could restrict mobility. Also, air hoses may become crimped, jammed or even disconnected. Be extremely cautious when using this type of respirator.*

### Self-Contained Breathing Apparatus (SCBA)

The advantage of this type of respirator, the self-contained breathing apparatus, is that it provides the user with an independent air supply that is not mixed with any outside air and there is no long length of air hose to be concerned with.

The self-contained breathing apparatus supplies air from pressurized tanks and provides the highest level of respirator protection and positive air pressure.

This is the main reason that this type of respiratory system is more commonly used in rescue and emergency situations. Positive air pressure and freedom of movement without a hose are the primary advantages of self-contained breathing apparatuses. Protection is provided for both oxygen deficiency and contaminants that are very immediate and dangerous to the worker's life or health. Table #3 provides some basic safety related facts regarding self-contained breathing apparatuses.

There are two kinds of self-contained breathing apparatuses:

***Closed - Circuit Rebreathing Units:*** which protect the user for several hours in situations such as mine rescue. In these unit's, the user's exhaled air is recycled, carbon dioxide is removed from the exhaled air, and oxygen from a smaller cylinder is added to the exhaled air, which is then suitable for return back to the user.

***Pressure - Demand Open Circuit Respirators:*** provide the most amount of respiratory protection, as the user carries 30 to 60 minutes supply of compressed air or oxygen in a self-contained pressurized cylinder. Air from the user is exhaled directly into the outside atmosphere and a positive pressure is maintained inside the user's facepiece. See illustration #32.

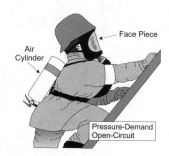

Face Piece

Air Cylinder

Pressure-Demand Open-Circuit

**Illustration #32 - Self-Contained Breathing Apparatus**

| | SELF-CONTAINED BREATHING APPARATUS FACTS |
|---|---|
| **Fact #** | **The Facts** |
| Fact #1 | BA provides compressed air (21% oxygen) to the user, not pure oxygen. |
| Fact #2 | BA protects you from: Hazardous airborne particles, Toxic gases, Asphyxiants, Hot gases, Irritants |
| Fact #3 | Use 5, 10, or 15 minute SCBA units for escape purposes only. |
| Fact #4 | Use a "minimum" 30 minute SCBA unit for rescue or for performing work.  Always try to work in pairs. |
| Fact #5 | Wearing SCBA:<br>1. Inspect unit (tank full, ready to use, clean, straps extended).<br>2. Put the cylinder (tank) and harness on.<br>3. Put the facepiece (mask) on and check the seal.<br>4. Connect the hose to the facepiece.<br>5. Turn on the air supply - full.<br>6. Check the gauge pressure (same as tank pressure?).<br>7. Test the SCBA alarm...shut off...breathe air pressure down...turn back on. |
| Fact #6 | Older SCBA units may have a "by-pass" valve.  It is only to be used in the event of a regulator failure. |
| Fact #7 | If there is a problem, remove the BA from service, and remember to tag it "do not use". |
| Fact #8 | SCBA will supply 1 minute of air for each 100PSI (689 kPa) pressure. |
| Fact #9 | Those who are not in good physical condition or are very nervous will use more air (approx. 30 - 40 seconds for each 100PSI (689 kPa)). |

**Table #3A - Self-Contained Breathing Apparatus Facts**

| SELF-CONTAINED BREATHING APPARATUS FACTS | |
| --- | --- |
| **Fact #** | **The Facts** |
| Fact #10 | Limitations of SCBA:<br>You must be close to clean shaven to properly wear SCBA.<br>Use only a positive pressure type system.<br>Not everyone's faceshape will fit the facepiece properly.<br>With some faceshapes there might be leaks at the facepiece.<br>Never assume the SCBA is safe until you fully test it.<br>Worker's voice communication will be poor.<br>SCBA units are heavy and can be awkward in tight places. |
| Fact #11 | Keep SCBA cleaned and hygenic - use soap and warm water. |
| Fact #12 | Sterilize the parts with a 10% bleach solution. |
| Fact #13 | Older models of SCBA may have an air valve and a by-pass valve at the regulator. |
| Fact #14 | Always leave the area immediately if the SCBA alarm is sounding. |
| Fact #15 | If using SABA, always have someone closely watching the air supply unit. |
| Fact #16 | SCBA parts include: cylinder, harness, regulator/gauge, facemask, high-low pressure air hoses.<br>SABA parts include: cylinders, long air hose, regulator/gauge, facemask, egress cylinder, connector couplings. |
| | **Note: BA (Breathing Apparatus), SCBA (Self-Contained Breathing Apparatus), SABA (Supplied-Air Breathing Apparatus)** |

Table #3B - Self-Contained Breathing Apparatus Facts (cont'd)

*Note: Some SCBA units can weigh as much as 40 lbs (18kg) and can put additional strain on the user's body. Wearing SCBA will increase physical exertion and can cause heat stress, increase in body temperature, dehydration and increased breathing. It is always recommended that a medical evaluation is conducted periodically to be sure that those who must wear SCBA are physically capable of doing so. Also, periodically observe the employee wearing and using the SCBA unit.*

*Caution: No respirator of any type will guard against toxins that may be absorbed through exposed skin. Be sure to wear the proper protective clothing along with the breathing unit.*

### Emergency Use of SCBA

Self-contained breathing apparatuses may be required while performing normal work activities or in those rare instances when there is an emergency situation requiring this type of protection. It is generally understood that the most frequent use of SCBA is in emergency situations. Several key points to consider regarding emergency use of SCBA include:

- SCBA for emergency use are usually stored in accessible locations just outside an area which is identified as having potential danger.
- Any person who is in the danger area while an emergency is sounded, must immediately leave the area. This person may be required to put on the SCBA unit and return to the danger area to perform rescue work or some type of repair or operational procedure. This action is usually done in pairs.
- Some danger areas within the work place may have SCBA units stored there for emergency use only when escape is necessary.

- In some dangerous work areas the workers must at all times carry an escape SCBA unit in case a safe and quick exit is required.

### Respirator Fit and Testing

Respirators rely on an effective face-to-mask seal for complete protection from hazardous atmospheres. Periodically, reviews should be conducted with workers to go over the requirements for ensuring good fit for respirators. All employees must realize that respirators which don't fit properly will allow contaminants to enter through the spaces and gaps between the facepiece and facial skin regions. This condition, if it were to occur, could be very hazardous to life and health. There are several key factors to consider in wearing respirators:

- Workers should try on and test several facepieces in order to find one which is most suited and fits well to their face shape.
- Beards, moustaches, long hair, low hairlines and eye glasses can interfere with the face-to-mask fit.

Four types of tests for respirator fit are:

***Negative Pressure Test***: This type of test must always be done just before entering any hazardous atmosphere. See illustration #33.

- Place your palms over the inhalation inlets or squeeze the breathing tube of the facepiece.
- Inhale gently so the facepiece collapses slightly.
- Hold your breath for about ten seconds.
- If the facepiece holds the suction created inside and no leaks are felt, the respirator fits the wearer well.

Press Hands
Over
Inhalation Pieces

Illustration #33 - Negative Pressure Test

***Positive Pressure Test:*** The positive pressure test should also be done before entering a hazardous atmosphere.   See illustration #34.

- Place your palm over the exhalation valve to block it off.
- Blow outward gently and hold for ten seconds.

- If the positive pressure is maintained and no leakage is felt, the respirator is fitting well.
- To make sure the facepiece maintains a good seal in a variety of positions: move your head up and down, turn side-to-side, breathe in and out deeply, and move your jaw to speak.

Positive Pressure
Should be
Maintained

Press Hand
Over
Exhalation Valve

Illustration #34 - Positive Pressure Test

***Qualitative Test:*** The qualitative test is sometimes better known as the odor or irritant test. See illustration #35.

- The person wearing the respirator is exposed to an odor or irritant agent (smoke, vapor, aerosol).
- If the odor or irritant is noticed, either through smell, taste or nasal irritation, the unit must be refitted or another one tried.

***Caution: This type of test is only as accurate as the user's sense of smell, taste or sensitivity to irritants.***

Odor or Irritant

Tight Seal Maintained

**Illustration #35 - Qualitative Test**

***Quantitative Test:*** The quantitative fit test is a very accurate way of measuring the fit of a respirator before the user enters into a highly toxic atmosphere. See illustration #36.

- The respirator which will be used in the highly toxic area will be worn by the user in a sealed testing booth.
- The wearer will be then exposed to a testing agent.
- The respirator is connected to sensitive test instruments which measure the amount of testing agent leaking by and entering into the user's facepiece.

**Illustration #36 - Quantitative Fit Test**

*Note: Your life depends on whether or not the seal is considered "air tight." Do not take unnecessary chances or risks!*

### Respirator Maintenance and Inspection

There are three basic procedures for effective respirator maintenance:

a. Inspection
b. Decontamination
c. Storage

*Inspection:* Workers who will be wearing respiratory protection devices are responsible for inspecting the unit. When inspecting the respirator, check for:

- Broken or loose hose connectors or fittings.
- Scratched or cracked facepiece.
- Holes or cracks in the filters.
- Tears in the headstraps.
- Missing components or parts.
- Loss of comformability and elasticity on the face mask.

- Residue and grime in the valves, general cleanliness.

*Note: Any respirators routinely used for non-emergency purposes must be inspected before and after each use and it is always recommended to inspect this equipment at least once a month if not in use. Never, ever use less than perfect operating respiratory protection equipment. Never attempt any do-it-yourself repairs on this equipment, unless fully qualified to perform such repair tasks.*

*Decontamination:* It is important to properly clean all respiratory protection equipment after each use in order to ensure flawless operation and performance. Practice the following decontamination tasks:

- Remove all respirator components and parts where grime can accumulate.
- Use mild detergent and warm water and scrub the parts thoroughly.

- Rinse off all cleaned parts with warm water.
- Select the correct disinfectant and treat the respirator parts with it.
- Again, rinse off the parts with clean water and make sure that all detergent and disinfectant is removed.
- Do not dry any rubber parts under any direct heat source or sunlight, only air-dry the parts.
- Never use any type of solvent to clean respiratory components or parts.
- After the decontamination process is completed, place the cleaned and assembled respirator in an individual plastic storage bag which can be sealed.

*Storage:* Respiratory protection devices must always be protected from moisture, dirt, dust, chemicals, sunlight, heat and cold.

When respiratory equipment is called upon for use, the user wants it to be there and needs it fully operational and fail-safe. Several storage tips include:

- After the respirator has been cleaned and decontaminated, place it in an individual plastic storage bag which can be sealed.
- Always try to store face masks with the exhalation valve and breathing hoses in a loose, natural, undistorted position, not all tangled together.
- Conduct periodic inspections of the storage areas and locations to ensure compliance and orderliness.
- Consider using separate compartments with a cabinet for storing air-purifying respiratory units.
- Wall-mount storage is recommended for emergency self contained breathing apparatuses, as this allows quick access and fitting.

## Hand Protection

The hand is one of the most complex and useful parts of the body. The hand's intricate design and structure gives people the sensation of touch, provides grip and dexterity to perform the most finite tasks. For most workers, it is their hands which they rely on everyday to perform hundreds of single, multiple, simple, and complex tasks. The hands of a worker make them highly skilled and valued in their trade or profession. Yet each year there are thousands of hand injuries in the workplace because of job related accidents and hazards.

Where there is a risk of hand injury from workplace hazards, suitable hand protection must be provided and worn in order to prevent hand related accidents. Hand protection must be worn to protect against the following conditions:

- Hazards from harmful chemicals and liquids which can absorb into the skin.

- Serious cuts or lacerations from sharp tools, equipment, parts, components and other sharp or jagged objects.
- Severe abrasions from rough objects.
- Deep puncture wounds from pointed objects.
- Burns from chemicals, solutions and harmful hot and cold temperature extremes.
- Effects of vibration and repetitive motions to the hand and fingers.
- Allergic reactions to various products being handled.

### Reasons for Hand Injuries

Employers must recognize that there are many ways for hand injuries to occur in the workplace. It is imperative that employers and workers participate in hand protection education programs to minimize hand injuries. Hand education and training should consist of:

- Identifying types of hand injury hazards.

- Determining when hand protection is necessary, and identifying what type of hand protection is required.
- Instructing workers how to properly fit, remove, adjust and wear hand protection.
- Being aware of what the hand protection limitations are.
- Discussing proper care, maintenance, life, storage and disposal of hand protection.

Hand injuries, being so common in the workplace, have been studied and researched for many years. It has been identified through various studies and data analysis that a worker's hands are generally exposed to four basic kinds of hazard categories:

***Mechanical Hazards***: These hazards are present whenever machinery, equipment and tools are in operation or used. Injuries resulting from mechanical hazards typically include: cuts, bruises, abrasions, crushing, punctures, sprains, breaks and amputation.

***Environmental Hazards:*** These hazards are usually related to those work conditions where hands are subjected to extreme hot or cold conditions, dangerous chemicals and liquids or electrical hazards.

***Irritating Substances:*** There are many examples of skin conditions, such as allergies and rashes, which are directly related to the hands being in contact with irritating agents such as chemicals, bacteria, fungi and viruses. Any of these substances, if conditions and exposure levels are high and long enough, have the potential for entering into the blood stream either directly through the skin or through abrasions or cuts to the hands.

***Human Error***: Many hand injuries are certainly caused by such hazards as mechanical, environmental or from an irritant, but in many of these accidents there was plenty of warning and signals that danger existed.

Many times the hand injury is really a result of someone not paying close enough attention to their work and the activities being performed. Human error like this is often attributed to: boredom of routine or repetitive tasks; inattentiveness to details and specific safety precautions; and to distractions which impair the worker's concentration level.

### Common Workplace Hand Hazards

***Pinch Points***: Places where fingers or the hand can get caught between two objects, where one is stationary and the other is moving, or between two moving objects. Avoid placing fingers and hands in these dangerous pinch point zones. See illustration #37.

***Rotating Machine Surfaces:*** Common to most work and shop areas are rotating types of tools and equipment. It is very easy to injure a hand or finger when working around any type of open or unguarded rotating equipment. Always use extreme caution and be alert when working with rotating equipment. See illustration #38.

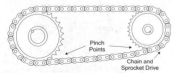

Illustration #37 - Pinch Points

Illustration #38 - Rotating Machine Surfaces

***Automated Tools and Machinery***:  Automated tools and machinery may unexpectedly start up and easily catch the unaware or unprepared worker off guard.  Much of this type of equipment has delay and relay type of switching for controlling start, stop, and move functions.  Always remember to be alert to the functions of automated tooling and equipment and remember to disconnect, lock out, and tagout any of this equipment if work has to be done on it.  Protect your hands and yourself.  See illustration #39.

***Loose Clothing and Jewelry***:  Loose fitting and baggy clothing, as well as certain designs of jewelry can easily become caught in moving parts or pinch points.  Many companies have rigid policies regarding suitable clothing and jewelry to be worn in the workplace.  Always remove all jewelry which has even the slightest chance of getting caught up in something.  Roll up loose or baggy shirt sleeves to avoid the clothing from being caught in machinery, therefore trapping your hand or arm.  See illustration #40.

Keep Hands Away

**Illustration #39 - Automated Tools and Machines**

Loose Fitting Shirt

**Illustration #40 - Loose Clothing**

***Hot and Cold Spots:*** Certain types of machinery and work areas can be quite hazardous to the hands and fingers because of extreme heat or cold temperature conditions. Hot and cold spots can cause serious burns to the fingers and hands. Always remember to wear protective gloves when working with hot and cold objects or in those areas where extreme heats and cold temperatures may exist. See illustration #41.

Protective Gloves

Hot Oil

**Illustration #41 - Hot Fluids**

***Chemicals and Dangerous Liquids:*** There are numerous dangerous chemicals and liquids found in the modern workplace. It is imperative that appropriate hand protection be worn at all times when handling and working with these dangerous and corrosive substances. See illustration #42.

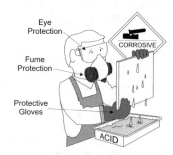

Eye Protection

CORROSIVE

Fume Protection

Protective Gloves

ACID

**Illustration #42 - Chemicals and Dangerous Liquids**

### Protection Tips For Using Handtools

It is important to always select the proper tool for the job and to ensure that its used correctly. Using the wrong tool for the job can easily lead to serious hand and finger injuries. Occasionally inspect tools for defects and repair or discard broken or worn tools. The following tips are recommended for preventing hand injuries when using common hand tools.

#### Knives

- Keep blades well sharpened.
- Always cut away from your body.
- Use a type of retractable knife blade whenever possible.
- Don't use a knife as a screwdriver or prybar.
- Be extra careful when working with a co-worker who is using a knife.
- Store knives separately from other tools, keep blades covered or turned down.
- Don't leave knives laying around.

- Consider wearing a type of hand protection device when using a knife.
- When carrying a knife sheath on your belt, secure it on your belt over the hip with the knife blade facing back.

#### Wrenches

Always choose the right size wrench for the job.

- If possible, use box-end wrenches instead of an open-end wrench to avoid slippage.
- Always pull on a wrench. Try not to push on the wrench.
- Refrain from using snipes or other extension devices with wrenches.

#### Screwdrivers

- Don't uses screwdrivers as prybars.
- Keep screwdriver points in good condition to minimize slippage.
- Secure objects in a vise or place on a flat surface instead of trying to hold the object in one hand and use the screwdriver with the other.

- Don't use the screwdriver handle like a hammer.
- Keep screwdriver handles in good shape, free from rough edges and nicks.

### Other Hand Hazards

Extra hand care must be taken when working around overhead hoists and cranes.

- Wear gloves when handling any type of wire rope and/or chain.
- Take extra hand care precautions when performing welding and oxy-acetylene operations.
- Keep hands out of door jambs and other door closure areas.
- Be careful of pinch points when using lifting jacks and blocking.

### Machine Guards

Every machine or piece of industrial equipment that has exposed moving, rotating, electrically charged or hot parts or processes; transports; supports or handles materials and objects that is deemed a potential hazard to an employee, must be equipped with a practical machine guard that:

- prevents the worker or any part of the body from coming into contact with the parts or material;
- prevents access by the worker to the area of exposure to the hazard during the operation of the machine; or
- in some machine designs, makes the machine inoperative if the worker or any part of their clothing is in or near a part of the machine that is likely to cause injury.

*Note: Many designs of machine guards have built-in safeguards in order to protect the worker's hands. In some machine designs, if the machine guard is removed, the machine will be inoperable. Never remove the machine guard from a machine which is in operation mode. Never remove the built-in safeguards, and never operate any machinery that has had any of its machine guards removed.*

***Don't override any built-in safety devices linked to the guarding mechanisms.***

Illustration #43A shows an example of a machine guard installed to protect workers from a large belt drive on piece of heavy equipment. Illustration #43B shows a machine guard used to cover the high speed shaft coupling of the electric motor drive. Illustration #43C identifies a specially designed machine guard to protect the hands from the rotating parts of the machine tool.

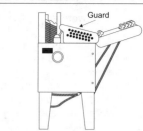

**Illustration #43B - Motor Coupling Guard**

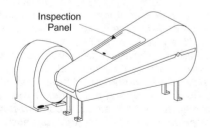

**Illustration #43A - Machine Guard**

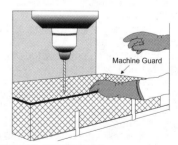

**Illustration #43C - Hand Protection**

### Types of Hand Protection Equipment

There are several common types of hand protection equipment used for various tasks and in certain work conditions. Hand protection equipment can help reduce the frequency and severity of hand and finger injury. Fingers are probably one of the most difficult body parts to protect, but yet, they can be shielded from many common injuries. Personal hand protection is available in the form of gloves, mitts, finger cots, thimbles, hand pads, sleeves, hand lotions and barrier creams. Gloves are probably the most common protectors for the hand and fingers.

### Protective Gloves

There are four glove classifications:

***General Purpose***: These gloves are usually used by workers for many types of job activities. There is no single glove which will offer protection against all hazards.

General purpose types of gloves are made of either leather or cotton and they offer minor protection from abrasions, cuts, punctures, snags, rough edges, and small temperature variations. Leather being a heavier and thicker material offers more overall protection than cotton. Leather gloves are commonly used in conditions where there is heat and sparking. See illustration #44.

**Illustration #44 - General Purpose Gloves**

***Cut-Resistant***: These gloves are made from specially designed materials which are reinforced to provide excellent cut resistant qualities. Materials which are commonly used for this category of glove include: metal mesh and extreme heat and cut resistance yarns and fabrics. Metal mesh gloves are commonly worn by workers in the meat packing industry who are using sharp knives and saws. See illustration #45.

***Special Purpose:*** These gloves are manufactured according to the service for specific types of hand protection required. An example of a special purpose glove would be specially insulated gloves suitable for welding, cutting, foundry and casting work. Another example of special purpose glove would be electrically insulated gloves worn by workers handling high voltage equipment or lines. See illustration #46.

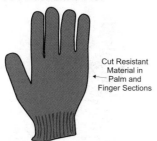

Cut Resistant
Material in
← Palm and
Finger Sections

**Illustration #45 - Cut Resistant Gloves**

**Illustration #46 - Special Purpose Insulated Gloves**

***Chemical Resistant:*** These special gloves are designed to prevent serious hand injury which could be caused by absorption of hazardous chemicals and other toxic type fluids through the skin and into the body. These gloves need to be non-porous and are usually made from different synthetic materials such as nitrile, neoprene or butyl rubber. Natural rubber may not offer good protection from some hazardous chemicals and fluids. See illustration #47.

Latex or vinyl disposable gloves, which are very thin and tight fitting, are commonly used in the medical field by doctors, nurses, and first-aid attendants. These gloves protect the hands and skin from bodily fluids, bacteria, viruses, and various liquid type solutions. Some people may be allergic to latex gloves. The employer can provide hypoallergenic gloves, glove liners or powderless gloves as alternative hand protection. See illustration #48.

Illustration #47 - Chemical Resistant Gloves

Illustration #48 - Vinyl Disposable Gloves

*Note: Depending on what materials and substances the gloves were worn for, it may be a requirement to properly dispose of the glove to prevent the spread of contamination or to protect other workers from being in contact with the residues of dangerous materials on the gloves. There should be a policy for proper glove disposal in these types of circumstances.*

*Note: Never wear gloves when working near open machinery which is operating, such as gears, sprockets, rollers and pulleys. It is very easy to get glove fingers caught in these moving machine parts.*

### Cautionary Tips

a. Wear gloves whenever working around infectious, chemical or radioactive hazards.

b. Health workers and medical care givers may have hand contact with blood, or other potentially infectious bodily fluids, mucous membranes or non-intact skin. Gloves must be worn when cleaning surfaces contaminated by blood or other body fluids including clothing, linens or the bedside commode, protective gloves must be worn.

c. All cleaning and janitorial staff handling garbage and refuse must wear protective gloves and should refrain from reaching into any receptacle to pick out garbage and trash. Infectious needles and other sharp objects which may be contaminated could easily cut a finger or other part of one's hand.

d. Protective gloves must be worn when picking up any type of medical waste bag which may contain blood, or other bodily fluids or blood and soaked bandages and wraps.

## How To Properly Fit and Remove Disposable Gloves

Before donning latex gloves, especially those workers in the medical field, it is recommended that you wash your hands thoroughly first.

It is best to not wear any petroleum based hand creams when preparing to wear latex gloves.

Cover any cuts, scratches or open sores with bandages, in case the glove leaks or tears.

Slip each hand into a clean glove, pull snug over the fingers and as far up the wrists as possible.

In the medical field, only use latex gloves once on a single patient, then discard properly.

Gloves used for utility type applications may be cleaned or decontaminated for reuse. If utility use gloves are torn or cracked, replace immediately.

If gloves become punctured, torn, cracked, or leak and become contaminated, remove as soon as possible and discard them properly.

It is generally recommended to not wash, decontaminate or reuse latex gloves. When removing contaminated gloves, be careful not to touch the outside surface of the glove with a bare hand or finger. See illustration #49.

- With both hands gloved, peel one glove off from the outside top to the bottom. Hold it with the gloved hand (Step 1).
- With the exposed hand, peel the second glove off from inside the top, tucking the first glove inside the second (Step 2 and 3).
- Dispose the used gloves promptly in an approved waste receptacle. Wash your hands after removing the gloves (Step 4).

*Note: No type of glove is 100% effective.*

Step 1.

Step 2.

Step 3.

Step 4.

**Illustration #49 - Removing Disposable Gloves**

### Other PPE For The Hands and Fingers

The following points identify several other types of specialty hand protectors:

*Mitts:* are similar to gloves, but have a division or part for the thumb and one for the fingers. Mitts may reduce fine motor skill and manual dexterity.

*Finger Cots:* provide protection for only a single finger or finger tip.

*Thimbles:* are used to protect the thumb or the thumb and the first two fingers.

*Hand Pads:* are used to protect the palm of the hand from cuts and friction. These pads are also used to protect against burns caused by hot or cold objects. Hand pads may greatly limit manual dexterity.

*Sleeves or Forearm Cuffs:* are worn to protect the worker's arms and wrists from heat, splashing liquids, impacts or cuts.

*Skin Barrier Creams:* Special skin barrier creams and lotions can be used by themselves or in association with other types of hand protection to reduce hand injury. To be effective, skin creams or lotions should be applied frequently.

Often, skin barriers are recognized as the last line of defense for protecting hands from noxious substances such as petrochemical solvents, acids, irritable powders, paints, glues, dyes, water cleaners, soaps, detergents, UV radiation, gasoline, diesel, hydraulic fluid, fiberglass, and other problem substances. The following list identifies four categories of skin barriers which are commercially available:

- Water Resistant Barrier Lotion (Apply before work, barrier against water and other aqueous substances).
- Oil Water Lotion (Helps with the skin regeneration process).
- Medicated Skin Cream (Smoothes skin, helps reduce infection, relieves irritation).
- Protective Solvent Resistant Cream (Combats growth of bacteria).

## Hearing Protection

Occupational hearing protection is one of the most important items for the worker's personal protection equipment. This section will explain what hazardous noise levels are in the workplace, how the ear works and the importance of hearing protection. When working in an environment where there is excessive, unwanted noise, it is absolutely necessary to wear some type of approved hearing protection. In some work situations and certain jurisdictions, it is mandatory that hearing protection be worn. Regulations governing the allowable levels of noise and hearing protection requirements for companies and workers are issued by CSA Standard Z94.2-M1984, Hearing Protectors, CSA Standard CAN/CSA-Z107.56-M86, Procedures for the Measurement of Occupational Noise Exposure, and OSHA 29 CFR 1910.95, Occupational Noise Exposure. Specifications for Sound Level Meters are ANSI SI.4-1971 (R1976), and Specifications for Audiometers are ANSI S3.6-1969.

### What is Sound?

One common definition of sound is as follows: "Sound is vibratory energy or waves of motion". Everything that moves makes sound. The vibrations have their own unique characteristic effect on the total amount of sound (noise) produced. Public concern over the issue of noise in the workplace and consistent noise - induced problems in the community has grown over the past two decades in North America. Federal, provincial and state regulations govern the maximum noise levels workers can be subjected to in the workplace.

### *Sound Frequency*

Sound frequency is defined as being the number of complete cycles or rise and falls in pressure in a given time period.

Sound frequency is expressed in cycles per second (CPS) or Hertz (Hz).

Frequency is important in all sound measurements. Sound frequency can be referred to as "pitch", and high frequency (high pitch) sound can be more damaging to hearing than low frequency (low pitch) sound. Sound frequencies associated with the human ear fall into three distinct categories:

*Infrasonic:* Sounds which are at frequencies below the range of human hearing, less than 20 CPS.

*Audio-sonic:* Sounds which are at frequencies within the range of human hearing, 20 to 20,000 CPS.

*Ultrasonic:* Sounds which are at frequencies above the range of human hearing, 20,000 CPS and greater.

*Note: The audio-sonic sounds are of primary concern to industry, as exposure to these sounds for prolonged periods of time will affect the worker's hearing.*

## Sound Measurement

Sound intensity (amplitude) is measured using the logarithmic decibel (dB) scale which is considered the most convenient method for measuring sound intensity. Sound intensity is really the "loudness" of a sound. Sound intensity that exceeds 85 dB over an eight hour work day may cause hearing damage. According to OSHA standards, workers may not be exposed to more than an average of 85 dB over an eight hour period without hearing protection being provided.

The human ear is sensitive enough to pick up various sound intensity levels. Illustration #50 provides common examples of noise typical to home and the workplace. Each of the identified sounds can vary in intensity measured, as there are several factors which can alter sound measurement.

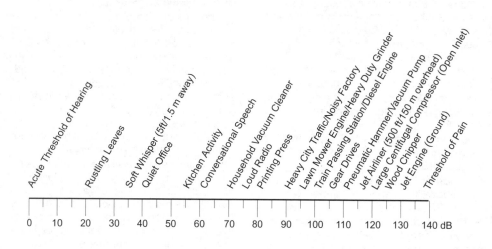

Illustration #50 - Sound Thresholds

Table #4 identifies the sound intensity levels (dB) to which the human ear responds.

| SOUND INTENSITY AND THE HUMAN EAR | |
|---|---|
| **Change in Sound Intensity** | **Human Ear Response** |
| 1 dB | Detect change under controlled conditions |
| 3 dB - 5 dB | Noticeable difference in loudness |
| 6 dB | Significant increase in loudness |
| 10 dB | Appears almost twice as loud to the human ear |
| 10 dB - 20 dB | Unbelievably louder |
| Example: a 6 dB change in sound intensity will be a significant increase in loudness or a 10 dB change in sound intensity is 3.162 x sound pressure, or almost twice as loud as the original sound heard. | |

Table #4 - Sound Intensity and The Human Ear

For example, the distance between the microphone and the sound source can significantly affect the sound measurement level. Other factors which make it difficult to establish specific noise levels in the workplace include:

- The nature of the immediate surroundings.
- Machinery and equipment location within the building.
- Machine proximity to other machines.
- Type of building and insulation materials used.
- Design/type of machinery and equipment foundation and support structures.
- Machinery load, feed rates, speed, or any reciprocating actions.
- Effects of noise reverberation and frequency.
- Types and design features of power transmission drives and components.

## Noise Exposure

Protection against effects of noise shall be provided when the sound levels exceed those shown in table #5 when measured on the "A" scale of a standard sound level meter at slow response. This table is referenced in OSHA 1910.95, Occupational Noise Exposure standard. When employees are subjected to sound exceeding those listed in table #5, appropriate administrative and engineering controls must be utilized to ensure adequate worker protection. If such controls fail to reduce sound levels within the acceptable levels, personal protective hearing equipment must be provided and used to reduce sound levels within the levels of the table.

| PERMISSIBLE NOISE EXPOSURES (OSHA 1910.95) | |
|---|---|
| **Duration Per Day in Hours** | **Sound Level dB Slow Response** |
| 8 Hours | 90 dB |
| 6 Hours | 92 dB |
| 4 Hours | 95 dB |
| 3 Hours | 97 dB |
| 2 Hours | 100 dB |
| 1.5 Hours | 102 dB |
| 1 Hour | 105 dB |
| 0.5 Hour | 110 dB |
| 0.25 Hour or less | 115 dB |

Table #5 - Permissible Noise Exposures

**Acceptable Noise Level Characteristics**

- Tasks involving exactness and sustained worker concentration are significantly effected by bothersome noise or high noise levels.
- Long term jobs requiring constant vigilance are especially susceptible to noise levels.
- Noise is more likely to cause a higher rate of work related errors and possibly accidents than an actual reduction in total production.
- Moderate noise can cause the pupil of the eye to dilate, effecting the ability to focus properly.
- High frequency sounds are usually more annoying than are lower frequency sounds.
- Hearing, particularly in the higher sound frequencies, deteriorates with age.
- Loud noises and high frequency noises interfere with normal voice communication.

- As noise levels increase, the worker's attention span lessens.
- Noise is more likely to lead to increased errors in work if the noise continues to be above 85 - 90 dB.
- Ear protection is recommended for continuous exposure to noise levels above 85 dB.

Exposure to intense noise may produce hearing damage. Some of the hearing loss may be temporary, with partial or complete recovery in time. The amount of hearing damage depends on: the loudness of the exposure; the length of exposure time; and the noise frequency.

**Protective Hearing Equipment**

Hearing protection for workers reduces their exposure to harmful noise while allowing them to hear signals, machine and process warnings and alarms and to maintain a functional level of conversation.

Employers must provide hearing protection to their workers and are responsible for training their employees on how to correctly use hearing protection equipment. As well, employers are responsible for providing regular hearing tests for their employees.

The type of hearing protection a worker selects really depends upon the noise level, the worker's comfort, and the duration and type of job they will be performing. There are two broad categories of hearing protection equipment, these are:

1. Earplugs
2. Earmuffs

### Earplugs

Earplugs are lightweight and can be comfortable to the wearer for long periods of time. In order to be effective, earplugs must fit snug in the ear canal so that no noise can get through. Most earplugs, as shown in illustration #51A, are tapered and pre-shaped to provide a comfortable fit.

Earplugs are made of soft, non-irritating and non-allergenic foam to best conform and fit to the shape of the ear canal comfortably. This design also allows for easy insertion and easy grasp for removal. Earplugs with an attached cord are useful in order to prevent loss and provide easy access. See illustration #51B. To insert foam earplugs, as shown in illustration #51C, follow the recommended procedure:

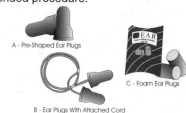

A - Pre-Shaped Ear Plugs

C - Foam Ear Plugs

B - Ear Plugs With Attached Cord

Illustration #S02-051A,B,C - Types of Earplugs
**Illustration #51A, B, C - Types of Earplugs**

- Make sure hands and earplugs are clean and dry, as dirt and moisture in the ear canal may cause ear infection.
- Carefully roll the earplug between the thumb and forefinger until completely compressed.
- With the opposite hand, pull the outer ear upward and back, then insert the earplug as far into ear as possible.
- Hold finger against the earplug until you feel the foam expand.
- Then switch hands and carefully insert the other earplug in the same way.
- If using "preformed" earplugs, pull outer ear upward and back, then insert the plug by twisting and pushing until it fits snugly and it feels as if a good tight seal is made.

*Note: This type of earplug is probably one of the most widely accepted form of hearing protection in industry. This design is very effective as it is a true "custom fit" for sealing out harmful noise.*

*Note: Custom molded earplugs can be made to fit the exact shape of the worker's ear canal. Silicone or a plastic molded compound is placed in each ear and allowed to set. After the setting period is completed, the worker has his or her own custom fitted earplugs.*

**Earmuffs**

Earmuffs are purposely designed to fit over the whole ear to best seal out noise. Earmuffs, if properly fitted and worn, can reduce noise levels to the ear by 20 to 25 dB. A typical earmuff, and there are many different designs and types, are made up of three basic parts: cups, cushions and headband. As shown in illustration #52A, the cups are usually made of lightweight, but durable molded plastic and are designed to hold the cushion which rests snugly against the entire ear. The cushions are covered with plastic and filled with foam, liquid or air.

The headband attaches to the cups and secures the earmuffs to the wearer's head. The headband can be worn over the head, behind the neck, under the chin, or worn over or integrated with the wearer's protective hard-hat, as shown in illustration #52B.

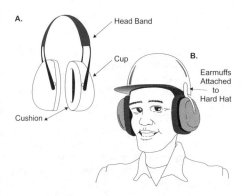

Illustration #52A, B - Ear Muffs

Always wear the earmuffs so that each cup completely covers the entire ear. Push away or remove anything which may interfere with the seal, such as earrings, hairclips, hair or a beard. The arms of safety glasses can interfere with the earmuff fit. The wearer may get a better earmuff fit if they used goggles instead of regular safety glasses.

***Rule of Thumb:*** A good rule of thumb for knowing whether hearing protection is required is if you have to raise your voice to be heard by someone who is less than 3 feet (1 m) away.

***Note: For maximum hearing protection, wearing both earplugs and earmuffs may be necessary to reduce noise levels below 85 dB. Caution though, workers must be assured that any necessary voice communication can be heard in the work area, and also be able to hear machine operation and process and equipment signals and alarms.***

## Signs of Hearing Loss

Workers must be aware of certain signs which may indicate that they may be experiencing hearing loss. Workers should never believe that they will get used to high noise levels and for some workers, they probably have hearing loss, but really are unaware of the seriousness of their condition. Even if a person has no symptoms at all and feels no pain or discomfort, one's hearing may be in the early stages of deterioration.

The human ear, as outlined in illustration #53, must channel the sound waves from the outer ear down through the ear canal and when the waves reach the eardrum they cause it to vibrate. The vibrations pass through three very small connected bones (hammer, anvil, stirrup) in the middle ear and on to the fluid-filled section of the inner ear called the cochlea.

Tiny hairs in the cochlea change the vibrations to nerve impulses that are transmitted to the brain through nerve fibers in the auditory nerve.

When the hair cells are repeatedly exposed to excessive noise and lose some of their resilient characteristics, sensorineural or noise induced hearing loss occurs. Several signs of hearing loss include:

- Catching only some words or part of phrases, or failing to catch words or phrases at all.
- Constant ringing or buzzing in the ears, commonly known as tinnitus.
- Muffled hearing for several hours after leaving the noisy area.
- Shouting or raising your voice without realizing it.
- Having problems discerning high frequency sounds.

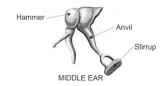

Outer Ear    Middle Ear    Inner Ear

Cochlea

Ear Canal    Eardrum

Hammer

Anvil

Stirrup

MIDDLE EAR

**Illustration #53 - The Human Ear**

## Hearing Loss Prevention

There are several methods employees and employers can utilize to help prevent hearing loss in the work place, other than wearing approved hearing protection equipment and training the workers how to use it properly. Other methods worth discussing include: Monitoring; Audiometric Testing; Administrative and Engineering Controls.

***Monitoring:*** By performing regular checks to measure the noise levels in the work area, employees and the employer will be up-to-date and aware of the various noise levels which may be harmful. Accurate monitoring of noise in the workplace is typically done with:

***Sound Level Meter:*** which identifies those specific work areas where employee exposure exceeds established permissible exposure levels. A Sound Level Meter measures noise in decibels (dB).

***Noise Dosimeter:*** which is worn on the worker's body and measures the employee's actual noise exposure during a work shift. The results provided can indicate representative exposure for other workers who were or are in the same work areas or performing similar jobs.

***Audiometric Testing:*** An audiogram is a common method for testing hearing loss. The worker being tested will receive a "baseline" audiogram which establishes the threshold or "softest" levels of noise he or she can hear in each ear. An audiogram examination is an effective method for early detection of hearing loss. Several audiometric test guidelines include:

- Workers who are scheduled to be tested should not be exposed to high noise levels at home or work for 14 hours before the baseline hearing test is conducted.
- Workers must always tell the person performing the test about any past or current hearing condition problems and about any exposure to loud noises or high frequency sounds on or off the job.
- Workers should always feel comfortable and relaxed when being tested.
- If workers don't understand any part of the test procedures, they must seek an explanation in order to have the test results as accurate as possible.

After the baseline test has been performed, at least annual audiograms are usually conducted to determine if there are any changes to the person's hearing. Any significant change is commonly referred to as a "Standard Threshold Shift" (STS). Workers who have experienced an STS are typically notified shortly after the test. Those workers who weren't wearing hearing protection will normally be fitted with suitable hearing protection and trained in its use. Those workers who have been wearing hearing protection will usually be refitted with hearing protection and offered some refresher training on hearing protection.

### Engineering and Administrative Controls

Another method for reducing or eliminating hearing loss is to implement effective administrative and engineering controls. Typically, this is best done through the combined ideas, solutions and efforts of the workers and management. Administrative controls usually focus on:

- Rotating employees in and out of high noise areas several times during their shift.
- Only allowing noisy types of jobs to be performed when fewer people are around.
- Setting limits for exposure time in the noisy areas.

Engineering controls usually are changes or modifications made to the machinery or physical structure to reduce the noise.

Common ways this is done include:
- Installing insulation or acoustical type of barriers or panels.
- Enclosing noisy processes in isolated sound absorbing rooms or enclosures.
- Using carpeting, curtains, sound-absorbing materials for walls and ceilings.
- Using rubber cushions or bumper types of materials to quiet the loud impact noises in chutes and slides.
- Replacing noisy metal parts with quieter parts made of synthetic or other non-metalic materials.
- Minimizing vibration noise by mounting heavy vibratory equipment on resilient pads.
- Ensuring equipment and machinery is properly maintained, aligned and lubricated.

*Remember: It is your eyes, your ears, your hands, your feet, your lungs and your head - protect them and keep them!*

# SECTION THREE

# FIRE PREVENTION AND SAFETY

## Introduction

Fire in the workplace will usually occur quickly, and is often catastrophic. Work related fires take the lives of many people and injure countless others each year in North America, they can however, be prevented.

This section of the handbook will provide useful fire safety and prevention methods, and will discuss fundamental characteristics of physics and chemistry related to fire. The best defense against a fire is to prevent the fire from starting. Everyone in the work place needs to know what to do to keep fires from starting, as well as how to respond with the emergency of an accidental fire. Because of the deadly danger of fire, it is to everyone's benefit to know how to size up a fire and how to respond in a fire emergency.

## Fire Codes and Regulations

### Occupational Safety and Health Administration (OSHA) - (USA)

Occupational Safety and Health Administration (OSHA) regulations for general industry have been issued in the United States in the Code of Federal Regulations (CFR), Title 29, Part 1910. Individual and specific regulations are issued as 29 CFR 1910.

The Occupational Safety and Health Administration (OSHA) regulates several aspects of fire prevention and emergency response in the United States.

Emergency planning, fire prevention plans, and evacuation that would be required in the event of a serious or hazardous fire are all specifically addressed in OSHA 29 CFR 1910.38. In addition, the provision of fire extinguishers and other fire protection is addressed in OSHA 29 CFR 1910.157.

### National Fire Protection Association (NFPA)

The National Fire Protection Association (NFPA) in the United States has classified fires into four classifications. Each fire classification is based on the combustible materials involved and the type of extinguisher required to suppress and extinguish the fire. The four fire classifications are A, B, C and D. Each classification, as designated and regulated by the NFPA, has its own unique symbol and color identification.

### National Fire Code of Canada (NFC)

The National Fire Code of Canada 1995 (NFC) is prepared by the Canadian Commission on Building and Fire Codes (CCBFC) and is published by the National Research Council of Canada (NRC). The NFC is prepared in the form of a recommended model code to permit adoption by an appropriate authority. The NFC comprises a model set of technical requirements designed to provide an acceptable level of fire safety within the community. Life safety is a primary objective of the NFC and property protection requirements are included to the extent that they make a direct contribution to life safety.

The NFC contains fire safety measures for both the occupant of the building and the fire fighter. In the NFC, measures for property protection are typically employed for the purpose of safe evacuation in fire emergencies and for the rescue of people within buildings. These measures may also assist in containment or control of a fire.

The NFC establishes a satisfactory standard for fire prevention, fire fighting, and life safety in buildings, including standards for the conduct of activities causing fire hazards, maintenance of fire safety equipment, standards for portable fire extinguishers, limitations on building contents and the establishment of fire safety plans, including the organization of supervisory staff for emergency purposes.

In addition, the NFC establishes the standard for prevention, containment and suppression of fires originating outside buildings which may present a hazard, and sets standards for the storage and handling of dangerous goods, and flammable and combustible liquids.

Under the terms of the Constitution Act, regulation of fire safety in Canada is the responsibility of provincial and territorial governments.

The NFC has received extensive use as the basis for most municipal bylaws and provincial fire codes.

The National Research Council of Canada publishes other code related documents that are often closely associated with fire codes. These include:

***National Building Code of Canada 1995:*** A code of minimum regulations for public health, fire safety and structural sufficiency with respect to public interest.

This code establishes a satisfactory standard of fire safety for the construction of new buildings, the reconstruction of buildings, including extensions, alterations, or changes in occupancy and upgrading of buildings to remove an unacceptable fire hazard.

***National Farm Building Code of Canada 1995:*** A model set of minimum requirements affecting human health, fire safety and structural sufficiency for farm buildings.

***Supplement to the National Building Code of Canada 1990:*** Chapter 3 provides explanatory materials on specific measures for fire safety in high buildings.

***National Plumbing Code of Canada 1995:*** Contains detailed requirements for the design and installation of plumbing and piping systems in buildings.

## General Classes of Fires

*Note: Fires are classified as A, B, C and D.*

*Class A:* This type of fire is the most common. The combustible materials are wood, cloth, paper, trash having glowing embers, rubber and plastics.

*Class B:* This type of fire consists of flammable liquids such as oils, gasoline and paints, and greases.

*Class C:* This type of fire is considered an electrical fire, where electrical equipment and wiring is burning.

*Class D:* These types of fires arise primarily from combustible metals, such as magnesium, titanium, zirconium and sodium.

Illustration #54 identifies the standard symbol and color code for each of the four classes of fire. They are recognized throughout business and industry in North America.

**CLASS A FIRES**
WOOD, PAPER, TRASH
HAVING GLOWING EMBERS

ORDINARY
**A**
COMBUSTIBLES
(GREEN TRIANGLE)

**CLASS B FIRES**
FLAMMABLE LIQUIDS, GASOLINE,
OIL, PAINTS, GREASE, ETC.

FLAMMABLE
**B**
LIQUIDS
(RED SQUARE)

**CLASS C FIRES**
ELECTRICAL EQUIPMENT

ELECTRICAL
**C**
EQUIPMENT
(BLUE CIRCLE)

**CLASS D FIRES**
COMBUSTIBLE METALS

COMBUSTIBLE
**D**
METALS
(YELLOW STAR)

Illustration #54 - Four Classes of Fire

## Elements of Fire

Fire is described as a chemical reaction involving rapid oxidation or burning of combustible materials accompanied by a release of energy in the form of heat and light. In order for "fire" to occur, four elements are required:

*Fuel:* can be any combustible material, in solid, liquid or gas form.

*Oxygen:* it supports combustion and typically fire only requires an atmosphere with 16% oxygen, while the air we breathe and require is approximately 21% oxygen.

*Heat:* is necessary to increase the temperature of the fuel to a point where sufficient vapors are given off for ignition to occur and be sustained.

*Chemical Chain Reaction:* A type of chain reaction can occur when the three elements (fuel, oxygen, heat) are present in the proper conditions and amounts. Fire occurs when this rapid oxidation, or burning takes place.

*Note: If any one of these elements is taken away (fuel, oxygen, heat), the fire cannot exist.*

## Three Sided Fire Triangle

The three sided figure of the Fire Triangle has, until recently, adequately described fire combustion and extinguishment theory. The triangle consisted of oxygen, heat and fuel, and when these three elements were in proper proportions a fire was created. This model stated that if any one of the three elements were removed, a fire could not exist. Illustration #55 provides the details for explaining each of the three elements of the three sided fire triangle.

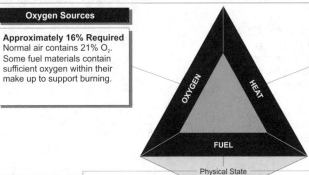

**Oxygen Sources**

**Approximately 16% Required**
Normal air contains 21% $O_2$.
Some fuel materials contain
sufficient oxygen within their
make up to support burning.

**Heat Sources**

**To Reach Ignition Temperature**
Open Flame - The Sun
Hot Surfaces
Sparks and Arcs
Friction - Chemical Action
Electrical Energy
Compression of Gases

OXYGEN

HEAT

FUEL

Physical State

**Gases**

Natural Gas
Propane
Butane
Hydrogen
Acetylene
Carbon Monoxide
Others

**Liquids**

Gasoline        Paint
Kerosene       Varnish
Turpentine     Lacquer
Alcohol          Others

**Solids**

**Bulky - Dust
Finely Divided**
Coal       Plastic
Wood      Sugar
Paper      Grain
Cloth       Hay
Wax        Cork
Grease    Others
Leather

**Illustration #55 - Fire Triangle**

## The Fire Tetrahedron

Recently, the Fire Tetrahedron is more commonly used to explain fire combustion and extinguishment theory. In today's workplace there are many newly developed chemicals, resins, materials and metals which burn differently and seemingly have varying types of chemical chain reactions which do not typically fit the traditional fire theories as was originally represented in the three sided fire triangle.

The Fire Tetrahedron, as described in illustration #56, is a four-sided solid geometric figure which resembles a pyramid. One of the four sides serves to represent the chemical chain reaction which occurs in fire. The removal of one or more of the four sides will make this tetrahedron incomplete and result in extinguishment of the fire. The four sides of the tetrahedron represent fuel, oxygen, heat, and chemical chain reaction.

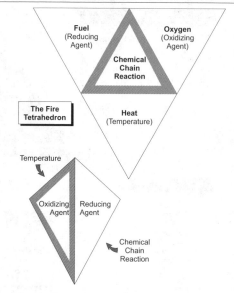

Illustration #56 - The Fire Tetrahedron

This model hasn't replaced the traditional fire triangle, it has simply added a fourth component or condition, the chemical chain reaction.

The four sides of the tetrahedron are explained as follows:

*Fuel (Reducing Agent):*  The fuel side of the tetrahedron is similar to the description for fuel used in the three sided fire triangle. It is defined as "a material that can be oxidized." The term "reducing agent" has reference to the fact the fuel reduces the oxidizing agent.

*Oxygen (Oxidizing Agent):*  The term oxidizing agent is used in place of oxygen or air. This term can be more useful for explaining why some materials, such as sodium nitrate and potassium chlorate, can burn in an atmosphere free of any outside source of oxygen.

Examples of some of the more common oxidizing agents include: oxygen, hydrogen peroxide, fluorine, chlorine, bromine, nitric acid, sulfuric acid, manganese dioxide, lead dioxide, nitrate, carbon dioxide, chromates and chlorates.

*Heat (Temperature):*  The term "temperature" is used in the tetrahedron to explain heat. Heat, at some temperature, is required to make fire.

*Chemical Chain Reaction:*  To have fire, typically there must be fuel, heat and oxygen. The fuel must be heated to give off gases and vapors, and sufficient heat must be present to ignite the gases and vapors. In the burning of either liquids or solid fuels, the vapors, which are distilled off and carried into the flame, contain atoms or molecules which may have not been totally consumed in the initial burning process. These free or liberated particles may be charged and could either attract or repel other particles.

Lesser burning takes place near the fuel source due to lack of oxygen molecules to react with the fuel particles. This area, between the vapor or gases and the visible flame, is referred to a "flame interface." Immediately above this area, oxygen molecules exist in sufficient number to produce energy reactions which create light, typically in the form of visible flames. This area is fed by the oxygen drawn into the fire. Throughout the flame, from the interface to the uppermost flame region, the fire process is continuous, and the chain reaction occurs simultaneously in varying degrees of intensity throughout the flame. The final byproducts of the fire finally are released or escape the flame as smoke and steam. Carbon, from the burning of hydrocarbons, is one of the elements released typically from many types of industrial fires, and since carbon is difficult to ignite, most of the visible smoke of these types of fires consists of unburned carbon particles.

## Fire Extinguishment

Included in the theory of the traditional three sided fire triangle were three methods of fire suppression:

1. Remove the fuel
2. Exclude the oxygen
3. Reduce the temperature

***With the introduction of the Fire Tetrahedron, a fourth suppression measure, "Interrupt the Chemical Chain Reaction" may be added.***

With the introduction of vaporizing liquids and dry chemical extinguishing agents, certain characteristics occurred which were not explained by the more common three fire extinguishing methods. When vaporizing liquids or dry chemical agents were used on fires they are observed to extinguish fire more rapidly than would the same quantity of some other types of smothering materials.

Certain activities in the flame area was enough evidence that some unexplained secondary reaction was taking place. Subsequent investigations disclosed that in heating these agents a chemical reaction takes place which is very similar to that explained in the chemical chain reaction section of the fire tetrahedron, with the difference being the nature of the compounds formed. The atoms released by the extinguishing agents would combine with the molecules already involved in the fire's chain reaction, and would form molecules which would not unite with the oxygen of the air, thereby breaking the chemical chain reaction and effectively suppressing the fire.

Illustration #57A provides a quick reference for identifying which types of fire extinguishers are typically recommended for the four classes of fires.

*Note: Always remember to refer to local regulations for a more thorough and complete listing of fire extinguishing methods and laws.*

## Portable Fire Extinguishers

"Incipient Stage Fire" refers to a fire which is in the initial or beginning stage and can be controlled or extinguished by portable fire extinguishers, Class II standpipe or small hose systems without the need for protective clothing or breathing apparatus.

Each portable fire extinguisher typically displays a rating on the faceplate showing the class of fire it is designed to control or extinguish.

Portable fire extinguishers, as shown in illustration #57B, are rated for Class A, B, C, and D fires. There are certain types of portable fire extinguishers that are marked with multiple ratings, such as AB, BC, and ABC.

|  | WATER TYPE | | | |
|---|---|---|---|---|
| **A**<br>(Green Triangle)<br><br>**B**<br>(Red Square)<br><br>**C**<br>(Blue Circle)<br><br>**D**<br>(Yellow Star) | STORED<br>PRESSURE | CARTRIDGE<br>OPERATED | WATER PUMP<br>TANK | SODA ACID |
| **CLASS A FIRES** ORDINARY<br>WOOD, PAPER, TRASH<br>HAVING GLOWING EMBERS COMBUSTIBLES | **YES** | **YES** | **YES** | **YES** |
| **CLASS B FIRES** FLAMMABLE<br>FLAMMABLE LIQUIDS, GASOLINE,<br>OIL, PAINTS, GREASE, ETC. LIQUIDS | **NO** | **NO** | **NO** | **NO** |
| **CLASS C FIRES** ELECTRICAL<br>ELECTRICAL EQUIPMENT EQUIPMENT | **NO** | **NO** | **NO** | **NO** |
| **CLASS D FIRES** COMBUSTIBLE<br>COMBUSTIBLE METALS METALS | **SPECIAL EXTINGUISHING AGENTS APPROVED BY** | | | |
| **USUAL OPERATION** | UPRIGHT<br>SQUEEZE HANDLE<br>OR TURN VALVE | TURN UPSIDE<br>DOWN AND PUMP | UPRIGHT AND<br>PUMP HANDLE | TURN UPSIDE<br>DOWN |
| **RANGE** | 30' - 40' | 30' - 40' | 30' - 40' | 30' - 40' |
| **SERVICING** | CHECK<br>AIR PRESSURE | WEIGH GAS CARTRIDGE<br>ADD WATER<br>IF REQUIRED | CHECK PUMP<br>AND FILL WITH WATER<br>ANNUALLY | DISCHARGE<br>ANNUALLY<br>AND RECHARGE |

**Illustration #57A - Fire Extinguisher Reference**

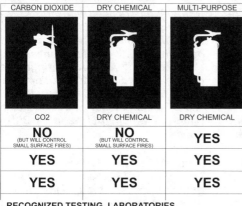

| CARBON DIOXIDE | DRY CHEMICAL | MULTI-PURPOSE |
|---|---|---|
| CO2 | DRY CHEMICAL | DRY CHEMICAL |
| **NO** (BUT WILL CONTROL SMALL SURFACE FIRES) | **NO** (BUT WILL CONTROL SMALL SURFACE FIRES) | **YES** |
| **YES** | **YES** | **YES** |
| **YES** | **YES** | **YES** |

**RECOGNIZED TESTING LABORATORIES**

| SQUEEZE RELEASE | RUPTURE CARTRIDGE SQUEEZE NOZZLE TO RELEASE | RUPTURE CARTRIDGE SQUEEZE NOZZLE TO RELEASE |
|---|---|---|
| 3' - 8' | 5' - 20' | 17' - 25' |
| WEIGH SEMI-ANNUALLY | WEIGH GAS CARTRIDGE AND CHECK CONDITION OF DRY POWDER | WEIGH GAS CARTRIDGE AND CHECK CONDITION OF DRY POWDER |

LETTERS indicate class of fuel on which the extinguisher will be effective.

| | |
|---|---|
| **A** | Ordinary Combustibles |
| **B** | Flammable Liquids |
| **C** | Electrical Equipment |
| **D** | Combustible Metals |

NUMBERS

Used with Letters on Class A and Class B Extinguishers only.

Indicate the relative effectiveness of the extinguisher.

- A 2-A Extinguisher will extinguish twice as much fuel as a 1-A Extinguisher.
- A 20-B Extinguisher will entinguish 20 times as much fuel as a 1-B Extinguisher.
- ABC is a mutiple purpose fire Extinguisher.

**Illustration #57A - Fire Extinguisher Reference (cont'd.)**          **Illustration #57B - Class *A* and Class *B* Extinguishers**

**Class A Fire Extinguishers:** Class A extinguishers are effective on ordinary combustibles such as wood, paper, and trash. The extinguisher works to cool the temperature (heat) of the burning combustible material below its ignition temperature. Class A fire extinguishers can use pressurized water, foaming agents, or multiple purpose dry chemical agents. Class A extinguishers may carry a numerical rating that indicates the effectiveness of the fire extinguisher.

**Class B Fire Extinguishers:** Class B extinguishers should be used on flammable liquids or gases, such as oils, paint, gasoline and greases. Class B extinguishers may come in several types including foam, carbon dioxide, ordinary dry chemical, multiple purpose dry chemical, halon or halon replacement extinguishers. Class B extinguishers may carry a numerical rating similar to Class A extinguishers which indicates the effectiveness of the fire extinguisher.

*Note: Numbers used with letters are only found on Class A and Class B portable fire extinguishers. These numbers indicate the relative effectiveness of the extinguisher. A "2-A" extinguisher is generally rated at extinguishing twice as much fuel as a "1-A" extinguisher. A "20-B" extinguisher will extinguish 20 times as much fuel as a "1-B" extinguisher.*

*Note: Although halon extinguishers (Halon 1211 and 1301) are effective in extinguishing certain fires, halon has been shown to be harmful to the environment and people and therefore is no longer being produced. However, there may still be halon extinguishers in your facility.*

*Note: "Halon 1211" means a colorless, faintly sweet smelling, electrically non-conductive liquefied gas (chemical formula CBrC1F(2)) which is a medium for extinguishing fires by inhibiting the chemical chain reaction of fuel and oxygen. It is also known as bromochlorodifluoromethane. "Halon 1301" means a colorless, odorless, electrically nonconductive gas (chemical formula CBrF(3)) which is a medium for extinguishing fires by inhibiting the chemical chain reaction of fuel and oxygen. It is also known as bromotrifluoromethane.*

***Class C Fire Extinguishers:*** Class *C* extinguishers are to be used specifically on electrical fires.   Class *C* extinguishers may contain carbon dioxide, ordinary dry chemical, multiple purpose dry chemical, halon or halon replacement agents.

Carbon dioxide, halon and halon replacements generally should not leave any harmful residue and are therefore preferable for sensitive electrical equipment and computer components. Never use water extinguishers or any other extinguishing agent which is capable of conducting electricity on Class *C* fires.

***Class D Fire Extinguishers:*** Class *D* extinguishers should only be used on metals which are considered combustible. Class *D* extinguishers are made with special agents specifically designed for the metal involved. In most cases, the extinguishing agent for Class *D* fires attempt to absorb heat and cool the metal below its ignition temperature. Class *D* fires will react extremely violent to water and other types of chemical extinguishing agents. Do not attempt to use these on Class *D* fires.

Class *D* extinguishers are considered to be unique, as they carry special extinguishing agents approved by recognized testing laboratories, those specializing in extinguishing metal based fires. Many of these extinguishers will include some reference to their effectiveness on certain types and amounts of specific metals.

Illustration #58 identifies a label from a multiple purpose portable fire extinguisher. This type of extinguisher uses a dry chemical extinguishing agent which is suitable for Class *A*, *B*, and *C* fires.

*Note: The extinguishing agent known as "Dry Chemical" means an extinguishing agent composed of very small particles of chemicals such as, but not limited to, sodium bicarbonate, potassium bicarbonate, urea based potassium bicarbonate, potassium chloride, or monammonium phosphate supplemented by special treatment to prevent packing and moisture absorption (caking) as well as to provide proper flow capabilities. Dry chemical does not include dry powders.*

*Note: "Foam" means a stable aggregation of small bubbles which flow freely over a burning liquid surface and form a cohesive blanket which seals combustible vapors and thereby extinguishes the fire.*

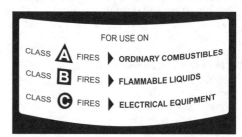

Illustration #58 - Label From a Multi-Purpose Unit

## General Requirements For Portable Fire Extinguishers:

- Portable fire extinguishers must be provided in the workplace and must be mounted in identifiable locations where they are readily accessible to employees without subjecting people to possible injury.

- Only approved portable fire extinguishers shall be used to meet the provincial, state and federal requirements.

- Carbon tetrachloride and/or chlorobromomethane extinguishing agents must not be made available or used in the workplace.

- Portable fire extinguishers must be maintained in a fully charged and operable condition and kept in their designated places at all times except during use.

- Employers must be responsible for all inspection, testing and maintenance of portable fire extinguishers.

- Employers must ensure that all portable fire extinguishers are subjected to an annual maintenance check at minimum. Records must be kept which identify the inspection, testing and maintenance dates and who completed the work.

- If portable fire extinguishers are removed from their station for service, maintenance or recharging, alternate or equivalent protection must be provided.

- Wherever portable fire extinguishers are provided, the employer is fully responsible for training and educating all employees with the general principles of fire extinguisher use and application and the hazards involved with incipient stage fire fighting.

## Portable Fire Extinguishers

- Emergency preparedness and emergency plans must also be included in the education program.
- Hydrostatic testing of portable fire extinguishers will be undertaken, dependent upon local and federal regulations, and can only be performed by trained and qualified personnel with suitable testing equipment and facilities. Table #6 identifies the test interval schedule for various types of portable fire extinguishers recommended by OSHA.
- In addition to an external visual examination of the portable extinguisher, an internal inspection of the shell and cylinder components must be done before performing a hydrostatic test.

| Types of Portable Fire Extinguishers | Test Interval (years) |
|---|---|
| Soda Acid (stainless steel shell) | 5 |
| Cartridge Operated Water and/or Antifreeze | 5 |
| Stored Pressure Water and/or Antifreeze | 5 |
| Wetting Agent | 5 |
| Foam (stainless steel shell) | 5 |
| Aqueous Fill Forming Foam (AFFF) | 5 |
| Loaded Stream | 5 |
| Dry Chemical with stainless steel shell | 5 |
| Carbon Dioxide | 5 |
| Dry Chemical, stored pressure, with mild steel, brass or aluminum shells | 12 |
| Dry Chemical, cartridge type or cylinder operated with mild steel shells | 12 |
| Halon 1211 or Halon 1301 | 12 |
| Dry Powder, cartridge type or cylinder operated with mild steel shells | 12 |

Table #6  - Test Intervals for Portable Extinguishers

*Note: In the United States all portable fire protection regulations may be referenced in section 1910.155 and 1910.157 of 29 CFR Part 1910.*

*Note: In Canada all portable fire extinguishers must be selected and installed in conformance to NFPA 10, "Portable Fire Extinguishers" and with the National Fire Code of Canada 1995.*

## Using a Portable Fire Extinguisher

It is very important and a requirement that all employees be trained on how to use the portable fire extinguishers located in their place of work. There are various models and designs of extinguishers, some are manually operated such as the water pump type, while others are more automatic in design, such as the pressurized or charged dry chemical extinguishers. The following description and illustration describes and demonstrates how a charged or pressurized portable fire extinguisher operates.

Typically, the "PASS" method is employed for charged or pressurized portable fire extinguishers. "PASS" refers to:

**P -** Pull the pin.

**A -** Aim the extinguisher nozzle at the base of the flames.

**S -** Squeeze the trigger while holding the extinguisher upright.

**S -** Sweep the extinguisher from side to side, covering the base area of the fire with the extinguishing agent.

*Caution: Only use a fire extinguisher when it is safe to do so. If the fire is too large, or if the flames are spreading, or there is a threat that your path of escape is blocked - LEAVE THE AREA IMMEDIATELY.*

## Using a Portable Fire Extinguisher

Illustration #59A demonstrates the four basic steps of PASS for using charged or pressurized portable fire extinguishers.

Illustration #59B serves as a reminder for how to use a fire extinguisher.

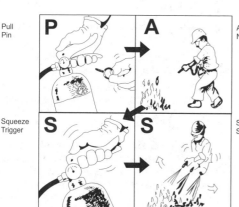

Pull
Pin

**P**

**A**

Aim
Nozzle

Squeeze
Trigger

**S**

**S**

Sweep
Side-To-Side

HOLD
UPRIGHT

PULL
PIN

STAND
BACK
8-10 ft

AIM AT
BASE
OF FIRE

**Illustration #59A - How to Use a Portable Fire Extinguisher**

**Illustration #59B - Reminder for Using a Fire Extinguisher**

## FIRE PREVENTION/SAFETY

Illustrations #60A and #60B demonstrate how a fire extinguisher is used.

Illustration #60B is a label commonly located on small portable fire extinguishers.

Sweep Side-To-Side at Base of Fire

**Illustration #60A - Fire Extinguisher Use Instructions**

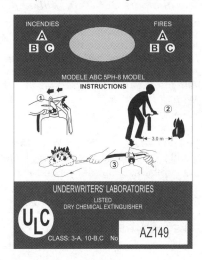

**Illustration #60B - How a Fire Extinguisher is Used**

*Note: Try not to panic. When a fire starts, think of your own safety FIRST, THEN the safety of others SECOND. Although fire is an extreme situation, when one panics, dangerous mistakes can be made. The calm person is the one who assesses the extent of the fire, calls the fire department, and acts quickly to contain or extinguish the blaze. This person is acting responsibly.*

Remember:
- Should your path of escape be threatened,
- Should the extinguisher run out of agent,
- Should the extinguisher prove to be ineffective or not function adequately,
- Should you no longer be able to safely protect yourself and fight the fire:

*LEAVE THE AREA IMMEDIATELY!!*

**Never Fight a Fire:**
- If the fire is spreading beyond the location where it first started.
- If you can't fight the fire with your back to an accessible escape exit.
- If the fire has potential for blocking your only escape.
- If you don't have adequate fire fighting equipment.

*If any of these conditions exist, don't fight the fire yourself, call for help immediately. If necessary, do not hesitate to use the fire extinguisher to clear an escape path.*

## Personal Cautions and Safety

Always be especially aware of smoke and noxious fumes from fires. These fumes enter into the lungs and can leave a person unconscious and in great danger as the flames advance. All fires consume oxygen in order to sustain burning. Most victims of a fire suffocate from lack of oxygen and eventually will die. Usually they are already unconscious or dead before the flames consume them.

Inside a building or enclosed space which is in flames, try to shut all the doors or seal off any open places that are within your reach. If trapped, and you can make your way to an exit or opening, get down to your hands and knees and crawl. This is very important because smoke and heat rises rapidly, and you will inhale less smoke near the floor. Outside, get away from the direction of the flames and smoke to avoid inhaling noxious fumes and particles.

## Extinguish a Small Fire

***Class A Fires:*** Extinguish ordinary combustibles, such as wood, paper and trash, by cooling the material below its ignition temperature and soaking the fibers and loose material to prevent re-ignition. Use pressurized water, foam, or multiple purpose dry chemical fire extinguishers for Class *A* fires. See illustration #61.

Burning Paper,
Wood, Trash

**Illustration #61 - Class *A* Fires**

***Class B Fires:*** Extinguish flammable liquids, greases or gases by removing the oxygen, preventing the vapors from reaching the ignition source or inhibiting the chemical chain reaction. Foam, carbon dioxide, ordinary dry chemical and multiple purpose dry chemical fire extinguishers may be used to fight Class *B* fires. See illustration #62.

Burning
Flammable
Liquids

**Illustration #62 - Class *B* Fires**

***Class C Fires:*** Extinguish energized or non-energized electrical equipment and computer systems using an extinguishing agent which is considered nonconductive, (is not capable of conducting electric current). Carbon dioxide, ordinary dry chemical and multiple purpose dry chemical fire extinguishers are recommended for use on Class *C* fires. Never use any water type extinguishers to fight an energized electrical or computer system fire. See illustrations #63 and #64.

***Note: Multiple purpose dry chemical extinguishers may leave residues which may be quite harmful to sensitive electrical and electronic components and computer equipment. Carbon dioxide fire extinguishers are preferred for usage on Class C fires where sensitive and expensive electric and computer equipment is protected from the threat of fire. Carbon dioxide leaves very little residue. Halon was used, and may still be used in some locations, as it too, left very little residue, similar to carbon dioxide.***

Electrical Fire

**Illustration #63 - Class *C* Fires**

**Class D Fires:** Extinguish combustible metals and materials such as magnesium, titanium, potassium and sodium with dry powder extinguishing agents specially designed for specific metals and materials involved. Typically, and in most cases, the extinguishing agent absorbs the heat from the burning metal or material, cooling it in the process to below its ignition temperature. See illustration #65.

*Note: Time is of essence in fire fighting. The smaller the fire the easier it is to extinguish. Know the location of alarms and extinguishers. Know the nearest fire exit or have knowledge of the escape routes. Always remember to proceed to fire exits and escapes in a quiet, orderly fashion.*

Never Use Water On Computer Fires

**Illustration #64 - Class *C* Fires**

## How To Prevent Fires

***Preventing Class A Fires:*** Class *A* fires can be normally prevented and avoided through simple, regular, routine housekeeping and cleanup activities:

- Keep storage and work areas free from trash, paper, cloths, fibers, sawdust and pieces of wood.

- Place oily and greasy rags, cloths and similar debris in covered metal containers away from any flame producing source.

- Regularly empty trash containers and do not let them become overfilled.

- Sweep up or hose down the floor with water occasionally, to ensure your work area and floor is free from combustible materials.

Burning Metal Materials

**Illustration #65** - Class *D* Fires

**Preventing Class B Fires:** Class B fires can generally be prevented by taking special precautions when working with and around flammable liquids and gases:

- Keep flammable liquids stored in tightly closed, secured, self closing, spill-proof containers, and only pour from the storage container the amount of liquid required.
- Never refuel gasoline powered equipment in a confined space, or in areas where there is a presence of open flames, such as furnaces, hot water heaters and boilers.
- Never refuel gasoline, propane or natural gas powered equipment while the equipment is hot or running.
- Always store flammable liquids away from spark - producing sources.
- Use flammable liquids only in well vented areas.

- Try to limit storage container capacity for flammable liquids to 5 gallons (20 liters).
- Make sure outside storage containers for flammable liquids are at least 20 feet (6 metres) away from other buildings and structures.

**Preventing Class C Fires:** Class C fires, where electrical equipment is used or misused, are usually one of the major causes of fire in the workplace. Class C fires can be very difficult to prevent, fight and control. Extra care must be taken in fighting any Class C fire, as the electrical equipment involved could be energized, therefore making this a very hazardous condition. Always assume that the electrical equipment is energized when preparing to fight these types of fires. Water must never be applied to energized electrical fires. Other considerations for preventing Class C fires include:

## How To Prevent Fires

- Carry out visual inspections of old, worn, damaged or broken wiring and fittings associated with electrical equipment.
- Keep electric motors clean and dust free and try to prevent them from overheating.
- Report any hazardous conditions with electrical equipment immediately to your supervisor or to the electrical specialists.
- Do not let water or moisture of any kind get anywhere near electrical panels and electrical control rooms. These areas must also be kept clean and dust free.
- Plan to investigate any electrical appliance, tool or equipment that gives off a strange smell. Unusual odors can be the first sign of overheating, melting or burning.
- Don't overload wall outlets; one wall outlet should have no more than two plugs.

- Never install a fuse rated higher than specified for an electrical circuit.
- Keep electrical control rooms free of flammable liquids, metal tools and equipment, rags, cloths, and anything else that does not belong there. These rooms are not storage places.
- Don't let forklifts or other wheel equipment drive or roll over extension cords and other types of electrical wiring.
- Make sure utility lights have some type of approved guard or cage over them. Direct contact with an uncovered light bulb can easily ignite most combustible materials.

***Preventing Class D Fires:*** Class *D* fires can be extremely difficult to contain and extinguish. One of the best ways to prevent a Class *D* fire is to always follow the specific working and handling guidelines identified by the manufacturer or your organization for these special combustible metals.

Failure to follow such guidelines can quickly lead to serious situations. Some of the more common metal materials to be cautious with include: magnesium, titanium, aluminum, potassium, and sodium.

## Inspecting Portable Extinguishers

Regularly scheduled inspections of portable fire extinguishers must be carried out by qualified personnel. It is important to have records for these inspections and a set routine of inspection items.

The following list identifies several key inspection considerations:

- Make sure the class of the extinguisher is safe to use on those fires likely to occur in the immediate area.
- Check for any visible leaks or seal breaks in and around the nozzle, hose and fittings.

- Look at the indicator gauge to determine whether the extinguisher is full and charged. Feel the weight to anticipate when it needs to be recharged.
- Has the extinguisher been tampered with or used previously?
- Are all the extinguishers in their properly assigned locations and are they adequately mounted, positioned and secured?
- Make sure that the extinguisher pin, nozzle and nameplates are intact and functional.
- Report any missing, empty or damaged fire extinguishers, and replace immediately.

Each fire extinguisher should have some type of tag attached to it which identifies the certification number for the extinguisher. Normally, on the reverse side of this tag is an area for recording the monthly inspections.

Refer to illustration #66A and #66B for an example of this type of extinguisher certification and inspection record tag.

Fire codes normally state that each portable fire extinguisher shall have a tag securely attached to it showing the maintenance or recharge date, the servicing agency, and the signature of the person who performed the service.

## Sprinkler Systems

Sprinkler systems refer to a piping system designed in accordance with local, and federal fire protection engineering standards and installed to control or extinguish fires. The system must include an adequate and reliable water supply and a network of specially sized piping and sprinklers which are correctly interconnected. The system must have a control valve and a device for actuating an alarm when the system is in operation.

**Illustration #66A and 66B - Extinguisher Certification Tag**

One of the general requirements for sprinkler systems is regular inspections and maintenance of the system. A usual requirement is periodic testing by provincial, state and federal regulations to ensure that the system is functioning properly. Testing of the system normally includes:

- Flushing of underground connections.
- Hydrostatic testing of system piping and connections.
- Air testing in dry pipe systems.
- Testing of all valve operations.
- Testing of drainage facilities.

Additionally, to ensure that the sprinkler fire protection systems are effective at all times, consideration must be given to the following factors:

*Water Supply:* There must be provision of adequate water supply to each sprinkler head, and that the water supply is capable of providing design water flow for at least 30 minutes.

An auxiliary water supply or equivalent protection must be provided when the main water supply is out of service.

*Hose Connections:* In some sprinkler systems it may be necessary to attach hose connections to standpipes for fire fighting use to wet sprinkler systems provided that the water supply is sufficient to satisfy demand for the sprinklers and the standpipes.

*Protection of Piping:* For those operations and services where freezing can occur, protection for the piping must be provided to ensure that there is no freeze-up within the sprinkler system. Also, some type of exterior corrosion protection is required to maintain the integrity of the piping, valving and connections.

*Drainage:* There has to be some method included in the sprinkler system so it can be completely drained if required.

*Sprinklers:* In order to meet provincial, state and federal regulations, only approved sprinklers can be used in the sprinkler fire protection system. Any older style sprinkler heads may eventually have to be replaced with newer designed ones. Regular inspection and service of sprinkler heads must be performed and that no mechanical damage or operational faults are present.

*Sprinkler Alarms:* Depending on local regulations, there may be a requirement for having an audible water alarm system which sounds a signal on the premises upon water flow through the system.

*Sprinkler Spacing:* Sprinklers must be spaced to provide maximum protection and coverage per area of each sprinkler and there must be minimum interference to the discharge pattern by building or other structural elements.

Local provincial, state and federal regulations will identify spacing and clearance distances for sprinkler head locations.

*Sprinkler Guards:* It is recommended that sprinkler heads be protected by sprinkler guards where there is a possibility of mechanical damage.

*Note: In the United States the design and installation of sprinkler systems for fire protection is referred to in the general industry standards of 29 CFR part 1910.159 Automatic Sprinkler Systems.*

*Note: In Canada the design and installation of sprinkler fire protection systems is stated in section 6.5.1.1 of the NFC and also must be to conformance under the National Building Code of Canada 1995.*

## Standpipe Systems

Standpipe systems are commonly used for industrial and commercial fire protection. They primarily are used to provide a sufficient water supply to various locations and floors in and around buildings and equipment.

Illustration #67 - Standpipe and Hose Cabinet

The placement and location of standpipes is often determined by local fire regulations. Illustration #67 identifies a type of standpipe typically located in buildings and plants. The fire department or emergency response team would remove the hose from the enclosed case, and the valve would be opened to supply pressurized water for extinguishing the fire

In other types of standpipe designs, there would be no hose. The fire department or emergency response team would connect their hose to the standpipe and use the standpipe for their water supply to fight the fire.

The typical hose connections on these types of standpipes are classed as "fire department" connections and are there so the local fire department can hook up their hoses into a reliable water supply.

The fire department, with the aid of pumps off their "pumpers" will boost the water supply pressure to a desired pressure in order to successfully fight the fire.

*Note: In United States, the requirements for standpipe systems are under section 1910.158 of 29 CFR Part 1910.*

*Note: In Canada, inspection, testing and maintenance of standpipe and hose systems must conform to NFPA 14, "Installation of Standpipe and Hose Systems."*

*Note: In section 6.6.1.1 of the NFC it is stated that water supplies for fire protection, including hydrants, shall be maintained so as to be capable of providing the flow and pressure of water for which they were designed.*

*Note: OSHA, Section 1910.158 requires that hemp or linen hose on existing systems must be unracked, physically inspected for deterioration, and reracked with a different fold pattern at least annually (the hose will rot in the fold if not used).*

## Ventilation

The need for ventilation is very important when a fire occurs. Ventilation is typically described as the removal of hot gases and smoke from the fire area and nearby surroundings and replacing it with cooler air from an outside source. The removal of hot gases and smoke from the fire area will improve the visibility and breathing for the fire rescue operations and extinguishing attack. Proper and timely ventilation may also help to stop the spread of the fire too.

When fire burns in a confined area, the smoke and heat will rise. In burning buildings, the smoke and heat typically rises to the ceiling area quickly. This smoke and possible toxic gases become super heated and with the introduction of oxygen, can cause a serious situation known as "back draft."

This is why it is very important to consider ventilation when extinguishing fires, especially in confined spaces and buildings.

The best place to ventilate a fire in a building is to do this as close as possible over the top and above the fire area. Many factors will have a bearing on fire ventilation. For example, consideration must be given to location and size of natural openings, wind direction, building construction, equipment and machinery location, and the extent and area of the fire.

## Smoke Explosions or Back Drafts

During a fire, flammable gases are vaporized from the combustible materials. When these gases are heated to their ignition temperature, they too will burn if there is sufficient oxygen. If there is insufficient oxygen, the unburned gases may collect in spaces and areas within the building or structure, or may even completely fill the entire building or structure.

Such a condition needs only the admission of sufficient fresh air at the right moment to cause immediate and rapid burning of these gases, and the subsequent expansion of these gases may be sufficient to cause an explosion. Such an explosion is commonly referred to as a "back draft."

The degree of intensity of a back draft depends upon the amount of confinement, the amount of heated gases, and the rate and volume of fresh air admitted from the outside. This type of serious condition can be made safer by providing proper ventilation. If the building or structure is opened at the highest point possible, the heated gases and smoke can be more easily expelled, thus reducing the chance for having serious explosions.

Illustration #68A and illustration #68B demonstrate how back draft conditions occur and what the end result can be if improper ventilation is provided.

Low oxygen
High heat
Smoldering fire
High fuel vapor concentrations

PRE BACK DRAFT

Illustration #68A - Pre Back Draft

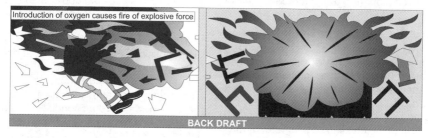

Introduction of oxygen causes fire of explosive force

BACK DRAFT

Illustration #68B - Back Draft

## Emergency Procedure Plans

It is very important that organizations in business and industry have a written, up-to-date Emergency Procedure Plan for their workplace employees in case of emergencies such as fire. The plan must provide specific and detailed instructions on how to evacuate the building and how people are to conduct themselves in emergency situations. These plans and procedures must be easily read and understood by everyone.

It is imperative that the employer provide all employees with training in the emergency procedures. It is everyone's responsibility to know and understand the emergency procedures for their workplace.

Typically, business and industry identifies certain individuals or teams to take charge and to lead the emergency procedures.

The written emergency procedures really serve as an "action plan" and should include the following types of information:

- The plan must identify who the designated fire wardens, emergency action leaders or individuals are who have been assigned "take charge" duties and responsibilities during the emergency. Their roles must be clearly understood by everyone.

- The plan must contain information about evacuation and escape routes from the building and/or vicinity. Primary and secondary routes must be included.

- Maps or diagrams which display floor plans and evacuation and escape routes must be posted and include simple emergency instructions. It is important to periodically review these with all employees and to make certain that nothing has changed.

- It is imperative that the plan include a warning to not have stairways, doorways, or other exit areas blocked off, locked or cluttered up with parts and equipment that do not belong anywhere near these areas.

- Any disabled worker or those with a history of certain medical conditions should be assigned to capable individuals or emergency leaders who can guide them to safety during the emergency.

- Emergency Fire Drills should be scheduled periodically to test the emergency procedure plan and to help determine any shortcomings or areas where improvements could be made. The Fire Drill should be used to find problems before the fire happens, not learning the hard way about problems after the real fire occurred. It is best to treat Fire Drills as the "real thing."

## Responsibilities of the Fire Warden

All assigned Fire Wardens or Emergency Action Leaders have specific duties and responsibilities to carry out before, during and after the fire emergency evacuation. The following list identifies several considerations:

- All Fire Wardens request that if anyone has an outside visitor with them and an evacuation is taking place, then this employee is responsible for escorting the visitor to the designated marshaling area.

- Fire Wardens or Emergency Action Leaders must be responsible for assisting disabled workers out during the evacuation, and offer assistance to those workers having a history of medical problems.

- Fire Wardens or Emergency Action Leaders will sweep (check) their designated areas to ensure everyone has safely cleared the area.

- They may be advised to close certain doors.
- Emergency Action Leaders must have an alternate.
- They must know the location of the designated marshaling area(s).
- They must do their personnel count (head count) at the marshaling area and report this information to those in charge of the emergency evacuation.
- The person(s) who is in charge of the complete emergency evacuation will advise the wardens or action leaders on further action required.
- It is important to close doors as the sweep is done.
- The Fire Warden or Emergency Action Leader may instruct workers to return to their work areas when advised to do so, as the person in charge of the evacuation has determined the areas to be safe.

## Evacuating Safely

1. Know and follow the procedures outlined in your organization's Emergency Procedures Plan.

2. During an emergency evacuation, proceed calmly, but be quick.

3. Never ever use an elevator to evacuate yourself and others. If there was a sudden power loss, you and others will be trapped inside the building.

4. Close the door if you are last out of a room. Do not lock it. Locked doors hinder search and rescue operations.

5. If you and others have to use a stairwell, go directly there and proceed down to the ground floor and exit the building immediately. Help people who are experiencing difficulty going down the stairs.

6. Keep low to the ground to avoid smoke, toxic gases and noxious fumes.

7. Remember to cover up your nose and mouth with a damp cloth to help breath if there is smoke or fumes in the air.

8. Once you are outside the building or structure, report immediately to the marshaling area so others know that you are not trapped inside. You now can be part of the "head count" and have been accounted for.

9. Remain calm and try not to be too noisy, as you may miss out on any further instructions. Help to comfort others and to keep them calm. If you display panic, others will panic.

**What To Do If You Are Trapped**

1. Don't panic. Your ability to think clearly could ultimately save your life.

2. If you are trying to escape an area, never open a door without feeling it first.

3. Use the back of your hand to prevent burning your palm.

4. If the door is too hot, try another exit.

5. If there is no other exit, attempt to seal off the cracks and narrow openings all around the door and vents with anything available.

6. If you are having trouble breathing, remain close to the floor. If possible, ventilate the room by opening or even breaking a window.

7. If trapped, and if possible, look for a telephone or radio to call outside, giving them your exact location. Remain there and try to breathe slowly and stay calm.

8. If you hear people outside the area you are trapped in, attempt to communicate with them.

**What To Do If You or Others Catch On Fire**

1. If your clothing catches on fire, stop, drop and roll. Do not run! This will only feed the fire with more oxygen, allowing it to burn faster.

2. If a co-worker catches on fire, smother the flames by grabbing a jacket, blanket, rug, or tarp and wrapping it around him or her quickly.

3. Always try to comfort the co-worker after this type of incident. They are usually quite traumatized by this experience. Seek medical attention immediately.

## Fire Inspection

Due to the very extreme consequences that result from a fire in the workplace or home, it is prudent upon the employer or worker to perform fire inspections on a regular basis. Fire inspections must be part of the organization's "due diligence" plans, as successful inspections can help prevent accidents, unnecessary damage and loss to property and people.

When fire inspections are conducted, there are two primary areas to inspect:

1. Fire Fighting Equipment
2. Fire Hazards

### Fire Fighting Equipment Inspection

Inspections carried out would include at minimum the following fire fighting and protection equipment:

- Portable fire extinguishers.
- Sprinkler systems.
- Standpipes and hydrants.
- Pumper unit (fire truck).
- Fire fighting tools and hoses.
- Fire detection and alarm systems.
- Emergency procedures and plans.
- Signs, floor plans, color coding.

Each type of fire fighting and protection equipment would require a specific type of detailed inspection and frequency for the inspections. Each type of equipment should have a check list for ensuring consistent items of the various equipment is inspected.

The person who performs these equipment inspections must realize the importance of inspection functions. There is nothing more serious than having a piece of fire fighting equipment checked off as being in good working order when actually it is inoperable or malfunctioning.

Training the people to do these types of inspections is imperative. The inspector must be familiar with all the components of the equipment. Typically, a qualified person from the safety department or fire protection group would undertake inspections and be responsible for ensuring that the fire fighting and protection equipment is in proper order.

### *Fire Hazard Inspection*

After the fire fighting and protection equipment inspection is completed, the next part of the fire inspection is to check for conditions commonly referred to as "fire hazards."

Particular attention must be paid to the following conditions which could lead to or have the potential for serious fire related consequences if problems exist:

- Storage of flammable liquids.
- General shop and plant housekeeping.
- Combustible materials (paper, scrap, rags, lumber).
- Electrical hazards.
- Chemicals and acid storage.
- Spills, leaks, runoff of flammable liquids.
- Storage and handling of explosives.
- Storing batteries.
- Lubrication storage and handling.

- Accumulation of dust, dirt, fibers.
- Smoking, cigarette butts.
- Storage and handling of pressurized cylinders and tanks.
- Protection from welding, cutting, air arcing, grinding sparks.
- Friction from parts or machinery wearing together.
- Overheating of machinery.
- Dangers from open flames from processes and operations.

*Note: What must always be kept in mind when conducting fire inspections is to take the job seriously, don't rush, and be thorough as you inspect each area for hazardous conditions or pieces of fire fighting and protection equipment.*

Fire Inspections are conducted in order to find problems and assess their risks before fire related incidents or accidents and other losses occur. A well managed fire inspection program can meet the following goals:

- Identify potential problems.
- Identify equipment deficiencies.
- Identify improper employee actions.
- Identify effects of changes in processes or equipment.
- Identify inadequacies in remedial actions.
- Provides you with valuable self-appraisal information.
- Demonstrates commitment and proactiveness.

## Glossary of Common Fire Terms

*Auto-ignition Temperature:*
The lowest temperature at which a flammable gas or vapor-air mixture will ignite without the introduction of a flame, spark or other ignition source; ignition is influenced by different reactions and compositions within the substances and materials involved.

*Blaze:*
Free burning, spectacular fire characterized by a generous amount of wild, high, erratic flame.

*Body of Fire:*
Intense mass of flame accompanied by heavy smoke under pressure, indicating heat of fire.

*Combustible:*
Materials which ignite and burn at temperatures in the presence of oxygen; the material is consumed by the fire.

*Combustion:*
Rapid oxidation of a flammable material, typically accompanied by flames and heat.

*Explosive Range:*
The range of vapor or gas and air mixture which will burn or explode.

*Extinguish:*
To completely control and put out the fire; so no abnormal heat or smoke remains; to quench.

**Fire:**
Rapid oxidation of combustible materials which produces heat and light.

**Fire Point:**
The lowest temperature at which a substance will give off sufficient vapors which can sustain continuous burning when ignited.

**Flame:**
Emitted light from burning vapors or gases and incandescent particles coming from the fire.

**Flashover:**
The stage of a fire at which all surfaces and objects are heated to their ignition temperature and ignition (burning) occurs almost at once over the entire surface.

**Flash Point:**
The lowest temperature at which a substance will give off enough vapors to form a flammable mixture of vapors which will ignite with the introduction of an ignition source; will not sustain continuous burning; may only be momentarily.

**Fuel:**
Combustible material required in order to produce fire; combined with oxygen and heat, fire occurs.

**Heat:**
Temperatures above the normal temperature produced by the burning or oxidation process; required to produce fire; combined with oxygen and fuel.

*Ignition Temperatures:*
Lowest point at which a combustible material will begin to burn.

*Oxidation:*
Any chemical reaction in which electrons are transferred; act or process of oxidizing.

*Oxygen:*
A gas which is present in the atmosphere, at 21% concentration; essential element required in fire, combined with fuel and heat; required to sustain breathing and human life.

*Oxygen Deficiency:*
Insufficient oxygen to support life or combustion; where the oxygen content of the atmosphere falls below 16%, flame production will be reduced and asphyxiation of humans can occur.

*Smoke:*
Combination of gases, carbon particles, steam, vapors and other products of incomplete combustion; hinders breathing, obscures vision, can delay access to contain the fire.

*Suppression:*
The total and complete work of extinguishing the fire after its discovery.

*Volatility:*
The tendency of a liquid or solid to vaporize; the lower the flash point, the more volatile the substance; for example, gasoline is very volatile.

# SECTION FOUR

# CONFINED SPACE ENTRY

## Confined Space Hazards

Every year, thousands of workers are exposed to possible illness, injury or death in what is commonly referred to as "confined spaces." Every confined space, and there are many types in any work place, exposes the person entering to an unpredictable environment which can be deadly, and not have any apparent sign of being so. To ensure that every worker enters and exits a confined space safely, the employer in most cases must establish safe work procedures which are tailored to meet specific hazards of each identified confined space.

They can appear safe at first glance, but confined spaces often contain unseen risks and hazards. Some types of confined spaces can be difficult to enter and even more difficult to exit. Poor ventilation can expose workers to unseen dangers, such as accumulations of deadly gases or insufficient oxygen for breathing.

In many cases, all that is required to protect workers who must enter these potentially dangerous zones is appropriate education and training and a strict set of enforced confined space entry procedures.

Employers have a strong responsibility under law, both in Canada and the United States, to establish effective confined space entry procedures and to educate their workers and supervisors in identifying hazards, using the proper monitoring and protective equipment, and for having emergency response systems in place for rescuing any trapped or downed workers without endangering others. It then becomes the worker's responsibility to comply with the established procedures. The safety and environmental departments of many industries are responsible for developing the confined space entry procedures as well as providing training for the employees.

In the United States, the regulations governing confined space entry are specified by the Occupational Safety and Health Administration (OSHA). These regulations are identified by OSHA as 29 CFR 1910.146 Permit Required Confined Spaces.

Briefly, the standard requires employers to, among other things, to inspect their work places for confined spaces, evaluate any identified spaces for potential hazards, develop a written confined space entry program which includes a permit system, develop safe procedures to control identified hazards and educate employees in proper procedures for safe entry. OSHA estimates that implementation of their Permit Required Confined Space standard will prevent dozens of fatalities and thousands of lost work days per year in the United States.

In Canada there is both federal and provincial occupational health and safety legislation and acts which are issued to regulate confined space entry. The Canada Labour Code includes confined space entry in the Canada Confined Spaces Regulations. Always be sure to know what the various federal and provincial confined space entry regulations are for the type of confined space workers will be exposed to. The intent is to be in compliance with these confined space entry requirements and to prevent unauthorized entry into confined spaces and to protect the health and safety of those who must enter confined spaces.

Under current requirements for confined space entry, the basic elements of a managed confined space entry program would include:

- Identification of locations or situations where confined space entry and work is required;
- Potential hazards present in each type of confined space must be identified and/or classified;
- Use of an entry and work permit system to ensure that only authorized, trained personnel enter a confined space;
- Provision of appropriate procedures for carrying out work in the confined space, including, but not limited to procedures for related activities such as lockout/tagout, air monitoring, respiratory protection, fire protection, and emergency response and rescue;
- Education and training of workers who perform work or supervise work being performed in confined spaces.

The National Institute of Occupational Health and Safety (NIOSH) reported recently that during a six year study period from 1983 - 1989, 37% of confined space deaths resulted from untrained rescuers who had entered a confined space to assist someone else who was in trouble. Confined space accidents are not common, but when they do occur, they are often fatal. There are many case studies in Canada and the United States to back this statement up. Typically, a confined space accident will involve more than one fatality due to an untrained person attempting to rescue a co-worker who has either become trapped or has collapsed inside the confined space.

There are several similar definitions of "confined spaces", as applied to an industrial setting.

The OSHA definition for confined space means a space that:

1. Is large enough and so configured that an employee can bodily enter and perform assigned work.

2. Has limited or restricted means for entry or exit (for example, tanks, vessels, silos, storage bins, hoppers, vaults, and pits are spaces that may have limited means of entry).

3. Is not designed for continuous employee occupancy.

A second definition of confined space means an enclosed or partially enclosed space that:

1. Is not designed or intended for human occupancy except for the purpose of performing work.

2. Has restricted means of access and egress.

3. May become hazardous to an employee entering it due to:

a. The design, construction, location or atmosphere.

b. The materials or substances in it.

c. Any other conditions relating to it.

A third definition of confined space means a tank, process vessel, underground vault, tunnel, trench, pit, excavation, or other enclosure not designed or intended for human occupancy, except for the purpose of performing work.

1. That has a limited number of openings for entry and exit.

2. That has poor natural ventilation.

3. In which there may be an oxygen deficient atmosphere.

4. In which there may be an airborne hazardous substance.

Some examples of confined spaces are identified in illustration #69.

## Confined Space Entry Program

*One of the most important points to remember for both employers and workers when setting up confined space entry programs is that each confined space is unique to itself. There is no blanket procedure for entering and working safely in all confined spaces. It would be impossible to impose one procedure for every situation. It won't work and can, in fact, be very dangerous.*

*It is important to keep in mind that each confined space entry program must be tailored to the particular hazards found in each confined space in the workplace*

Employers should consider taking the following steps for planning, developing, implementing and managing their confined space entry program:

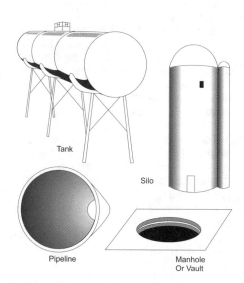

Tank

Silo

Pipeline

Manhole
Or Vault

**Illustration #69 - Examples of Confined Spaces**

**The steps are:**

***Step One:*** *Know The Legislation and Regulations*

An employer's first step in developing a confined space entry program is to research the company's responsibility to its workers according to the law. Industries in each province of Canada are governed by their own occupational health and safety regulations for confined spaces, as are certain industries which are under federal jurisdictions. In United States, OSHA provides specific regulations for confined space entry under the standard 29 CFR 1910.146. The regulations whether for Canada or United States, become the framework for confined space entry procedures and for employee training programs.

***Step Two:*** *Identify Confined Spaces*

The next step for the employer is to conduct a workplace audit to identify all confined spaces which can be encountered at the worksite. A confined space usually has limited or restricted entry and exit because of its design, structure, or location and may contain or produce dangerous accumulations of hazardous gases, have insufficient oxygen, or present dangerous conditions such as those found in trenches, ditches and other pits or holes commonly found at construction worksites.

***Step Three:*** *Identify Potential Hazards*

For each confined space identified by the workplace audit, the employer and workers must work together to determine the potential atmospheric and general safety hazards found in each particular confined space.

*Step Four:* Develop Confined Space Entry Program Procedures

Upon completion of the identification steps, as outlined in Steps Two and Three, the employer will prepare specific procedures for various confined space entry requirements. Procedures must be developed for entry requirements, exit requirements, atmospheric testing and monitoring, breathing apparatus, other personal protective equipment, fire protection, escape procedures, rescue procedures and an outline which specifies the employee education and training program requirements.

*Step Five:* Educating the Employees

If the Confined Space Entry Program is to be fully effective, the established procedures must be communicated to the workers.

One of the best methods for doing this is to provide a comprehensive training program on the confined space entry program, and incorporate not only classroom training, but include on-the-job training sessions in a controlled environment in various confined space locations. This training should be given to both workers and supervisors, also include members of the occupational health and safety committee, the rescue team and the fire protection team.

Employees who work in confined spaces must be given specific instructions on: basic hazard and risk assessment; lockout/tagout and blanking off procedures; use of monitoring and testing equipment; ignition control; use of respiratory equipment and other personal protection equipment; fall protection; emergency entry/exit procedures and rescues; communication systems; first aid and cardiopulmonary resuscitation.

A summary of the more common hazards to evaluate in the workplace audit are found below. This listing is not complete, but serves as an excellent reference to determining the potential atmospheric and general safety hazards particular to a confined space. Use this summary when preparing the details identified in Step Three, Identifying Potential Hazards.

*Note: As mentioned previously, no confined space entry procedure is suitable or practical for all confined spaces. Procedures vary depending on the characteristics of the space and its potential hazards. But there usually are specific standards, practices and rules that must be incorporated into every written confined space entry procedure.*

## Potential Hazard Assessment In Confined Spaces
### Explosive Atmospheres
Explosive atmospheres in confined spaces are typically caused by the presence of combustible and explosive gases. Common gases include: sewer gases, methane, natural gas, propane, kerosene, diesel fuel, solvents, and paints.

### Toxic Gases
Toxic gases are harmful to workers as they can be irritable, cause nausea, restrict breathing and cause respiratory failure. Toxic gases include: carbon monoxide, carbon dioxide, nitrogen dioxide, and hydrogen sulphide.

**Potential Hazard Assessment In Confined Spaces Cont'd.**

### Fumes, Mists and Dusts

Examples common in this category include welding fumes, burning metals, grinding particles, coal dust, grain dust, sand and dirt, various spray applications such as paints, insecticides and herbicides.

### Smoke

Smoke is a combination of gases, vapors, fumes and dusts as a result of combustion. Examples include burning materials, metal welding and cutting processes and excessively heated lubricants and flammable liquids.

### Oxygen Deficiency

Oxygen deficiency is caused by the displacement of oxygen by other gases, or by biological or chemical reactions, such as rusting or burning

### Oxygen Enrichment

Oxygen enrichment creates an explosive atmosphere where too rich of an oxygen mixture is provided in the environment. This oxygen enriched environment can easily lead to serious explosive conditions.

### Poor Ventilation Systems

Improper ventilation systems can result in oxygen level variations, build up of toxic gases and the introduction of biological agents and explosive gases.

**Potential Hazard Assessment In Confined Spaces Cont'd.**

### Biological Agents

Biological agents refer to bacteria and viruses, often located near health facilities, hospitals, food industries or industrial settings which are processing biological agents.

### Hazardous Entries and Exits

There are many types of hazardous entries and exits, often caused by openings being too small, too narrow, too high, or very difficult to negotiate. Extra care must be taken in situations like this to plan for emergency evacuations and for the use of respiratory equipment in these tight or awkward conditions.

### Mechanical Equipment

Includes all powered machinery and equipment such as gears, belts, chains, pulleys, drive shafts, couplings, agitators, fans, mills, refiners and scrapers. This equipment must be immobilized and de-energized before entry into the space where the equipment is located

### Piping and Valve Systems

There are many types of pipe and valve systems where workers must enter to perform various work functions. Pipes and valves include all main lines, supply lines and secondary lines which run in and out of confined spaces and each must be cut off (blanked/closed off) before entry.

**Potential Hazard Assessment In Confined Spaces Cont'd.**

*Residual Materials*

Residual materials include corrosive and toxic materials/chemicals remaining in the confined space. Sometimes these materials are easily identified, but care must be taken with certain substances as they may be embedded or absorbed into the structure's material and can be released suddenly, with the application of heat for example, such as in welding, cutting or grinding processes.

*Temperature Extremes*

Temperature extremes must be considered in any safe entry procedures of confined spaces. Examples include extremely cold temperatures in coolers, freezers, condensers, and types of heat exchangers which can easily cause frostbite and hypothermia. There are many examples in confined spaces where extremely hot temperatures may cause burns and heat stress and exhaustion. (boilers, heat exchangers, steam pipes, kilns, process tanks and vessels).

*Humidity*

Humid conditions inside a confined space can easily cause poor visibility, irritation to the eyes and skin, slippery surfaces, heat loss and chill effects.

*Noise*

Unusual noise or noise which is excessive can lead to hearing impairment and communication problems; sources include jack hammers, air chisels, grinders, air arcing and gouging, high pressure wash systems, and ventilation fans and blowers.

**Potential Hazard Assessment In Confined Spaces Cont'd.**

*Vibration*

Vibration conditions can be common in many confined spaces as sources of vibration outside the confined space area can be easily transferred to the confined space where workers are located. These sources include operating machinery and equipment outside the confined space, vibrating piping and valves, impact tools and grinding/milling processes. Vibration can cause disorientation, nausea, poor circulation, tingling, and nervous system disorders.

*Radiation*

Radiation includes non-ionizing sources such as ultraviolet and infra-red light and sunlight, and ionizing sources of radiation such as x-ray equipment.

*Hazardous Animals and Insects*

Hazardous animals include rats, mice and pigeons, which are common to many industrial settings. They leave excrement which can be very hazardous, or deadly to human beings. Insects which are hazardous include types of stinging insects and ants which can inflict serious bites or cause severe skin rashes.

## Entry Program Characteristics

### 1. Using The Buddy System:

Working in confined spaces should never be attempted alone. The number one rule for any worker assigned to perform work in a confined space is to pair up with another worker who is trained in all aspects of confined space entry and rescue. All workers involved in the work should agree on a communication system and be familiar with the emergency response procedures and systems in place for contacting the fire department, rescue team and the police in the event of an emergency. At least one worker should be standing on guard, monitoring the situation within the confined space and be ready to initiate emergency response procedures should a co-worker become injured or appears overcome or is acting strangely.

*When the entry way to the confined space is above the workers, there should be at least two people stationed there in case it is necessary to haul an injured or ill worker out.*

### 2. Develop a Permit System:

A work permit system is one of the best methods for ensuring that the potential hazards of a particular confined space have been identified and assessed, that the necessary preventive procedures have been established, and that workers are aware and reminded of these procedures before each entry to the confined space. A work permit is really a checklist which is filled out before any entry is made to the confined space and it is used to anticipate any problems that might arise as a result of the work to be performed. Illustrations #70A-D provide an example of a typical confined space entry work permit.

The permit should be used to record the following types of information:

- Time, date, location and description of work to be done;
- Types of hazards which might be encountered;
- Sources of hazards to be isolated by closing off, blanking off and/or disconnecting;
- Sources of electrical, hydraulic or mechanical hazards to be locked out;
- Personal protective equipment and clothing to be used, and any other safety gear required;
- Pre-entry atmospheric test readings for toxic substances, oxygen levels, explosive or flammatory levels, and any other types of tests, if necessary;
- What type of atmospheric monitoring to be performed while work is in progress;
- Recognition that all personnel who are working in the confined space are trained and qualified to work in the type of hazardous condition present;
- Names of stand-by workers and associates are clearly identified who will be monitoring from outside of the confined space the work and conditions within the confined space;
- Authorization by the supervisor(s) for work to be done;
- The emergency procedures which are in place and location of a first aid station and fire protection systems.

Typically, work permits for confined space entry are dated and valid for only one shift. The permit must be checked over and authorized by the workers' immediate supervisor before any work can be undertaken in the confined space. After the work permit is authorized, the supervisor then issues the official entry permit for the job.

Before any worker enters the confined space, the workers must post this permit outside the entrance of the confined space to warn others that work activities are proceeding inside the confined space.

*Note: Any additional permits, such as for "hot work", may be issued to authorize this type of work in the confined space. Hot Work Permits are issued by employers giving authorization to perform operations such as welding, cutting, grinding, riveting, burning and heating which are capable of providing a source of ignition.*

| Confined Space Entry Permit | |
|---|---|
| Description **A** | |
| Hazards **B** | Equipment **C** |
| Preparation **D** | Participants **E** |
| Emergency Services **F** | |
| Testing **G** | Approvals **H** |

**Illustration #70A - Confined Space Entry Permit**

| Name of Space To Be Entered: | Permit Number |
|---|---|

Location/Site/Building: _____     Purpose of Entry: _____

**Authorized Duration of Entry Permit:**

Date: _____     to: _____

Time: _____     to: _____

**A**

---

**Permit Space Hazards**

☐ Oxygen Deficiency (less than 19.5%)

☐ Oxygen Enrichment (greater than 23.5%)

☐ Flammable Gases/Vapors/Liquids/Solids

☐ Toxic Gases/Vapors/Liquids/Solids

☐ Airborne Combustible Dust Particles

☐ Mechanical Hazards

☐ Electrical Hazards

☐ Materials Harmful to Exposed Skin

☐ Engulfment

☐ Other:

**B**

**Type of Equipment Required for Entry and Work**

**Please Specify As Required**

1. Personal Protective Equipment

2. Respiratory Protection

3. Atmospheric Testing/Monitoring

4. Communication System

5. Emergency Rescue Equipment

**C**

**Illustration #70B - Confined Space Entry Permit**

**Preparation For Entry**
**(Check After Steps Have Been Taken)**

Notification of Affected Departments of Service Interruption

**Isolation Methods:**
☐ Lockout/Tagout     ☐ Atmospheric Testing
☐ Purge/Clean        ☐ Ventilation
☐ BlankOff/Blind     ☐ Inert          ☐ Barriers

**Personnel Awareness:**
Pre-entry Briefing on Specific Hazards
& Control Methods
Notify Contractors of Permit
& Hazard Conditions

**Additional Permits Required:**
Hotwork   Line Breaking   Other:

**D**

Communication Procedures (Used By Entrants & Attendants)
_____
_____
_____
_____
_____
_____

Authorized Entrants (List By Name Or Attach Roster)
_____   **E**  __
_____        __
_____        __
_____

**Emergency Services:**

Name of Service _____ Phone Number _____ Contact Name **F** Method of Contact ____
Name of Service _____ Phone Number _____ Contact Name     Method of Contact ____

Illustration #70C - Confined Space Entry Permit

| Tests Performed | Acceptable Conditions | Result: AM/PM | Result: AM/PM | Result: AM/PM | Authorization By Entrant Supervisors: *I certify that all precautions have been taken and necessary equipment is provided for safe entry and work in this confined space.* |
|---|---|---|---|---|---|
| Minimum Oxygen | >19.5% | | | | Printed Name: |
| Maximum Oxygen | <23.5% | | | | Signature: |
| Flammability | <10% LEL/LFL | | | | Date & Time: |
| $H_2S$ | <10 ppm | | | | Comments: |
| Toxic (specify) | | | | | Printed Name: |
| $Cl_2$ | <0.5 ppm | | | | Signature: |
| CO | <35 ppm | | | | Date & Time: |
| $SO_2$ | <2 ppm | | | | Comments: |
| Heat | °F/°C | | | | **THIS PERMIT MUST BE POSTED ON THE JOB SITE, AT THE CONFINED SPACE LOCATION, AND IS GOOD ONLY ON DATE INDICATED.** |
| Tester Initials | | | | | |

Illustration #70D - Confined Space Entry Permit

### 3. Prepare The Site:

It is strongly recommended that the site surrounding the entrance and exit area of the confined space be cleared of anything that might be flammable or combustible. All equipment and tools to be used around the confined space should be grounded, free of leaks and explosion proof. Welding and cutting hoses and lines should only be brought in to the area when needed and removed immediately after the work is completed.

Warning signs and barriers should be installed around the confined space area to notify unauthorized personnel to not be in the entrance and exit region. This is very important when work is being undertaken in the vicinity of open manholes, where traffic must be diverted to protect both workers and the public. As well, to further reduce the risk of fire and explosion in flammable or combustible areas, no smoking or other open flames are allowed.

In cases where there is risk of toxic contamination, no one should be allowed in the region who is unfamiliar with the risks and safety procedures.

### 4. Lockout/Tagout or Blank Off Hazardous Sources:

All mechanical equipment and electrical systems inside the confined space must be locked out. This means that each type of machine or equipment inside the space must be disconnected from its electrical power source in order to prevent accidental start up. All workers who are performing work inside the confined space must follow the company's lockout and tagout procedures. This means that all workers who are participating in the work activities in and around the confined space must put their own lock and tag on each machine's electrical control/isolator device.

All pipe lines and circuit systems leading in and out of the confined space which could allow hazardous or toxic substances to enter the confined space must be closed off, which may include blanking off or blinding. Blanking off or blinding means the absolute closure of a pipe line, duct or valve by fastening a solid plate that completely covers the opening bore with a gasket, and is capable of withstanding the maximum pressure of the pipe, line, duct or valve with no leakage beyond the plate.

### 5. Atmospheric Testing and Monitoring:

Before any worker sets foot inside a confined space, extensive testing and monitoring must be done to ensure that there is no build-up of or discharge of dangerous gases and other emissions. The three main hidden hazards to test for, and regularly monitor for are:

- Combustible Gases
- Toxic Gases
- Oxygen Deficiency

Two types of commonly used detectors are shown in illustrations #71A and B. Illustration #71A is an oxygen detector and illustration #71B is a combined oxygen/combustible gas detector.

Illustration #71A - Oxygen Detector

Illustration #71B - Oxygen/Combustible Gas Detector

Guidelines for acceptable levels of airborne toxic chemicals are found in various occupational health and safety regulations. Another good reference source is the Material Safety Data Sheets (MSDS) for the toxic materials in question. Many regulations refer to the "threshold limit values" (TLVs) set out by the American Conference of Governmental Industrial Hygienists.

The toxicity test measures the level of toxic or poisonous materials in the air. Concentrations of toxic chemicals must not exceed the "permissible exposure limit" (PEL). The confined space entry permit will indicate which toxic substances to test for and what the PEL is for each one. Always make sure that the testing equipment can measure all the toxic materials listed on the entry permit. The manufacturer's instructions will explain how to operate the testing instrument.

Four toxic materials especially dangerous in confined spaces are carbon monoxide, nitrogen dioxide, sulphur dioxide and hydrogen sulphide. Most confined spaces should be tested for these materials.

*Oxygen Deficiency* in confined spaces can be caused by corrosion and rusting of metals, combustion and the displacement of oxygen by other gases. Normal air that humans breathe contains approximately 21% oxygen. An oxygen deficient atmosphere means an atmosphere containing less than 19.5% oxygen by volume. An oxygen enriched atmosphere means an atmosphere containing more than 23.5% oxygen by volume.

Breathing oxygen deficient air can cause loss of coordination, fatigue, vomiting, unconsciousness and death. Air that has too much oxygen is oxygen enriched. This condition can lead to serious fire hazards, since combustibles burn violently in oxygen enriched air.

In confined spaces, oxygen deficiency may result from either consumption or displacement of the amount of oxygen present. Activities or processes which can "consume" oxygen include combustion (welding and cutting torches), decomposition of organic matter (rotting food or plant life), or oxidation of metals (rusting and corrosion). Oxygen can be "displaced" when inert gases such as nitrogen, carbon dioxide, helium, or even when steam is used to purge a confined space of residual chemicals, gases or vapors.

Oxygen in humans is consumed by a variety of cellular chemical processes which produce carbon dioxide as a waste product. All cells will die when deprived of oxygen but some are more critically affected than others. For example, brain cells begin to die within 4 - 6 minutes of being deprived of oxygen, and since the brain does not produce new cells, the damage is permanent.

Skin and liver cells, however, are less critically affected by oxygen deficiency because of their ability to generate new cells to replace those that die. Oxygen levels, therefore, must be maintained in confined spaces to within well defined limits - too much or too little oxygen can be catastrophic for life. The effects of oxygen deficiency, listed in table #7, are primarily health based, whereas oxygen enrichment increases the risk of fire and explosion. If oxygen levels deviate above 23.5% or below 19.5% it is considered a hazard. Oxygen deficiency (less than 19.5%) is probably the most common type of confined space hazard.

Most testing and monitoring instruments have three independent sensors which can detect combustible gases, detect toxic gases and materials and indicate oxygen levels. These instruments usually have audible and visual alarms. Readouts allow workers to record levels.

There are often two alarm sounds as well; one signals a lack of oxygen and the other signals the presence of a toxic or combustible gas.

| EFFECTS OF OXYGEN DEFICIENCY ON HUMAN BEINGS | | |
|---|---|---|
| **Oxygen Content (%)v** | **Symptoms** | **Physical Effects On Humans** |
| 19.5% - 23.5% | None | No physical effects are detected on humans. |
| 12% - 19% | Increased pulse rate | Lack of fine coordination in fingers and hands. |
| 10% - 12% | Rapid pulse rate, nausea, headache | Breathing difficulties, lack of coordination, tingling sensations, vomiting. |
| 6% - 10% | Rapid pulse rate, nausea, head ache, disorientation | Complete lack of coordination, inability to sense danger or to react to the danger, loss of consciousness. |
| 0% - 6% | Loss of breathing, heart stopped | Death |

Table #7 -Effects of Oxygen Deficiency On Human Beings

*Note: A good source of information on toxic and hazardous substances can be found in OSHA's Toxic and Hazardous Substances Tables Z-1-A, Z-2, and Z-3 of air contaminants, located in 29 CFR 1910.1000. These tables record "time-weighted averages" (TWA), "short-term exposure limits" (STEL) and ceiling concentrations not to be exceeded at any time for materials listed. According to OSHA, any materials listed in these various tables is considered hazardous.*

### 6. Regular Atmospheric Monitoring of the Confined Space:

The steps involved with performing regular monitoring of the confined space at predetermined intervals are as follows:

a. Pretest or calibrate the detection instrument being used to ensure it is in correct working order. These tests should be carried out according to the manufacturer's instructions.

b. Test for combustibles before entering a confined space where the opening of the entrance could possibly set off an explosion.

c. Tests should be taken in all areas of the confined space, from top to bottom and no corner, pipe, valve or duct should be missed as gases can easily accumulate in these areas. Some "heavier-than-air" gases like propane and butane sink to the bottom of enclosures, while "lighter-than-air" gases like methane rise to the top of enclosures. Testing only on the top will not necessarily detect the hazards present at the bottom, and vice versa.

d. Record all test results in permanent log books or record sheets. Once the area is shown to be safe, the confined space can be entered by the authorized workers who have been properly briefed on the job and wearing suitable personal protective equipment and have with them the required safety gear.

It is generally recommended that the worker wear a safety harness attached by a life line to a hoist over the confined space entry point. The outside attendant can operate the hoist in case there is any indication of danger or if the monitor alarm sounds. While work is being performed inside the space, the air must be regularly monitored for all suspected health hazards.

Table #8 identifies the composition of air that humans typically breathe. This table is a valuable source of information when determining whether there is sufficient oxygen available in the confined space for normal breathing, or if self-contained breathing apparatuses must be worn or made readily available.

*Note: The confined space entry permit will identify if continuous monitoring is needed. If it is not, the permit should indicate how often re-testing is required. Continuous monitoring is important if work inside the confined space can make the air unsafe.*

*Potentially hazardous work activities inside confined spaces which can make air unsafe include: scraping, grinding, welding, cutting, burning, scaling, using solvents and cleaners.*

*Note: Accurate continuous monitoring requires sensors to be placed in good locations. The best places to locate sensors include: worker's breathing zones and any area where potential contaminants could leak into the confined space. Pipe flanges, valve bodies and ducting are obvious places where leaks could occur.*

| COMPOSITION OF AIR | | |
|---|---|---|
| COMPONENT OF AIR | SYMBOL | CONTENT (% VOLUME) |
| Nitrogen | $N_2$ | 78.084% |
| Oxygen | $O_2$ | 20.947% |
| Argon | Ar | 0.934% |
| Carbon Dioxide | $CO_2$ | 0.033% |
| Neon | Ne | 18.2 ppm |
| Helium | He | 5.2 ppm |
| Kyrpton | Kr | 1.1 ppm |
| Sulphur Dioxide | $SO_2$ | 1.0 ppm |
| Methane | $CH_4$ | 2.0 ppm |
| Hydrogen | $H_2$ | 0.5 ppm |
| Nitrous Oxide | $N_2O$ | 0.5 ppm |
| Xenon | Xe | 0.09 ppm |

| COMPOSITION OF AIR | | |
|---|---|---|
| COMPONENT OF AIR | SYMBOL | CONTENT (% VOLUME) |
| Ozone | $O_3$ | 0.0 to 0.07 ppm |
| Ozone - Winter | $O_3$ | 0.0 to 0.02 ppm |
| Nitrogen Dioxide | $NO_2$ | 0.02 ppm |
| Iodine | $I_2$ | 0.01 ppm |
| Carbon Monoxide | CO | 0.0 to trace |
| Ammonia | $NH_3$ | 0.0 to trace |

Note: The above table is an average for clean, dry air at sea level. 1 part/million (ppm) = 0.0001%

Note: Nitrogen (78.084%) + Oxygen (20.947%) + Argon (0.934%) + Carbon Dioxide (0.033%) = 99.998% of Air Content

Table #8 - Composition Of Air

### 7. Provide Ventilation In The Confined Space:

Ventilation is used to control the atmospheric hazards of confined spaces by efficiently replacing unsafe air with clean, breathable air. For most confined spaces, ventilation must be provided mechanically, with fans or blowers. Ventilate a confined space whenever its atmosphere contains hazardous conditions such as:

- When the air contains too little oxygen.
- When the air contains too much oxygen.
- When the atmosphere is flammable.
- When the air is toxic.

Always remember to begin ventilating the confined space far enough in advance so that the air will be safe before anyone has to enter the confined space.

Before anyone enters the space, test the atmosphere to make sure the ventilation system has been working long enough.

After entry, continue ventilating for as long as anyone is in the confined space and at least until the oxygen level and the concentrations of hazardous materials are within safe limits. If work inside the confined space can make the air unsafe, such as hotwork, painting, coating, using cleaners or solvents, and sand blasting, ventilating must continue for as long as the work is in progress. The confined space entry permit should indicate if continuous ventilation is required.

There are two types of mechanical ventilation systems commonly used to provide ventilation for workers in confined spaces. The types are:

- Local Exhaust Ventilation
- General Ventilation

*Local Exhaust Ventilation* captures air contaminants near their point of origin and removes them. Local exhaust ventilation is probably one of the best ways to control flammable and toxic materials produced at a single source such as in welding and cutting operations, as shown in illustration #73. Whenever possible, use local exhaust ventilation during any type of hotwork and when using cleaners, solvents or paints inside a confined space. It is important to keep the local exhaust intake as close as possible to the work area where the contaminants are being generated. Local exhaust ventilation does not work very well when contaminants are dispersed over a wide area and sometimes the shape and location of the confined space make for difficulties in using a local exhaust system.

Illustration #73 - Hot Work

*General Ventilation* systems work to flush the atmosphere within the confined space by supplying and exhausting large volumes of air.

There are two types of general ventilation systems used in confined spaces: exhaust ventilation as seen in illustration #74A and supply ventilation as seen in illustration #74B.

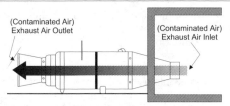

Illustration #74A - Exhaust Ventilation

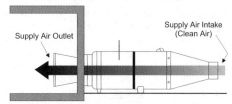

Illustration #74B - Supply Ventilation

Exhaust ventilation draws contaminated air out of the confined space area. This system is advantageous when the atmosphere is either flammable or toxic.

Supply ventilation systems provide a quantity of fresh air to be blown into the confined space. If there are toxics or flammables in the confined space, do not use a supply ventilation system because it would only spread the contaminants around inside the space.

General ventilation systems do not reduce the amount of contaminants released into the confined space, therefore there are limits on when and where it can be used.

For general ventilation to work effectively, workers should not be too close to the contaminating source. The contaminants must not be highly toxic, the concentration levels must be low, and the contaminants must be produced at a fairly uniform rate. The best uses of general ventilation systems in confined spaces are for providing extra amounts of breathing air to the confined space and to assist with controlling low concentrations of materials which are not highly toxic.

Always be careful if general ventilation systems are used during hazardous work, such as hotwork.

It is recommended that the atmosphere is periodically retested and that continuous monitoring be done. As well, it is a good idea to have a good respirator when general ventilation is used. Always have a back up in case something fails.

Several tips for ventilation safety include:

- With either local or general ventilation systems always ventilate with fresh air, never with pure oxygen.
- All electrical ventilation equipment should be equipped with durable electrical cable and connections, and be grounded to prevent any electrical discharge. Explosion proof ventilation equipment may have to be considered for certain types of confined space conditions.
- Place the intake of the air supply as far as possible from any flammable or toxic materials.
- The ventilation system may produce contaminated exhaust, therefore locate the exhaust outlet so that any contaminants won't be drawn back into the confined space.
- If possible try to place the exhaust outlet where there is a natural flow of air to carry and disperse the exhaust away quickly, without endangering nearby workers.
- In some cases the exhaust may have to be filtered to reduce the chances of air pollution in the vicinity.
- If the exhaust from the ventilation system is flammable, remove all ignition sources from the area, and try to pipe the exhaust system so that it is well away from the work area and other workers on the job site.

## Effective Ventilation

There are at least two main problems to consider when using ventilation systems to provide a constant supply of fresh air to all areas of a confined space. The two problems are:

1. There can be a chance that recirculated contaminated exhaust gets back into the confined space area. See illustration #75A.

2. There can be a chance that the ventilation system short-circuits the air flow directly from the inlet of the confined space to the exhaust outlet without proper ventilation reaching other areas of the confined space. See illustration #75B.

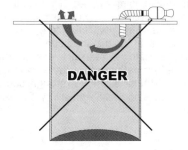

**Illustration #75A - Recirculation**　　　　　　**Illustration #75B - Short Circuiting**

There are several ways listed below to help avoid these ventilation problems.

- Use ventilation equipment which is powerful enough to throw or push the air far enough into the confined space to ventilate the whole area.
- Ensure that the ventilation system is able to capture and carry significant amounts of contaminants.
- Consider using a series of fans or blowers to move the air long distances or to provide sufficient ventilation to a large open area within the confined space.
- Try to locate the fresh air inlet and exhaust outlet properly so that the in-coming air and exhaust air move through separate openings located well away from each other.

- Use duct work effectively. Flexible ducting, as shown in illustration #76, can be used to direct air flow to specific areas of the confined space.
- Place the ducts so they are not damaged by the various work activities.
- Do not make duct bends too tight, and ensure that all connections are secure.

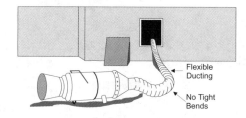

Illustration #76 - Flexible Ducting

Illustration #77 demonstrates one of the better methods to supply air to a long confined space. Blow the fresh air in at one end of the confined space and exhaust the stale or contaminated air at the other end of the space if possible.

Illustration #78 demonstrates one of the better methods to supply air in deep confined space. Blow the fresh air in near the bottom of the confined space and try to set it up so the exhaust outlet is near the top of the space so the stale or contaminated air can exit there.

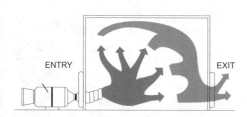

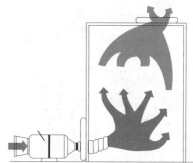

**Illustration #77 - Long Confined Space**

**Illustration #78 - Two Openings**

Illustration #79 demonstrates how short-circuiting of fresh air can be prevented in a confined space which has just one opening. In order to minimize the effects of short-circuiting in this type of space it is best to use a blower which is powerful enough to blow clean air into the entire space.

In the same space as just discussed, there also could be a chance of recirculating the exhaust air. In order to prevent this from happening, add additional duct work to the intake on the blower to keep it distant from the exhaust stream. See illustration #80.

Air Intake

**Illustration #79 - Single Opening**

Air Intake

Ducting

**Illustration #80 - Protecting the Air Supply**

Illustration #81 demonstrates how flexible ducting can be used to provide effective air circulation in a long confined space which has only one opening. The ducting is drawn far into to the confined space where suitable amounts of air can be blown to the far ends of the space and allowed to circulate back towards the opening.

Illustration #82 demonstrates how a short-circuit can be prevented if a confined space has two openings, but they are in a position that would leave some areas unvented. One way to deal with this problem is to use additional flexible duct work to direct fresh air into those hard to reach places.

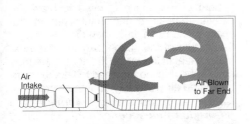

**Illustration #81 - Carry the Air Flow**

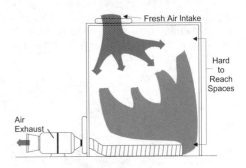

**Illustration #82 - Directing Fresh Air**

Illustration #83 demonstrates one method for removing lighter-than-air contaminants from a deep confined space which has two openings on the top. Place the flexible ducting at the inlet to bring fresh air down toward the bottom of the space and install a fan to draw the contaminated air from the top of the confined space at the second opening. It might also be best to run additional ducting from the exhaust outlet of the fan in order to draw any contaminated air farther away from the area around the openings.

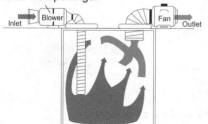

**Illustration #83 - Removing Lighter-Than-Air Contaminants**

Illustration #84 demonstrates the same type of confined space as shown in illustration #83, but in this example the intent is to remove heavier-than-air contaminants from the bottom of the confined space area. In this case at the opening on the left, the blower is bringing fresh air into the space, while the fan on the right with the length of flexible ducting coming from the fan's outlet down to near the bottom of the space is used to draw the heavier-than-air contaminants out of the space. The fresh air is then drawn down to the bottom of the space. Again, at the exhaust outlet of the fan on the right, there may have to be ducting attached to take the contaminated air well away from the work area.

***Note: Ventilation protects workers from hazardous atmospheric conditions found in confined spaces. It is important to ventilate properly and to consider ventilating any confined space which might contain hazardous materials.***

*Follow the basic rules for safe ventilation, use the right equipment, and locate it where it will provide the most effective circulation of fresh air through all areas of the confined space.*

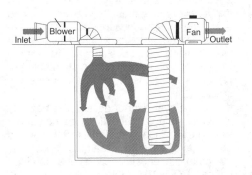

Illustration #84 - Removing Heavier-Than-Air Contaminants

## 8. Wearing Personal Protective Equipment and Using Safety Equipment:

It is typically required, and makes good sense, to wear personal protective equipment in confined spaces, even when initial testing indicates that the confined space is free of hazards. Because atmospheric conditions in a confined space can change quickly, a portable monitor can be attached to the worker's body. Evacuate immediately at the first alarm indication.

Appropriate personal protective equipment, such as hard hats, face shields, goggles, protective gloves and footwear, coveralls or encapsulated suits must be made available at the confined space site and listed on the entry permit. In the original site evaluation there may also have been a recommendation to have respirators or other types of breathing apparatuses made available.

If continuous communication between the attendant and the entrant(s) will be difficult or impossible, choose and list devices, such as radio or video equipment. Test this equipment before entering the confined space and list any special procedures necessary for communicating with the attendants and entrants.

Have spark proof tools and special light sources made available. Make sure these tools are safe and in good operating condition. Always remember to guard against shock, such as ground fault circuit interruptors (GFCI). Have ladders, scaffold sections, boatswain chairs and work platforms and hoists available, ready to go before anyone enters the confined space.

### 9. Never Enter If There Are Problems:

If there are problems with ventilation, or if the monitoring shows a hazard is present only the authorized supervisor should give the permission to subsequently enter the confined space. No worker must enter the confined space if there are problems. There must be sufficient work done to prepare the confined space so it is deemed safe to enter. This may mean additional ventilation for a length of time before the space is ready to enter again. Before anyone can enter the space, everything must be checked out and okay, then the supervisor can give the approval to re-enter the confined space and work can resume once again. Ventilation may be ongoing to allow for a constant supply of air while the workers are inside the space.

If the employer cannot assess the hazards within a confined space, if the space cannot be regularly monitored, and if the workers don't have suitable breathing apparatus available, no one is to enter the confined space. *DO NOT ENTER.*

### 10. Emergency Response and Rescue:

Before any work is undertaken in a confined space the employer and the workers must consider what the emergency response and rescue procedures will be. Every year, workers die needlessly when they enter confined spaces to rescue an unconscious colleague without first adequately protecting themselves. They may not be familiar with the emergency procedures, or they are not trained sufficiently to handle the rescue operations. Sometimes people just panic and they react to the situation by jumping in before considering their safety and what the process will be for performing the rescue.

Emergency rescue procedures must be developed for each confined space and thoroughly communicated to all workers.

**There are no generic rescue procedures that will address every potential complication during work performed in confined spaces.**

It is important for the employer and workers to work together to plan the most suitable rescue procedures for the type of confined spaces which will be encountered in the work setting.

In summary, before any worker enters any pit, excavation, tank, vessel, manhole, small room, or vault, he or she should get into the practice of asking themselves what might be inside. In any industry, whether it be chemical, food, refineries, manufacturing, material handling or transportation, workers can face flammable, asphyxiating, poisonous and toxic atmospheres, or a lack of oxygen. Storage tanks and vessels may contain cleaning agents, solvents or explosive vapors. Check to see that electric motors and drives are disconnected or isolated correctly so that they cannot be started up from outside, or valves opened to let in acids or other dangerous fluids or gases which can be harmful.

Never enter the confined space until satisfied it is safe to do so, and that you are adequately protected. Always be careful around manholes, especially those below ground, as they can be laden with sewer gas or natural gas. Be aware of the special procedures required for entering manholes, trenches and ditches. These can be obtained from a local occupational health and safety division.

## Asphyxiant Gases

There are many examples of asphyxiant gases common to workplaces. All employees must be made aware of the asphyxiant gases found in their work areas and should be trained on the characteristics and precautions required in order to minimize hazards and personal safety.

Asphyxiants are gases which can cause asphyxiation by either displacing the oxygen in the atmosphere or interfering with the body's ability to use oxygen. Those gases that are physiologically inert (i.e. produce no effect on the body) and are present in sufficient quantity to displace the air and, therefore, an adequate oxygen supply are called "simple asphyxiants." An example is nitrogen.

Substances which incapacitate the body's ability to utilize an adequate oxygen supply are called chemical asphxiants. Carbon monoxide is toxic, colorless and an odorless gas which combines with the hemoglobin of red blood cells. Carbon monoxide has a much higher affinity for hemoglobin than oxygen so it will attach preferentially and exclude oxygen. This greatly reduces the amount of oxygen available for life processes and can lead to death due to chemical asphyxiation.

*Carbon monoxide* is one of the most common asphyxiants encountered in the work place and in confined spaces. It is formed by incomplete combustion whenever fuel containing carbon is burned.

In addition to its presence as a by-product in many industrial situations, it is also produced in large amounts by internal combustion engines such as automobiles, fuel powered compressors, generators and welders, and fork lifts.

The allowable working limit for carbon monoxide is usually 10 ppm (0.0001%). The allowable working limit for carbon monoxide may vary by jurisdiction and industry.

*Hydrogen sulfide* is another chemical asphyxiant and it is one of the most vicious and deadly hazards encountered in confined work spaces. It goes by many names $H_2S$, Sour Gas or Sulphuretted Hydrogen. Workers in industries such as oil and gas, refineries, chemical plants, pulp and paper, mining and workers who perform sewer line maintenance must be specially aware of this deadly gas.

Workers should make sure they are able to recognize its presence, know how to protect themselves from its deadly effects and how to rescue and administer first aid to victims who are overcome.

Hydrogen sulphide is a highly toxic, colorless gas, heavier than air, with the odor of rotten eggs. If ignited, it burns with a blue flame and produces sulphur dioxide, which is a very irritating gas with a pungent odor. Hydrogen sulphide forms explosive mixtures with air, with the lower explosive limit being 4.3% hydrogen sulphide, and the upper explosive limit being 46.0%. Hydrogen sulphide is most frequently encountered in the production and refining of high sulphur petroleum, in the natural gases, in gypsum and sulphur mining, in rock strata and underground water because it is soluble in water, in blasting operations using black powder, in natural gas manufacture and in the manufacture of certain synthetic materials and other chemicals.

Hydrogen sulphide is generally recognized by a characteristic foul odor, however this odor cannot be used as an early warning sign.

Prolonged exposure to low concentrations of hydrogen sulphide will desensitize the sense of smell. Those workers who have been exposed to hydrogen sulphide for some time will fail to recognize its presence even if the concentration level suddenly increases. This can be fatal to those who think they can detect dangerous concentrations by the offensive odor. It quickly acts on the eyes and respiratory system, resulting in irritation. As hydrogen sulphide enters the blood stream it begins to paralyze the nerve centers of the brain. Soon thereafter, lung paralysis occurs, and the individual is asphyxiated. In high concentration levels, death due to lung paralysis probably occurs very quickly. The individual in this case would have probably never smelled the distinctive odor first, as there is no chance because of the quick effects of the gas upon the brain.

The Permissible Exposure Limit (PEL) for hydrogen sulphide is 10 ppm (0.0001%) for an eight hour work day over a five day work week.

The Short Term Exposure Limit (STEL) for hydrogen sulphide is 15 ppm. This is how much a person can safely be exposed to averaged over a 15 minute period. The STEL should be checked four times a day, when the worker's risk is likely to be greatest. The allowable working limit for exposure to hydrogen sulphide may vary by jurisdiction and industry. Breathing in hydrogen sulphide is the most dangerous route of exposure. How a person is affected depends on the concentration level a person is exposed to and the length of exposure. A person will lose their ability to smell within minutes if exposed to more than 100 ppm.

A person could also lose their ability to smell if they breathed in only 50 ppm over one hour's time.

To avoid exposure to hydrogen sulphide:

- Know where to find emergency exits.
- Be familiar with emergency phone numbers.
- Know how to use self contained breathing apparatus.
- Remain alert of winds and drafts.
- Pay attention to wind socks, streamers, flags, and banners.
- Make sure that there are sufficient fans and blowers used.
- Know how to use air monitoring instruments.
- Don't smoke around hydrogen sulphide because it is highly flammable and explosive.
- Be aware of the safety rules, warning signs and the company's hydrogen sulphide procedures.

- Take hydrogen sulphide seriously - it is a matter of life or death.

*Note: Working in a confined space may be a regular part of the job, or it may be a one-time emergency. Always think of confined spaces as dangerous. Workers can protect themselves. Workers must learn the hidden hazards and use safe work practices. It is the smart way to stay safe in confined spaces.*

## Welding Gases and Fumes

Often hotwork such as welding and cutting is performed inside confined spaces. Welding and cutting gases and fumes can be very hazardous to a person's health. The exposure time to welding gases and fumes, the type of welding being done, the work environment, and the protection being used determine the risks and how people will be affected.

All welding processes produce toxic gases. The heat in both the flame and the arc, and the ultra-violet radiation from the arc produce gases such as carbon monoxide, carbon dioxide, oxides of nitrogen and ozone. Gases are invisible to the eye, and may or may not have an odor. Other types of gases may be produced as products of decomposition of the residual solvents or from the coatings on the metals. Gases, when they are used for arc-shielding or as a fuel, are also given off during welding.

Fumes are also produced whenever welding is performed. Fumes are formed when hot vapors cool and condense into very small particles that stay suspended in the vapor or the gas. The particles may be of metal or metal compounds, and are very small. Welding smoke is an example of visible fumes. Even if the fumes cannot be seen, the small particles are present.

The air being breathed in by the workers inside the confined space will contain welding gases and fumes if welding operations are being undertaken. Welding gases and fumes will effect people differently.

Certain gases are considered to be relatively non-toxic, while others can be more toxic. Inhaling welding fumes have different effects on the body. Iron oxides, which are produced during most electric arc welding processes, are typically considered to be non-toxic and the effects, as currently known, are not permanent, unless one were exposed to rather large amounts over an extended period of time. The long-term effects can be shown in chest x-rays and can cause short term or in some cases longer term breathing problems.

For most substances produced from welding processes, the early symptoms resulting from harmful exposures are often quite similar.

These may consist of irritation in the eyes, nose, throat and respiratory system, and sometimes cause skin irritation and sensitivity. Coughing, tightness in the chest, chest pains, headaches, nausea, vomiting and general fatigue may also be persistent symptoms of prolonged exposure to various types of welding gases and fumes.

Consider the following points related to welding gases and fumes:

- The welding process, including the type of metal being welded, as well as the type of fumes produced, rather than its actual quantity, often determines the seriousness of the occupational hazard.

- For example, E6010 electrodes used on low carbon steel, generate a large amount of iron oxide particles, which are considered to be relatively non-toxic.

- But, an E316-15 electrode produces small quantities of highly toxic chromium fumes. The health hazards are higher for this electrode than for E6010.

- Some welding process variables include the type of shielding gas used, current, voltage, type of electrode, and polarity. Each can affect the quantity and type of welding gases and fumes produced.

- If the metal being welded is coated or painted, or has a residual solvent on its surface, toxic types of organic gases and fumes can be produced.

- The amount of available ventilation determines how long and how much of the welding gases and fumes remain in the worker's breathing area.

- The position and location of the worker's body relative to the welding job being performed is also a factor to consider. If the welder for example, is crouched low over the work while welding, gases and fumes will be breathed in directly.

- Also consider how many welders and welding operations are most suitable for the size and type of confined space where the work is being planned.
- Try to determine what materials will be welded and find out what types of substances were inside the confined space. Evaluate the work situation inside the confined space.
- When the risks of exposure to welding gases and fumes are high, use proper respiratory protective equipment.
- Always try to keep a good system of ventilation operating within the confined space in order to bring fresh air in to the area and to help push the welding gases and fumes out.

## Training and Duties of the Entry Team

*Supervisor:* The supervisor responsible for the work activities in the confined space must make sure that the conditions for entry into the confined space are safe.

Before entry, the supervisor must verify that the confined space entry permit is filled out completely and all safety steps and precautions identified on the permit are taken. Then the supervisor signs off on the permit.

During entry into the confined space by the workers, the supervisor checks conditions to make sure they remain safe throughout the time work is undertaken within the confined space. If conditions become unsafe, the permit is cancelled and all workers are ordered out of the space immediately. The supervisor must ensure that all workers have left the space and sees to it that no unauthorized people attempt to enter the space. When all the work is finished in the confined space, the supervisor cancels the confined space entry permit and concludes the work activities.

***Attendant:*** There may be one or more attendants involved with the work activities at the confined space (see illustration #85).

Each will have a designated role to play while the work is being done inside the confined space by their fellow workers.

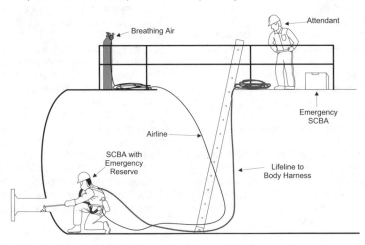

Breathing Air

Attendant

Emergency SCBA

Airline

SCBA with Emergency Reserve

Lifeline to Body Harness

**Illustration #85 - Precautions For Hazardous Entry**

Several important points for the attendant's role and responsibilities include:

- The attendant must stay at their post to observe and monitor conditions and to support the workers inside.
- The attendant must be familiar with the hazards inside the confined space and know the signs and symptoms of exposure to hazardous materials.
- The attendant must keep a current record of the workers who are entering and exiting the confined space and be able at any time to identify who is inside the space and who is not.
- The attendant must keep in continuous contact with the entrants.
- The attendant must be sure that only authorized workers are entering the confined space or the areas surrounding the space.

- The attendant orders workers out of the confined space in any of the following situations:

  a. when the attendant observes a condition not allowed by the confined space entry permit.

  b. when the attendant notices signs of exposure with any of the workers.

  c. when the attendant sees something outside the confined space which could cause danger inside.

  d. when the attendant must leave the post to perform rescue or emergency duties.

- The attendant must never leave the designated observation post for any reason, other than when required to do so because of an emergency. If this happens, they must first order those workers inside the confined space out immediately.

- If the workers need to escape the confined space, the attendant calls the emergency response or rescue team immediately.
- In case of an emergency, the attendant must not enter the confined space unless they are trained in confined space rescue, have proper emergency equipment and another attendant is there as backup.

***Workers - The Entrants:*** The workers who are designated to enter the confined space must also do their part to control the hazards of the confined space.

- The entrants must know the hazards of the confined space and the signs of exposure. For example, lack of oxygen can cause: loss of muscle control; mental confusion; difficulties with breathing; nausea; ringing in the ears; death.

- Entrants must follow the procedures closely for wearing the required personal protective equipment and having the correct safety equipment with them.
- The entrants must keep in contact with the attendant, and leave the confined space at once if they have been ordered to evacuate.
- The entrants must always be ready to evacuate quickly and, if possible, without assistance.
- If the entrant at any time feels that they are in danger, they are to leave the confined space immediately and tell the attendant what is happening.

*Note: A problem which periodically occurs with certain workers inside confined spaces is a condition called "claustrophobia", which is defined as a fear of being in closed, narrow or tight spaces. If a worker has this condition, it can be quite a challenge to get out of the confined space, or on the other hand they will quickly discharge themselves from the space because of their overwhelming fear. It is always important to discuss this condition openly and frankly with all the entrants before going inside a confined space. It may require additional support and communication from fellow entrants, the attendant and the supervisor to assist the person who has this condition to overcome their fears about being inside a confined space. It may be the best decision to not allow this person inside the space, but to have them perform duties outside the space.*

## Confined Space Rescue

In a confined space emergency, every second will count. The lives of each worker may depend on the knowledge, skill and performance of the attendants and workers. Each worker who is in the confined space has a role to play in the rescue, because the rescue team may not arrive on the scene in time to save the workers. As many as 60% of those people who die each year in confined spaces are "would-be-rescuers." These people are well intentioned, usually poorly trained co-workers who enter the confined space in a desperate attempt to help.

There are two common types of rescues in confined spaces, these are:

- Self-rescue
- Non-entry rescue

***Self-rescue*** is a procedure where the people inside the confined space evacuate the space by themselves at the first sign of trouble. Self-rescue requires teamwork among all those involved with the work activities in and around the confined space. At the first sign of trouble, the entrant notifies the attendant and begins the evacuation process immediately. Once the attendant learns of the evacuation by one entrant, the remaining entrants are quickly contacted and ordered to evacuate as well. At this time the attendant also notifies the rescue team.

***Non-entry rescue*** refers to a rescue retrieval system which the attendant uses to pull the entrant out of the confined space without entering into it. Note, neither the self-rescue or the non-entry rescue systems puts others at risk by entering the confined space. Both require advance training and on-going teamwork between the entrants and the attendant.

In the non-entry rescue system the attendants should be using a mechanical device like a hand-cranked, man-rated winch and tripod system to raise or pull the victim out of the space. OSHA for example, requires that a mechanical device be available to retrieve personnel from vertical entry confined spaces more than five feet deep (1.5 metres). A hand operated winch with a 25:1 mechanical advantage allows a 250 pound (113 kg) man to be lifted with a force of ten pounds (4.5 kg). In order to do this :

- The entrant wears a chest or full body harness connected to the retrieval line connected to the winch. A full body harness is considered safer, is considered more secure and there is less risk of injury from a fall because weight is more evenly distributed. See illustration #86.

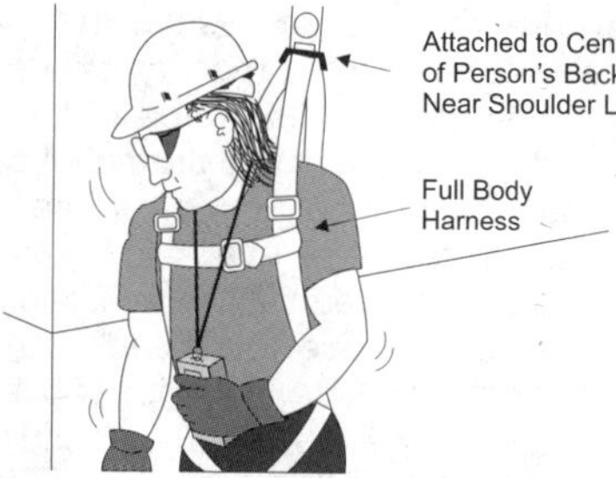

**Illustration #86 - Full Body Harness**

Attached to Center
of Person's Back
Near Shoulder Level

Full Body
Harness

- The attendant can crank the winch in order to lift the entrant out of the confined space in an emergency situation.
- The retrieval line should be attached at the center of the person's back near shoulder level. This will minimize slumping and makes the body as straight as possible when pulling it out.

- Another attachment device used to lift a person out of a confined space and through narrow entry ways is wristlets, as shown in illustration #87. OSHA allows the use of wristlets only if absolutely necessary, as wristlets can cause injury if the line is pulled too hard.

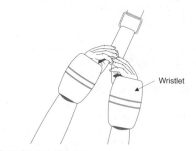

Wristlet

**Illustration #87 - Wristlets**

- Pulling an entangled person out of a confined space can also easily cause injury. Any extra pressure on the retrieval line means that the entrant may have become entangled in a ladder, piping, beams, scaffolding, or other obstacle inside the space area. If this occurs, stop cranking immediately, back off the cable somewhat, then try to move the cable around by hand to disentangle the person from the obstacle.

- Never use a motorized crane, overhead hoist or other powered hoist or lift to pull a person out of a confined space. The problem is that powered equipment can travel too far, too fast and may injure the entrant if they become seriously entangled inside the confined space. Powered equipment may also create dangerous sparks in a volatile atmosphere and will be useless in a power outage.

*Note: Obviously, never try to pull or lift an injured or unconscious worker out of a confined space unless it is a straight line pull with no corners or obstacles.*

*This is why non-entry rescue techniques often must be limited to fairly simple vertical type confined spaces.*

*Do not attempt to use a mechanical retrieval system when spaces contain projections, obstructions or turns and bends that prevent a pull on the line being transmitted directly to the entrant. Also be careful that the retrieval line does not get caught up in someone's air supply respirator or with electrical cords.*

In those emergency situations where neither self-rescue or non-entry rescue systems are suitable, a trained and qualified rescue team must be called in to perform the rescue in the confined space.

All members of these rescue teams are expected to maintain current certification in first aid and cardiopulmonary resuscitation (CPR). Trained rescue teams will have knowledge and skills in:

- Recognizing confined space hazards;
- Communication in confined space areas;
- Using personal protective equipment such as self contained breathing apparatus;
- Using specialized rigging and hoisting equipment for confined space rescue applications;
- Perform rescue techniques specific to those types of confined spaces found in the workplace.

*Note: One of the most important goals of confined space rescue training is learning to work together as a team. Every member on the team has an important role in the rescue effort and it is imperative that all members work together as a smooth functioning unit. Through effective teamwork, successful confined space rescues will be achieved.*

## Heat Stress

An important consideration employers and workers must keep in mind while planning and preparing for work inside certain types of confined spaces is "heat stress." High temperatures are often associated with confined spaces and this puts stress on the human body. When the body's cooling system has to work extra hard to reduce heat stress, it can become quite strained, and the physical strain, combined with other stresses from the work itself, loss of fluids and fatigue, may lead to severe heat disorders, disability or even death.

Those at greatest risk are people who live and work in warm or seasonally hot climates, or those who work in hot, humid environments.

They will be affected by heat stress, even when they are physically fit, young and healthy. In addition to the medical hazards of bodily (physiological) illness or injury caused by heat stress, there is also a higher frequency of accidents in hot and usually cramped work environments. Direct causes of accidents related to hot working conditions inside confined spaces include:

- Dizziness or fainting.
- Slippery and wet hands.
- Sweat (perspiration) in the eyes.
- Fogged lens on glasses, goggles and face shields.

As well as the above direct causes of accidents related to heat, there are also several indirect causes of heat related accidents:

- Physical and mental discomfort.
- Irritability, loss of patience.
- Unclear thinking, poor judgement.
- Loss of attention span.
- Slower reactions.
- Sleepiness, drowsiness, tired.

Heat disorders are common in many work environments, and can be prevented with consideration given to proper job planning, supervision and training.

Employers and workers can work together to better understand the effects of heat stress, as well as be knowledgeable about the symptoms and treatment for heat stress disorders. Personnel who are entering confined spaces which may be quite hot and humid must take personal precautions against heat disorders. This may mean limiting the time spent inside the space as well as getting sufficient fluids to prevent dehydration and loss of fluids.

To better understand the effects of heat stress there are several factors to be familiar with:

- The human body always generates internal heat, but the amount of heat that remains stored in the body depends on the person's surroundings; their level of physical activity; the type of work being performed; how much time is spent doing the work; and the recovery time between the periods of work activities.
- The human body is a heat control mechanism that tries to keep the inner temperature at a constant 98.6°F (37°C). The body gains or loses heat in four ways:

a. Radiation: transfers heat to or from surrounding objects that are not in direct contact with the body.

b. Convection: transfers body heat to or from air moving over the skin.

c. Conduction: is direct contact with objects that are colder or hotter than the body.

d. Evaporation: causes cooling when air absorbs body moisture from the lungs or skin.

- The amount and speed of heat gain or loss in the body depends on: temperature of the surrounding air and objects; air movement (wind, fans, blowers, drafts); and humidity levels (amount of water vapor in the air).

*Note: While resting, the human body loses approximately 75% of its heat through conduction, convection or radiation from the blood vessels at the skin surface. However, as internal body heat rises due to the result of work activities or high temperatures, surface blood vessels get bigger and the pulse rate increases, placing a strain on the heart and circulatory system.*

In order to prepare for work activities inside warm or hot confined spaces, supervisors, rescuers, attendants and entrants should learn a few key points about their body's cooling system. When the body is trying to cool itself, more blood is being pumped close to the skin for the cooling process, less blood, therefore, goes to the brain. Any strenuous activity, such as lifting, bending, squatting, or standing up suddenly can result in dizziness or even momentary blackout, which could greatly increase the chance for secondary injuries or accidents.

If the temperature of the air and surrounding objects in the confined space area rises above one's body temperature, then conduction, convection and radiation cause the body to gain heat instead of losing it. The evaporation of body sweat becomes the body's most important, and sometimes only effective cooling method. But heavy sweating can also make things worse for the person because there is increased loss of body fluid and minerals. Most people will lose about one quart (one litre) of sweat per hour while working in high temperature environments. This puts additional strain on the body's circulatory system since it actually lowers the amount of blood in the body. Even though a person is sweating, they may not be getting rid of heat, since sweat must evaporate to cool the body.

Normally, the faster the air moves over the heated body, the more the sweat evaporates. But if the air is too full of water vapor to absorb any more water, the person may not get any cooler.

If a human body's natural defenses against heat stress are pushed beyond their capabilities, they may simply shut down, leading to an uncontrolled and rapid rise in body temperature that can quickly lead to heat stroke and permanent damage to the central nervous system, and finally death.

## Heat Disorders

Several types of heat disorders include:

**Heat Rash:** Heat rash is also known by some as "prickly heat", and is another heat disorder which causes discomfort and can lower the body's ability to lose heat. Heat rash is usually associated with hot, humid environments. The sweat ducts become plugged, the sweat does not evaporate and the skin stays wet most of the time.

It is important to keep the skin clean and dry to prevent heat rash.

**Heat Cramps:** Heat cramps can occur alone or may be combined with one of the other heat stress disorders. Heat cramps are very painful, sometimes quite severe, and occur as cramps in the muscles of the legs, arms and stomach. Heat cramps are caused by excessive sweating and lower levels of salt.

It is best to get in a cool area, drink liquids with a tiny amount of salt, and seek medical attention if the cramps continue.

**Heat Exhaustion:** Heat exhaustion occurs when the body's heat control mechanism is overactive. The cause of heat exhaustion is related to surface blood vessels that are enlarged. Heat exhaustion symptoms include: heavy sweating; intense thirst; clammy and pale skin; rapid pulse; low to normal blood pressure; and fatigue, weakness or loss of coordination. Victims of heat exhaustion require immediate medical attention.

**Heat Stroke:** Heat stroke is a medical emergency requiring immediate attention. It is considered to be a very severe illness and has a high death rate. The cause of heat stroke is usually brought on by the body being depleted of salt and fluids, sweating stops and heat loss by evaporation of sweat is blocked. The body temperature increases quickly to fatal levels.

Heat stroke occurs more readily when the body has experienced previous heat disorders such as heat cramps and/or heat exhaustion. Symptoms of heat stroke include: rapid pulse; difficult breathing; constricted pupils; high blood pressure; headache/dizziness; confusion; delirious; weakness; nausea; vomiting; seizure or convulsions; loss of consciousness; and very high body temperatures. Treatment for heat stroke includes: lowering the victim's body temperature as fast as possible; immerse the victim in cool water; massage the body with ice; refrain from giving the victim liquids if they are unconscious; and call an ambulance and evacuate the victim to a hospital.

There are three precautions workers can take for controlling heat disorders:

*1. Acclimatization:* If the temperature or humidity in the confined space can't be controlled, the workers must become acclimatized to the work area by gradually getting themselves accustomed to the environment within the confined space. Being in good physical condition helps one to better acclimatize and for some workers the acclimatization period to get adjusted to the heat and humidity may take longer than for others.

*2. Work Procedures:* An important method for reducing the ill effects of heat stress is to have the workers follow scheduled work and rest cycles which prevent the workers from overexertion inside the confined space.

This means having minimal activity during rest breaks, alternating light and heavy work, sharing work both in and out of the confined space, and rotating the duties amongst the workers inside the space to protect them from heat, fumes, moisture, drafts, toxics and other heat stress factors.

**3. Food and Water Intake:** Hot food and heavy meals add directly to body heat and may reduce one's ability to get rid of heat because more of the blood flow is being directed to the digestive system instead of to the skin surface. Eat lighter meals during the work day, and save the heavier foods after the work day is over. Fluid intake should equal the fluid loss throughout the day. Consuming drinks designed to replace body fluids and electrolytes is okay, but never drink alcoholic beverages, since alcohol dehydrates the body.

Except when treating heat disorders, salt supplements are not recommended, since too much salt can cause higher body temperature, increased thirst and bring on nausea. If the worker's diet is normal it will usually have enough salt in it, but if the person is sweating continuously, they might want to put extra salt on their food. Salt tablets are considered harmful because the salt does not enter the body's system as fast as water or other fluids.

*Note: If salt is needed to treat heat disorders, make a 0.1% saline solution by adding approximately 1/4 teaspoon table salt per quart (litre) of water. If only salt tablets are available, break them into pieces and crush them into water so they will dissolve quicker to make the saline solution. Always discuss salt intake with your family physician.*

# SECTION
# FIVE
## SAFETY GUIDELINES FOR TRENCHING AND EXCAVATION WORK

## Trenching Regulations

Working in trenches and excavations can be very dangerous. Each year there are numerous worker injuries and fatalities because of unsafe work practices, and poor design and construction features. Any person who must perform work in a trench or excavation must protect themselves by learning more about safe work practices in these types of confined spaces, and they must have some basic knowledge of soil conditions, trench and excavation protection systems, atmospheric hazards and accepted emergency response methods.

Workers, employers and contractors should understand the laws and regulations applicable to trenching and excavation work in their local regions. The laws and regulations, as provided by province in Canada and through OSHA in the United States, are in effect for the express purpose of protecting those who work in any type of trenching and excavation situations. In the United States, all excavations shall be made with the rules, regulations and guidelines set forth in 29 CFR 1926.650, .651, and .652; the Occupational Safety and Health Administration's Standard on Excavations. In Canada, each province has its own laws and regulations for trenching and excavation work. The provinces will provide employers and contractors with guidelines for excavation work and specific regulatory requirements regarding excavation work would come under the Workplace Safety and Health Act.

## Trenching Definitions

***Accepted Engineering Practices:*** Refers to those requirements which are compatible with standards of practice required by a registered professional engineer.

***Actual Slope:*** Refers to the slope to which an excavation face is excavated.

***Aluminum Hydraulic Shoring:*** Refers to an engineered shoring system comprised of aluminum hydraulic cylinders (crossbraces), used in conjunction with vertical rails (uprights) or horizontal rails (walers). Such a system is designed specifically to support the sidewalls of an excavation and prevent cave-ins.

***Benching:*** Refers to a method of protecting employees from cave-ins by excavating the sides of an excavation to form one or a series of horizontal levels or steps, usually with vertical or near-vertical surfaces between levels.

***Cave-in:*** Refers to the separation of a mass of soil or rock material from the side of an excavation, or the loss of soil from under a trench shield or support system, and its sudden movement into the excavation, either by falling or sliding in sufficient quantity so that it could entrap, bury, or otherwise injure and immobolize a person.

***Competent Person:*** Refers to a person who is capable of identifying existing and predictable hazards in the surroundings, or working conditions that are hazardous or dangerous to others, and who has authorization to take prompt corrective measures to eliminate them.

***Crossbraces:*** Refer to the horizontal members of a shoring system installed perpendicular to the sides of the excavation, the ends of which bear against either uprights or walers.

***Deep Foundation:*** Refers to a foundation unit that provides support for a building by transferring loads either by end bearing to soil or rock at considerable depth below the building, or by adhesion or friction or both, in the soil or rock in which it is placed.

***Distress:*** Means that a cave-in is imminent or is likely to occur.

Distress is evidenced by such characteristics as the development of fissures in the face of or adjacent to an open excavation; the slumping of material from the face or the bulging or heaving of material from the bottom of an excavation; the spalling of material from the face of an excavation; and raveling, (i.e. small amounts of material such as pebbles or little clumps of material suddenly separating from the face and trickling or rolling down into an excavation).

**Excavation:** Refers to a man-made cavity or depression in the earth's surface formed by earth removal, and includes a trench, deep foundation, tunnel, shaft, or open excavation, but does not include borrow pits, gravel pits and quarries, unless specified by the local regulations or safety and health officer/inspector.

**Face:** Refers to the vertical or inclined earth or rock surfaces formed as a result of excavation work.

**Failure:** Refers to the breakage, displacement, or permanent deformation of a structural member or connection which will reduce the structural integrity and its supportive characteristics.

**Hazardous Atmosphere:** Refers to an atmosphere which is identified as being explosive, flammable, poisonous, corrosive, oxidizing, irritating, oxygen deficient, toxic, or otherwise harmful, which may cause illness, injury or death.

**Kickout:** Refers to the accidental or sudden release or failure of a crossbrace or other support device.

**Maximum Allowable Slope:** Refers to the steepest incline of an excavation face that is acceptable for the most favorable site conditions as protected against cave-ins, and is expressed as the ratio of horizontal distance to vertical rise (H:V).

*Mudsills:* Refer to a plate or flat section of suitable material used to prevent horizontal and/or vertical supports from sinking or embedding themselves into soft soil or mud.

*Open Excavation:* Refers to an excavation where the width is equal to or greater than the depth of the excavation.

*Pile or Caisson:* Refers to a slender deep foundation unit made of materials such as wood, steel, or concrete or combination thereof, which is either pre-manufactured and placed by driving, jacking, jetting or screwing, or cast-in-place in a hole formed by driving, excavation or boring.

*Protective System:* Refers to a method of protecting employees from cave-ins, from material that could fall or roll from an excavation face or into an excavation, or from the collapse of adjacent structures. Protective systems include support systems, sloping and benching systems, shield systems, and other systems designed to provided necessary protection.

*Ramp:* Refers to an inclined walking or working surface that is used to gain access to one point from another, and is constructed from earth, rock, or from structural materials such as steel, concrete or wood.

*Shaft:* Refers to a vertical or inclined opening excavated below ground level.

*Sheathing:* Refers to a continuous row of wood or steel sheets in close contact to provide a tight wall designed to resist the pressures exerted from the excavation walls and faces.

*Shield System:* Means a structure that is able to withstand the forces imposed on it by cave-in and thereby protect employees within the structure. Shields can be permanent structures or can be designed to be portable and moved along as the work progresses.

**Shoring:** Refers to structures such as metal, hydraulic, mechanical or timber shoring systems which can provide adequate support to the sides of an excavation and designed to prevent cave-ins.

**Short-term Exposure:** Means a period of time less than or equal to 24 hours that an excavation is open. This applies only to excavations in Type "A" soil less than 12 feet (3.7 m) deep.

**Sloping:** Refers to a method of protecting employees from cave-ins by excavating inclined sides or faces away from the excavation. The angle of the incline required to prevent a cave-in varies with differences in such factors as the soil type, environmental conditions of exposure, and application of surcharge loads.

**Stable Rock:** Refers to solid mineral material that can be excavated with vertical sides and will remain intact while exposed. Unstable rock is considered to be stable when the rock material on the side or sides of the excavation is secured against caving-in or movement by rock bolts or by other protective devices which have been designed by registered professional engineers.

**Trench:** Means an excavation having a depth which exceeds its width measured at the bottom.

**Trench Cage:** Refers to an approved steel support structure designed to resist the pressure from the walls of a trench and capable of being moved as a unit.

**Tunnel:** Means a generally horizontal excavation more than three feet (one meter) in length located below ground level.

**Uprights:** Means the vertical members of a trench shoring system in contact with the earth and usually positioned so that individual members are closely spaced, in contact with or interconnected to each other.

- *Waler:* Means horizontal members of a shoring system placed parallel to the excavation face whose sides bear against the vertical members of the shoring system or earth.

## Trenching Hazards

The question is often asked, "Why do serious injuries and fatalities to workers continue to occur in earthworks, utilities and construction industries?" There are several explanations as to why incidents and accidents continue to occur, but the most common mistake made is that both the employer and the employees often forget that when they remove (excavate) earth and rock from the ground, they are creating a situation where extreme pressures can be generated at the various openings and faces of the trench or excavation. If there is insufficient material available to support the walls of the trench or excavation, a failure of some type will occur sooner or later. It may catch some people off guard, with the high possibility of an injury or a fatality.

*Points To Remember:*

- No one can predict accurately if an excavation is safe to enter without a proper support structure being provided. A worker does not have to be completely buried in soil to be seriously injured or killed. *There are cases where workers have been only buried up to their waist and have died as a result of the significant pressures exerted by the soil on their bodies.*

- Excavations in or near "back-filled" or previously excavated ground are especially dangerous since the soil is "loose" and does not provide sufficient support within itself.

- Ground water and seepage increases the possibility of a cave-in or failure situation. The increased water pressure exerted on the soil can be the final factor in causing the trench or excavation walls to collapse.

- Clay soil conditions can be extremely treacherous if dried by the sun. Large chunks of material can break off a trench wall after having been stable and solid for a long period of time.
- It is not safe to assume that because the walls of a trench or excavation are frozen that it is safe to enter the area. Frozen ground and soil conditions is no alternative for proper shoring systems.
- A trench or excavation should be considered a "confined space" and appropriate evaluation and controls undertaken to ensure workers are not exposed to any hazardous conditions.
- Shoring must always be adequate to overcome any additional pressures from piles or mounds of excavated material or construction debris, adjoining structures, vehicular traffic, and nearby equipment.

## Soil Mechanics

Typically, in trenching and excavation practices, "soil" is defined as any material removed from the ground to form a hole, trench, or cavity for the purpose of working below the earth's surface at that point. This material is most often found to be weathered rock and humus known as clays, silts, and loams, but also can be materials such as gravel, sand and rock. It is necessary to have some knowledge of soil mechanics before commencing any type of trenching or excavation job.

*Note: Most occupational health and safety regulations stipulate the need to have a "competent person" to be in charge of all excavation and trenching activities at a job site.*

Soil scientists and geo-technical specialists can be helpful in both identifying and characterizing soil materials and specific conditions.

Soil is an extremely heavy material, and may weigh more than 100 pounds per cubic foot (1600 kg per cubic meter). A cubic yard of soil (3 ft x 3 ft x 3 ft), which contains 27 cubic feet of material, may weigh more than 2700 pounds (1227 kg). Furthermore, wet soil conditions, rocky soil or rock is usually heavier than just loose soil. The human body cannot support such heavy loads without being severely injured (internally/externally). See illustration #88.

Illustration #88 - The Body Cannot Support Heavy Loads

Illustration #89 shows a series of multiple columns of soil blocks used to demonstrate basic soil mechanics. These blocks are piled one on top of the other. Each solid block in this example measures one foot square and weighs approximately 100 lbs, and supports the weight of all the blocks above. This means that a block sitting at a five foot depth supports its own weight and the combined weight of the four blocks resting on it. The combined weight of this column is 500 lbs spread over a one square foot area. The five block column constitutes a 500 lb force exerted vertically on whatever lies below.

A column of soil, as shown in illustration #89, exerts not only a vertical force as just described, but also a horizontal force in all outward directions. The outward force is equal to one-half the vertical force. For example, the five block column in illustration #89 has a downward vertical force of 500 lbs (227 kg) at the base of the bottom soil block.

**Illustration #89 -Forces Exerted by a Column of Soil**

The horizontal force pushing out from the base of that same block is half of 500 lbs, or 250 lbs (114 kg), in all outward directions. As the weight of the column increases, the soil blocks at the bottom of the column theoretically have a tendency to compress and spread outward. In undisturbed soil conditions, this process is stopped by the presence of the surrounding columns pushing back with equal pressure.

These hypothetical columns press against each other, maintaining an equilibrium. Therefore, the horizontal pressures of all the columns are balanced, producing a stable relationship.

*Note: Soil that has not been disturbed is kept in place by horizontal and vertical forces. In a trench or excavation, soil will naturally move downward and inward, creating a potentially life threatening situation for the worker. See illustration #90.*

**Illustration #90 - Trench Can Collapse**

## Trench Failure

When a trench is excavated, the stable relationship described previously in soil mechanics no longer exists. As demonstrated in illustration #91A, the horizontal pressure on the soil along the trench wall is no longer in equilibrium, and soil near the bottom may not be able to support its weight and the weight of the soil above. At the point where the soil can no longer withstand the pressure, the wall will shear and break away from its stable position. The first failure occurs as the bottom of the wall moves into the trench area, as seen in illustration #91B. This movement creates an undercut area at the base of the trench as soil material along the wall falls into the trench. Usually there are subsequent movements in which even more material from the wall erodes away, as shown in illustration #91C. Finally the erosion of the trench leaves the upper part of the column only partially supported by cohesion. More soil falls away and soon a full column of material has fallen away into the trench as shown in illustration #91D. Many rescue attempts are unsuccessful because the rescuers attempt to save the victims before the second or third failure has occurred, often trapping the would-be rescuers along with the first victim(s).

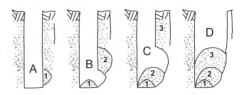

Illustration #91A, B, C, and D - Mechanics of Trench Failure

*Note: Typically, time elapses between the failure segments as just described. It is the uncertainty of when the next failure will occur that makes rescue or recovery extremely hazardous in conditions like this. Time is a major consideration. The longer the trench remains unsupported, the more potential there is for further trench collapse.*

Some employers and contractors believe that proper safety procedures for trenching and excavation work waste valuable time and money. However, accidents that occur because safety precautions are not taken can be extremely costly. In addition to the loss of life, the possible resulting financial costs of a trenching or excavation accident include:

- Work stoppage to rescue the trapped victim.
- Additional time and labor to re-excavate the collapsed trench.
- Increased worker's compensation costs and employee health and insurance premiums.
- Additional administrative work resulting from investigations and incident reports.

- And in some cases, employers are fined because of their negligence or failure to comply with the safety regulations and laws.

The combination of potential fines, loss of human life, personal lawsuits and poor public relations could mean the end of a once successful business.

## Types of Soil Collapse

Employers, contractors and workers as mentioned earlier in this section, should have some basic knowledge of soil mechanics and trenching hazards. Included in these topics is a general discussion on types of soil collapse common to trenching situations.

Five types of soil collapse situations are identified.

### General Zone of Exposure:

Illustration #92 identifies the major areas where workers would be exposed the most to mass soil and/or rock movement in a trench or excavation. The zone of exposure is greatest in the areas highlighted in the drawing.

### Spoil Pile Slide:

Illustration #93 shows how a spoil pile alongside an excavation can slide into the trench if poor excavating procedures are practiced. In this example, the excavated material (spoil) is not placed far enough back or away from the edge of the excavation.

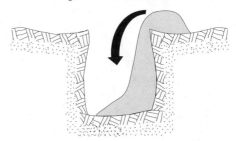

Illustration #93 - Spoil Pile Slide

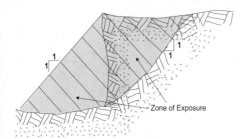

Zone of Exposure

**Illustration #92 - General Zone of Exposure**

## Side Wall Shear:

Illustration #94 shows a situation in an excavation where one of the side walls shears away from the soil mass and suddenly collapses into the excavation. This condition is common to clay type soils which are exposed to drying in the sun.

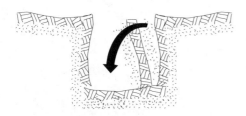

Illustration #94 - Side Wall Shear

## Cave-ins (Sloughing):

Illustration #95 shows a situation in an excavation where materials pull away from the bottom or mid section of the soil mass. This is usually a common problem to previously excavated material, sand, and gravel mixes. The soil conditions are generally quite loose and easily break away from the larger soil mass to cause cave-ins or sloughing of the material.

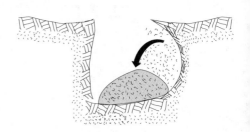

Illustration #95 - Slough-in (Cave-in)

### Soil Rotation:

Illustration #96 shows a situation where, in clay type soils that have become saturated with water, the soil will actually "rotate off" or peel in large sections.

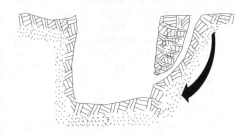

Illustration #96 - Rotation Effect

## Three Soil Classifications

Each soil and rock deposit at an excavation site must be classified by a qualified person.

In North America there are generally three soil classifications. It is important to know which soil types are in the region where any trenching or excavation work will be undertaken and to be familiar with the classifications used for soils by the local, provincial or state governments.

*Type A Soil (Category I):* Type A soil is considered the most stable class of soil. It is difficult to break up when dry and holds together when wet. Typically, Type A soil is very cohesive with an unconfined comprehensive strength of 1.5 tons per sq. ft.. Type A soils include clay, silty clay, sandy clay, clay loam and hardpan. No soil should be classified as Type A if it is fissured; subject to vibration from activities and conditions such as heavy traffic, pile driving, blasting or other impacts; previously disturbed; or part of a sloped, layered system where the slope is 4 x 1 (four horizontal to one vertical) or greater.

*Type B Soil (Category II):* Type B soil is cohesive with an unconfined comprehensive strength greater than 0.5 tons per sq. ft., but less than 1.5 tons per sq. ft.. Type B soils include granular type cohesiveness soils such as angular gravel, silt, silt loam, and medium clay, unstable dry rock, and material that is part of a sloped layered system where the layers dip on a slope less deep than 4 x 1.

*Type C Soil (Category III):* Type C soil is cohesive with an unconfined compressive strength of 0.5 tons per sq. ft. or less. Type C soils include granular soils such as gravel, sand and loamy sand; submerged soil; soil from which water is freely seeping; submerged rock that is not stable; or material in a sloped, layered system where the layers dip into the excavation at a slope of 4 x 1 or steeper.

*Note: OSHA refers to stable rock as a natural solid mineral material which can be excavated with vertical sides and remain intact while freely exposed.*

*Layered Geological Strata:* Refers to soils which are configured in layers. The soil must be classified on the basis of the soil classification of the weakest soil layer. Each layer may be classified individually if a more stable layer lies below a less stable layer, i.e. where a Type C soil rests on top of stable rock. If for example, most excavations are being done to repair or replace existing pipelines or other buried utility services (i.e. the soil has been previously disturbed), excavations should be made to meet the requirements for Type B or Type C soils only.

## Soil Testing

When a qualified person makes a site soil classification, several soil qualities are assessed in addition to the type of soil. Those qualities are:

- Grain size
- Saturation
- Cohesiveness
- Unconfined compressive strength

*There are four different grain sizes:*
- Gravel
- Sand
- Silt
- Clay

If a grain of soil is larger than the size of a typical pencil lead, it is classified as gravel. If smaller, it is sand. The naked eye is not capable of seeing particles of clay and silt. In general, and for safety precautions, the bigger the grains the less stable the soil and more care is thus required in order to prepare the trench or excavation for workers to safely perform their work while in it.

*Saturation* refers to how much water is in the void between the grains of the soil. When the voids fill with water, as shown in illustration #97A, the soil would be considered to be water saturated. When the voids in the soil fill with air, the soil would be considered quite dry, as shown in illustration #97B. A certain amount of water (moisture) can help to make the soil stable, but too much, or too little water, causes cave-ins.

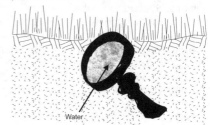

Illustration #97A - Soil Saturation

Illustration #97B - Soil Dryness

*Cohesion*, or stability of the soil refers to how well the grains in the soil hold together. This helps to predict how well the trench or excavation wall will hold together and what design or method of protection is required.

*Unconfined Compressive Strength* refers to how soil reacts under pressure. This is typically measured by the amount of weight required to collapse a standard size soil sample.

To classify soil, a qualified person will conduct both visual and manual tests.

## Visual Soil Testing

During the visual soil test, the qualified person should be observing the entire excavation site, including the soil conditions adjacent to the site and the soil being excavated. Several visual inspection tips include:

- Look for soil particle size and type.
- Does the soil clump together when dug up?
- Could the soil be some type of silt or clay?
- Are there visual signs of crack-line openings or fissures?
- Look for any signs of vibration.
- Look for existing utility lines or services that indicate that the soil has been previously disturbed.
- Observe the open side of the excavation for indications of layered geologic structuring.
- Look for signs of bulging, sloughing or shearing.
- Look for signs of surface or ground water seepage from the sides or bottom of the excavation.

*Note: Layered soil systems with adjacent hazardous areas such as buildings, foundations, roads and vibrating machinery may require a professional engineer for accurate soil classification.*

## Manual Soil Testing

Manual soil tests are required before it can be determined which type of excavation protection system is selected. There are several common types of manual soil tests. A soil sample must be taken from the soil dug out into the spoil pile and this sample should be tested as soon as possible to preserve its natural moisture contents. Manual soil tests are conducted either on-site or off-site. Manual soil tests include:

***Sedimentation Test:*** This test determines how much silt and clay are in sandy soil. A sample of saturated sandy soil is placed in a straight sided jar with about five inches (12.7 cm) of water. After the sample is thoroughly mixed and allowed to settle, the percentage of sand is visible. If the sample, for example, contains 80% sand, the solid would be classified as Type C. See illustration #98.

***Thumb Penetration Test:*** Attempt to press the thumb firmly into the soil being excavated. If the thumb penetrates the soil the full length of the thumb, it is probably Type C soil. If the thumb only penetrates to the length of the thumb nail, the soil is probably Type B. It should be noted that this type of soil testing is the least accurate testing method.

***Dry Strength Test:*** In this test, take a sample of dry soil. If it crumbles freely or with moderate pressure into individual grains it is considered granular or Type C soil. Dry soil that falls into clumps that subsequently break into smaller clumps, and the smaller clumps can only be broken with difficulty, is probably a soil which is clay in combination with gravel, sand, or silt (Type B soil).

Illustration #98 - Sedimentation Test

***Wet Shaking Test:*** This is another method used to test the amount of sand versus clay and silt in a soil sample. Place soil in the hand, as shown in illustration #99, shake a saturated amount to gauge the soil's permeability based on the following factors: shaken clay resists water movement through it; water flows freely through sand and less freely through silt.

**Illustration #99 - Wet Shaking Test**

***Thread Test:*** Take a moist sample of soil, mold it into a ball and then attempt to roll it into a thin thread approximately 0.125 to 0.250 inches (.3 to .6 cm) in diameter by two inches (5 cm) in length. The rolled piece is placed on a flat surface, as shown in illustration #100, then picked up. If the sample does not break when held by one end, it is considered cohesive.

**Illustration #100 - Thread Test**

*Ribbon Test:* This test is also used to determine cohesion, similar to the thread test. A representative soil sample is rolled out using the palms of the hands, as shown in illustration #101. The sample should be rolled to approximately 0.75 inches (1.9 cm) in diameter, and several inches in length. The sample is then squeezed between thumb and forefinger into a flat unbroken ribbon 0.125 to 0.250 inches (.3 to .6 cm) thick, which is allowed to fall freely over the fingers. If the ribbon sample does not break off before several inches are squeezed out, the soil is considered to be quite cohesive.

**Illustration #101 - Ribbon Test**

## Trenches and Excavations

A trench is defined as any excavation which is typically less than 15 feet (4.6 meters) wide and it is longer and deeper than it is wide. See illustration #102. Whereas open excavations are much wider, as in deep basements or one sided like in deep open pits.

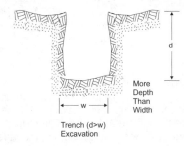

More
Depth
Than
Width

Trench (d>w)
Excavation

**Illustration #102 - Exposed Trench**

See illustration #103 for an example of an open excavation.

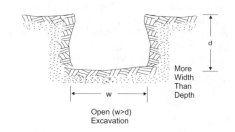

Open (w>d)
Excavation

**Illustration #103 - Exposed Excavation**

According to OSHA requirements, exposed trenches, as shown in illustration #102, that are more than five feet (1.5 m) high must be stabilized by either shoring, sloping the face of the wall back to a stable slope or some equivalent method to prevent cave-ins. Soil testing and rock stability tests may indicate the need for protection in excavations less than five feet (1.5 m) deep. If the trench is excavated in hard, compact soil materials more than five feet (1.5 m) deep, the walls must be supported. If the soil tests indicate soft loose soils in trenches less than five feet deep, then trench boxes, shoring, sheeting, bracing, sloping or other equivalents are required to prevent the trench wall from collapsing.

When employees are required to work in trenches or excavations, an adequate means of exit, such as a ladder, steps or ramp, must be provided. The trench must be braced and shored during excavation and before any personnel are allowed entry. Cross braces and trench jacks must be secured in horizontal positions and spaced vertically in order to prevent the trench wall material from sliding, falling or otherwise moving into the trench. Portable trench boxes (trench shields) or safety cages may also be used to protect employees instead of full shoring systems or bracing methods.

When in use, these devices must be designed, constructed and maintained in a manner that will provide at least as much protection as shoring and bracing, and extended to a height of usually no less than six inches (15 cm) above the vertical face of the trench.

## Trench and Excavation Protection

There are several types of trench and excavation protection systems. Each type has several design features which are suitable to certain types of conditions and soil classifications. There are several preliminary questions which need to be addressed in order to determine which type of protection system is needed.

- Is the trench or excavation more than five feet (1.5 m) deep?
- Is there any potential for cave-ins?
- Is the trench or excavation entirely in stable rock?
- Is the trench or excavation made entirely with vertical sides?
- Is the trench or excavation going to be sloped, shored or shielded?
- If the trench or excavation is to be sloped, how must it be designed?
- If the trench or excavation requires either shoring or shielding, how will it be safely done?

*Note: According to OSHA, protective systems for use in trenches or excavations more than 20 feet (6.10 meters) in depth must be designed by a registered professional engineer.*

## Preliminary Work

Anytime trench or excavation work is to be undertaken, consider the following points before beginning the job:

- Obtain clearance from the public utilities before any digging begins. Serious accidents have occurred in the past when excavators have made contact with a gas or energized electrical line causing fires, explosions, injuries and fatalities.

- An excavation cannot be started until all public utilities (including telephone, hydro, gas, steam, etc.) have been notified and the accurate location of all underground facilities has been determined.

- The employer may in some jurisdictions provide their employees with detection equipment to locate underground utility installations. Always check with local regulations before commencing the excavation and determine first who has the authority and responsibility for locating underground services.

- If damage to any pipe, cable, or other underground facility occurs once the excavation has started, the employer must contact the utility company immediately and advise them of the contact made. No further excavation work should proceed until the utility has undertaken an on-site inspection. The workers must be evacuated from the work site if an energized cable or ruptured gas line or other dangerous fluid or gas is released.

- Where a worker or any portion of an excavation machine is close to any type of overhead line or underground power line, the utility company must be contacted and let them determine the severity of the situation.

- Remove or adequately support loose or large objects in the trench or excavation area which could create a hazard to the workers. These may include rocks, boulders, lumps of frozen dirt, pieces of concrete, timbers, blocking, machinery parts, etc.

## Engineering Approvals

An employer must engage a professional engineer to provide design and construction information and approvals for shoring and support structures where workers are required to enter a trench or excavation. Approvals from engineers must be given when the trench exceeds 20 feet (6.1 m) in depth, this is in accordance to OSHA standards. In Canada, refer to the provincial regulations which state protection requirements at specific depths. Engineering approvals are also required if a shoring structure is required because of the nature of the soil conditions; where a trench cage is to be used; for all shaft and tunnel excavations; for all deep foundation excavations (caisson, pile); or where the excavation may affect the structural integrity of an adjacent building, foundation, utility pole or other structure.

## Dangerous Conditions

Always plan for dangerous conditions before commencing any trench or excavation work. A hazard assessment must be undertaken to determine the risks associated with workers entering the trench or excavation. Possible hazards include:

- Fires, explosions and toxic atmospheres
- Oxygen deficient atmospheres
- Restricted access and egress
- Water seepage, mud, and flooding
- Utility contacts such as electrical, gas, steam, and other dangerous or flammable gases or liquids
- Human factors such as phobias, mental and physical conditions

If a hazard assessment reveals that there is a confined space entry hazard in an evacuation situation, then a proper emergency response plan must be developed before any excavation work begins.

The employer must test the atmosphere prior to entry into the trench or excavation. If an unsafe atmosphere exists, ventilation must be provided to maintain safe working conditions.

If it is impossible to maintain a safe atmosphere by providing engineering controls such as ventilation systems, and the worker must enter the trench or excavation, then a proper supplied air respirator and full emergency procedures must be provided.

If other hazardous conditions such a potential flooding of the trench or excavation exist, then the employer must have a safe working procedure. This may include the provision of personal protection equipment such as safety harnesses and lifelines to allow workers to be removed from the excavation immediately, should a hazardous condition develop.

An effective training program is always recommended for safe trenching and excavation work. Prior to beginning excavation work, the employer must instruct each worker in proper and safe trenching and excavation work procedures. This includes hazard awareness and emergency procedures. The employer must ensure that an experienced and trained worker is designated to directly supervise each trenching or excavation project. This worker must be competent in all aspects of the work, from shoring requirements, soil classification, rescue procedures and site preparation work. The supervisor must directly supervise all excavation work during the entire period the workers are in the trench or excavation.

## Protection System Types

Once the soil is classified and the preliminary work just described has been completed, the most appropriate trench or excavation protection system is selected. There are two main types of systems:

- Sloping or benching
- Shoring or shielding

## Sloping or Benching

Sloping or benching are protection systems that cut the walls of an excavation back at an angle to its floor. Illustration #104 identifies a simple slope system which is easily identified by the angle cut in the wall face.

Illustration #105 identifies the bench system which is commonly used to prevent wall failure in large open excavations. The bench system consists of one or more steps cut into the soil mass of the excavation walls.

The angle used for sloping or the bench design is a ratio based on the soil classification and site restrictions. In both systems, the flatter the angle, the greater the protection provided for the workers.

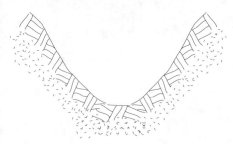

Illustration #104 - Sloping System

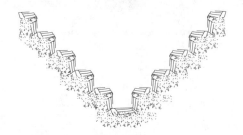

Illustration #105 - Bench System

For Type A soil, which is the most stable soil, the slope angle can be at a ratio of .75:1 and benched in steps of four feet (1.2 m) horizontal to five feet (1.5 m) vertical. Refer to illustration #106A & B.

For Type B soil, which is not as stable as Type A soil, the slope angle can be at a ratio of 1:1 and benched in steps of four feet (1.2 m) horizontal and four feet (1.2 m) vertical. See illustration #107A & B.

Illustration #106A - Slope Requirements - Type "A" Soil

Illustration #107A - Slope Requirements - Type "B" Soil

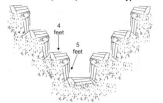

Illustration #106B - Bench Requirements - Type "A" Soil

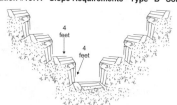

Illustration #107B - Bench Requirements - Type "B" Soil

Type C soil is the least stable. This soil is made up of gravel, loamy sand, soft clay, submerged soil or heavy, loose, unstable rock. Type C soil must be sloped at a ratio of 1.5:1 because of the soil instability. Refer to illustration #108. *Type C soil conditions are not benched.*

Table #9 provides information on allowable slopes for excavations less than 20 feet (6.1 m).

| Soil or Rock Type | Maximum Allowable Slopes (h:v)[1] for Excavations Less Than 20 Feet (6.1 m) Deep[2] |
|---|---|
| Stable Rock | Vertical (90 Degrees) |
| Type A[3] Soil | 0.75:1 (53 Degrees) |
| Type B Soil | 1:1 (45 Degrees) |
| Type C Soil | 1.5:1 (34 Degrees) |

Table #9 - Maximum Allowable Slopes

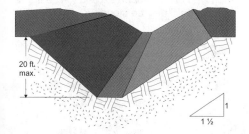

Illustration #108 - Slope Requirements - Type "C" Soil

*Notes:*

1. Numbers shown in parentheses next to allowable slopes are angles expressed in degrees from the horizontal. Angles have been rounded off.

2. Sloping or benching for excavations greater than 20 feet (6.1 m) deep shall be designed by a registered professional engineer, according to OSHA regulations.

3. A short-term maximum allowable slope of .5H:1V (63 degrees) is allowed in excavations in Type A soil that are 12 feet (3.7 m) or less in depth. Short-term maximum allowable slopes for excavations greater than 12 feet (3.7 m) in depth shall be .75H:1V (53 degrees).

## Sloping, Shoring and Shielding
### Sloping

Instead of a shoring structure, a safe method for protecting workers in an excavation is to slope the walls of the excavation at a grade of 1:1 (45 degrees) or flatter depending on the soil type. Illustration #109 identifies a common type of "V" sloped excavation designed to have a 45 degree slope.

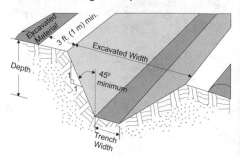

**Illustration #109 - "V" Sloped Excavation**

A combination 1:1 (45 degree) slope and vertical face may be used, as long as the vertical face does not exceed 3 feet (1 meter) and the overall depth of the excavation is not greater than 15 feet (5 meters). Refer to illustration #110.

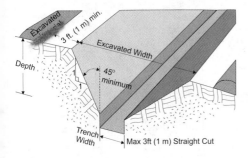

**Illustration #110 - Combination Vertical and Slope Face**

## Shoring

Shoring is designed to prevent cave-ins by supporting trench walls with vertical shores called uprights or sheeting. A series of crossbraces and horizontal supports (wales) complete the shoring framework which is designed to distribute the weight of soil. Illustration #111 identifies a typical shoring system using metal crossbraces and wooden horizontal wales supporting the sheeting which is up against the vertical trench wall.

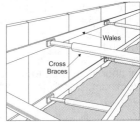

**Illustration #111 - Metal Cross Braces**

It is important to periodically inspect the shoring system in the trench and to watch for changes in the structure and surrounding ground conditions.

Illustration #112 demonstrates how timber shoring is placed in a trench. Uprights are placed vertically up against the trench wall, wales are placed horizontally to position the uprights and the crossbraces are secured tight up against the wales to make an effective timber shoring system.

In order to meet the shoring requirements for this trench or any other type, several factors must be considered:

- Soil classification
- Trench depth
- Trench width
- Type of shoring system to be used (timber, aluminum, trench jack screws, hydraulic, etc.)

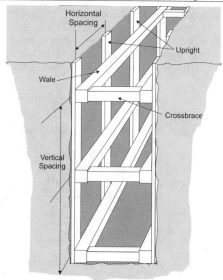

**Illustration #112 - Timber Shoring**

*Note: Always refer to the proper trench shoring specifications issued by OSHA or other occupational health and safety authorities before any shoring work is undertaken. The OSHA shoring specifications, for example, are designed to meet the conditions unique to each of the three soil classifications.*

Designs for aluminum hydraulic shoring systems, as shown in illustrations #113A & B, should be based on the manufacturer's specifications, recommendations and limitations. If this type of shoring system is to be used it is important to refer to the local occupational health and safety authorities before beginning the installation of this system. OSHA has specifications for aluminum shoring systems identified in their excavation and trenching standards and the illustrations shown use OSHA specifications for each shoring design.

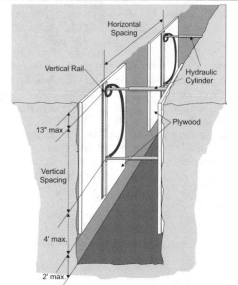

Illustration #113A - Vertical Aluminum Hydraulic Shoring

In illustration #113A vertical aluminum rails are placed up against sheets of plywood and special hydraulic cylinders are placed horizontally to support the complete shoring system. The dimensions and placements used in this example would meet OSHA requirements for Type B soil conditions.

In illustration #113B, horizontal walers made of aluminum are placed up against the wooden vertical uprights and the system is held firmly in place by the horizontally placed hydraulic cylinders. The dimensions and placements used in this example would meet OSHA requirements for Type C soil conditions.

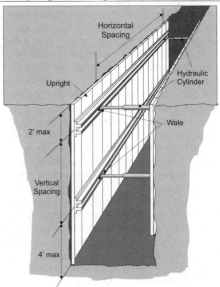

**Illustration #113B - Horizontal Aluminum Hydraulic Shoring**

### *Shielding*

Shielding is designed to give workers a safe work area by providing full protection from collapsing material. Shielding systems can either be built on the job or pre-manufactured. In either case, construction and design specifications must be followed in order to offer maximum protection for the workers in the trench.

Illustration #114 identifies one type of shield used in trenches. These shields can be referred to as trench boxes or a trench cage, and are usually portable steel structures positioned into the trench by heavy equipment. Shields, whether they are job built or pre-manufactured, must be designed to withstand soil pressures and protect the worker against soil cave-ins.

Illustration #114 - Pre-manufactured Shield

Where trench cages are designed to be "stacked", as shown in illustration #115, in deep excavations, each stacked section must be strongly secured to prevent any movement and provide equal load distribution between the cages.

- No worker is allowed to stand inside the trench cage while it is being raised or lowered into place.

- Hoisting hookup and drag points on trench cages must be engineered designed and approved.
- Any worker working inside a trench cage that is to be dragged forward, must be protected against rigging failure by suitable screening or other means.
- No workers are to work outside the protection of the trench cage.

If either shielding or sheeting is used along with sloping, as in illustration #116, it must extend some distance above the sloped portion of the excavation. This protects the workers from debris and loose materials rolling into the trench and falling onto the workers.

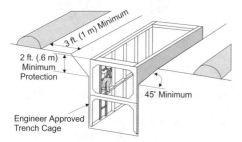

Illustration #115 - Stacked Pre-Manufactured Shield

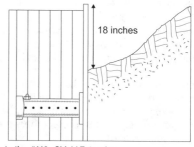

Illustration #116 - Shield Extension

## Installation of Shoring

When installing trench shoring and shielding systems, using excavation equipment, as shown in illustration #117, the bucket of the excavation machine must be placed in the trench directly in front of the shoring being installed.

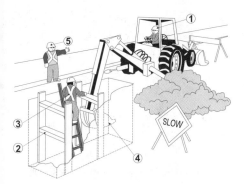

**Illustration #117 - Installing Trench Shoring**

The bucket will serve as additional protection if a cave-in occurs. A proper ladder must be provided in the trench and must extend at least 3 feet (1 m) above the ground level and be located within 10 feet (3 m) of the worker's working location.

**1.** Backhoe operator must place the bucket directly in front of the shoring to be installed and take care not to strike shoring in place.

**2.** Install the first and second strutjack on each set of uprights to stabilize the excavation walls prior to placing the lower strutjacks.

**3.** The worker installing the shoring is protected by a set of shoring behind and the backhoe bucket positioned in front.

**4.** The backhoe bucket is place between the vertical uprights while the worker is placing the strutjacks. This procedure must be followed with each set of shoring.

**5.** The "observer" keeps the excavation under surveillance at all times the worker is in the excavation.

It is essential that shoring crossbraces or struts/jacks be placed from the top of the trench down. It is important that the top (first) crossbrace be placed approximately 18 inches (0.5 m) below the top surface level, then the second crossbrace placed according to the specifications provided in the shoring tables used. The installation of the first and second crossbrace to support the vertical uprights is very important as it stabilizes the trench walls. Refer to illustration #118A.

When plywood or other types of sheeting are used, the crossbraces should never be installed directly onto the plywood or sheeting. The crossbraces must be positioned on the vertical uprights which support the plywood or sheeting. Once the worker has a minimum of two crossbraces placed on each set of uprights, the worker can proceed to install the bottom (lowest) crossbraces used on each shoring section.

This procedure is to be followed with each section of shoring. Using this installation method, the worker is protected by the bucket of the excavation machine and the shoring already installed.

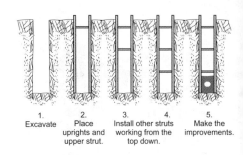

1.
Excavate

2.
Place uprights and upper strut.

3.
Install other struts working from the top down.

4.

5.
Make the improvements.

**illustration #118A - Sequence for Installation of Shoring**

## Removal of Shoring

When removing trench shoring, the reverse procedure is used. Refer to illustration #118B. The crossbraces are removed from the bottom of the trench first, with the top crossbrace being removed last.

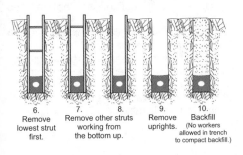

6.
Remove lowest strut first.

7.
Remove other struts working from the bottom up.

8.

9.
Remove uprights.

10.
Backfill
(No workers allowed in trench to compact backfill.)

**Illustration #118B - Sequence for Removal of Shoring**

Remember, there must never be less than two sets of vertical uprights in place and the worker must always remain within the shoring section for protection. If there is undue pressure felt when removing a crossbrace or jack, it may indicate that the soil has moved and the trench must be back filled up to the bottom crossbrace before it is removed; then up to the next crossbrace and so forth.

Refer to illustration #118C. Never attempt to remove a crossbrace with undue pressure, as it may cause a sudden collapse.

It is always preferable on the job-site to have the worker(s) who installed the trench shoring sections be the ones who removes them. That worker will know if there has been changes in the conditions, and if extra pressure is being placed against the crossbraces or other potentially dangerous conditions. Always back fill any trench or excavation immediately after the support systems are removed.

Shoring and shielding systems are only as good as the workers who build them and use them. Unfortunately, every year there are examples of where trenches collapsed because safe work procedures and practices were ignored.

Many workers die and many more are seriously injured in trench and excavation accidents.

Accidents occur when:
- Shoring or shielding is not installed.
- Shoring or shielding is not installed properly.
- Underground utilities are not marked correctly.
- Old underground utilities are not identified on current maps or plans.
- Soil conditions change, there is ground movement, or when loose materials are not secured.
- Severe rain falls occur and the water movement is rapid.

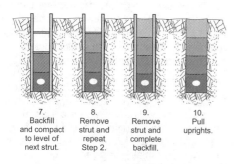

7.
Backfill and compact to level of next strut.

8.
Remove strut and repeat Step 2.

9.
Remove strut and complete backfill.

10.
Pull uprights.

**Illustration #118C - Removing Shoring Under Pressure**

## Shaft and Tunnel Excavations

Shaft and tunnel excavations are primarily used in sewer, water, and other utility work and include such procedures as vertical circular shafts, hand tunneling operations and fully mechanized tunneling systems using "mole" excavators.

Shaft and tunnel excavations are considered confined space entry situations and a thorough hazard assessment and risk control analysis must be performed before any work is started.

Illustration #119 identifies a typical vertical circular shaft where a cylindrical steel sleeve is used to shore the drilled shaft. The steel sleeve is used to prevent cave-ins of blocks of soil, rocks and wet silt layers.

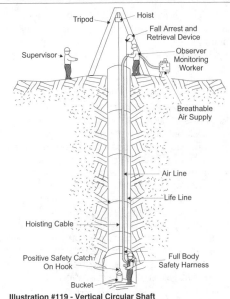

**Illustration #119 - Vertical Circular Shaft**

Due to the risks associated with this type of work, it is important to consider the following points:

- Have proper first aid supplies at the excavation site.
- It is recommended that at least one worker on each shift be a certified first aider with CPR training.
- A basket stretcher and blankets must be available at the work site.
- Full body harnesses must be used by workers in the shaft.
- All workers at the work site must be instructed on rescue procedures which will be employed in case of a serious accident or injury occurring in the shaft.
- Underground excavations and shafts must be provided with an adequate source of electrical lighting for the full length of the tunnel or shaft and at the working face of the excavation.
- In the case of electrical failure, an emergency lighting system must be in place.

- All electrical circuits in underground or shaft type excavations must meet the requirements of the electrical code.
- All light bulbs must be "caged" to prevent them from being damaged.
- Due to possible moisture accumulation in such excavations, it is essential that all electrical wiring be properly grounded.
- Only electrical equipment and tools that are double insulated or properly grounded can be used. It is recommended that "ground fault circuit interrupters" be used for electrical circuits underground.
- Adequate fire protection must be provided in each shaft or tunnel excavation.
- Any flammable or combustible liquids must be stored in compliance with the local fire codes and dispensed only from approved safety containers.
- Combustible scrap materials, such as wood, paper, and rags must not be allowed to accumulate in the excavation.

- All blasting operations must be undertaken by a certified blaster who is qualified to handle and use explosives. Explosives must be stored and transported in accordance to the local regulations.
- Vertical drilled shafts, shored with steel sleeves, are normally provided access by a straight fixed vertical ladder. In deep shafts, fall protection must be provided. This can be done by providing workers with a full body harness secured with a lifeline to a fall arresting device at the top entrance of the shaft.
- In shaft and tunnel operations, the worker accessway to a shaft must extend the full length of the shaft and should be separated from the hoistway in a manner so that the load or hoisting device cannot come into contact with the worker.
- There should be an observer positioned at the top of the shaft entrance way and be there to monitor the work and to keep regular communication channels open with the workers.
- A portable air supply system may be needed to supply fresh air to the workers.
- Regular checks should be made to determine air quality and to ensure that there are no dangerous or toxic gases, fumes or vapors present.
- Some type of ventilation system may also be required.
- All cranes and hoisting equipment used for excavation work shall be inspected and maintained in accordance with the local regulations and the manufacturer's specifications.
- All ropes, cables, slings, chains, blocks and other rigging attachments must be rated for the lifts required and regularly inspected to ensure the equipment is not damaged and can continue to be used safely.

- The employer shall establish a system of clearly communicated signals which are to be practiced for all hoisting operations.
- Haulage buckets or bins should not be overloaded or off-balance with mud or other materials in a manner where the material is likely to fall out and onto the workers below.

*Note: Due to the nature of the risks associated with workers entering a caisson or similar type deep shaft or tunnel excavation, it is essential that the employer develop a documented safe work procedure for this type of confined space entry work. A documented method of access and egress for the workers should be available at the work site prior to any worker entering the shaft or tunnel.*

*It is also essential that the shaft or tunnel be under constant supervision at all times when workers are inside the excavation.*

## Trench Collapse

If a trench collapses when workers are inside, there is extreme danger to the workers, as the ground may be very unstable and the trench may cave-in again, begin to flood, or expose dangerous utility lines to those both inside or outside of the excavation. Remember, trenches don't always cave-in from the top. External pressures applied on the trench surface can force sections of the inner walls to "belly out" or bulge in the middle as demonstrated in illustration #120.

If a trench collapses and someone is trapped in it:

- Do not stay in the trench yourself. The trench has proved to be unstable and if you stay in it you could easily become another victim. Get out and call for help immediately.

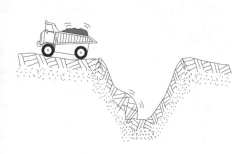

Illustration #120 - External Pressures - "Belly Out"

- It is best to not attempt a rescue by yourself, because any attempt to assist a trapped co-worker will likely result in another cave-in or lead to further injuries of the trapped worker.

- It is best to not try and dig out a trapped worker by yourself, as you could severely injure the person by using a shovel or you could cause more loose material to fall down on the trapped person and onto yourself. Get out and call for help immediately.

- Do not attempt to remove any equipment or tools which are partly submerged in the loose fallen material. Any movement may cause further materials to fall down.

- Be very careful with heavy equipment around a trapped victim, as the vibrations coming from the heavy equipment may cause the trench to collapse again. Never try to dig a trapped victim out or pull a victim out with heavy machinery.

# SECTION SIX

## WORKPLACE HAZARDOUS MATERIAL INFORMATION SYSTEM

## Introduction

The Workplace Hazardous Material Information System (WHMIS) was established in Canada to provide employers and employees with reliable information about the hazardous materials encountered in the workplace. The objective of WHMIS is to reduce accidents and incidents involved with handling, storing, use, and production or disposal of hazardous materials. WHMIS came into effect in Canada on October 31, 1988.

The purpose of WHMIS is to inform all workers about the hazards of chemicals and other dangerous materials in the workplace. It also provides information on how to protect people in the event of exposure to a controlled product.

## Controlled Products

Controlled products are classified into six groups:

- Class A: Compressed Gas
- Class B: Flammable and Combustible Material
- Class C Oxidizing Material
- Class D: Poisonous and Infectious Material
- Class E: Corrosive Material
- Class F: Dangerously Reactive Material

Controlled products are subject to regulations for labeling "Material Safety Data Sheets" (MSDS), and worker education, unless they are packaged for consumer use. Consumer packaged products used in the workplace require only worker education.

Other products in Canada requiring worker education are:

- Explosives
- Cosmetics, drugs, foods, and devices
- Radioactive products
- Pesticides

The following products are exempt from all aspects of WHMIS:

- Wood and products made of wood
- Tobacco and products made of tobacco
- Manufactured articles
- Products covered under the Transportation of Dangerous Goods (TDG) Act

## How is WHMIS Implemented?

WHMIS is implemented in Canada through a combination of federal and provincial regulations. These include:

1. The Controlled Product Regulations, issued pursuant to section 15(1) of the Hazardous Products Act, contain requirements that specify the form and content of supplier labels, the type of information on the MSDS, conditions of exemptions and the definition of what constitutes a controlled product (classification).

2. The Hazardous Products Act (federal), requires suppliers of hazardous materials to provide supplier labels and MSDS's as a condition of sale and importation.

3. The Ingredient Disclosure List, issued pursuant to section 17 (1) of the Hazardous Products Act, contains the names of (toxic) chemicals that must be identified if they are present in controlled products above specified concentrations.

4. The Canada Labour Code and the Canada Occupational Safety and Health Regulations establish requirements for WHMIS in federally regulated workplaces.

5. (Provincial) WHMIS Workplace Regulations, require employers to provide labels, MSDS's and worker education in the workplace, and to help provide uniform provincial WHMIS regulations across Canada.

## Three Elements to WHMIS

*1. Labels:* All hazardous materials must carry labels that clearly identify risks and recommend precautions that should be taken for safe handling.

*2. Material Safety Data Sheets (MSDS):* MSDS must be provided for every hazardous material in the workplace. The MSDS provides detailed information about the material, more than is typically provided just on the product label. Carefully read the MSDS before handling a hazardous material.

*3. Worker Education:* The employer must train their employees how to interpret and use the information which is provided on product labels and MSDSs.

WHMIS applies to the workplace only, it does not regulate:

- Hazardous products that are used in the home.
- The disposal of hazardous waste.
- Hazardous materials in transport (TDG).

Under the current WHMIS regulations, both suppliers and employers are responsible for providing hazard information. The supplier is responsible for:

- Labeling hazardous materials supplied to the workplace, and
- Providing the correct MSDS for the supplied product.

The employer is responsible for:

- Ensuring that MSDSs are current and readily available;
- Ensuring that hazardous materials are correctly labeled, and
- Training workers on how to handle hazardous materials safely.

Workers have responsibilities as well, and these include:

- Workers must learn how to access and interpret hazardous product information;
- Workers must learn to handle, store and dispose of controlled products, and
- Workers must report unsafe conditions.

*Note: Controlled products which are not properly labeled represent an unsafe condition.*

## WHMIS and TDG

TDG (Transportation of Dangerous Goods) and WHMIS in Canada are complementary hazard communication systems.

- The purpose of WHMIS is to help workers safely handle hazardous materials in the workplace.
- The purpose of TDG is to protect the general public from hazards associated with dangerous goods during transportation.

No overlap is intended between WHMIS and TDG. Where one system leaves off, the other system takes over.

Anyone in Canada who ships, receives or transports dangerous goods, must be trained and carry a Certificate of Training, or work under the direct supervision of someone who is trained in the transportation of dangerous goods.

## WHMIS Hazard Symbols

Each class of controlled product under WHMIS is depicted by a distinguishing hazardous product symbol. Controlled products, those subject to WHMIS, are included in six classes. Table #10 identifies each product with its own unique hazard symbol.

*Note: A material which is classed as a controlled product must be labeled. The Supplier Label must display one or more of the hazard symbols to identify what class the material belongs to and to indicated the risks associated with the product.*

| WHMIS SYMBOLS | | |
|---|---|---|
| Hazard Symbol | Class & Division | Description |
| | Class A | *Compressed Gas* |
| | Class B | *Flammable & Combustible Material* |
| | Division 1 | - Flammable Gas |
| | Division 2 | - Flammable Liquids |
| | Division 3 | - Combustible Liquids |
| | Division 4 | - Flammable Solids |
| | Division 5 | - Flammable Aerosols |
| | Division 6 | - Reactive Flammable Material |

| WHMIS SYMBOLS | | |
|---|---|---|
| | Class C | *Oxidizing Material* |
| | Class D | *Poisonous & Infectious Materials* |
| | Division 1 | - Materials causing immediate and serious toxic effects |
| | Division 2 | - Materials causing other toxic effects |
| | Division 3 | - Biohazardous infectious materials |
| | Class E | *Corrosive Material* |
| | Class F | *Dangerously Reactive Material* |

Table #10 - WHMIS Symbols

## Class A: Compressed Gas

Compressed gases are dangerous because they are stored and kept stable under pressure. Compressed gases are materials which can be stored as pressurized gas, pressurized liquid, or refrigerated liquid. Examples of compressed gases common to most workplaces include: compressed air, carbon dioxide, chlorine, hydrogen, argon, helium, nitrogen, and propane. Several safety features for compressed gases include:

A cylinder of compressed gas that is mishandled or damaged may rupture or break and can be extremely dangerous to anyone in the immediate vicinity.

- If a compressed gas cylinder is heated or exposed to temperature variations, it may become unpredictable and explode.
- Leakage in a compressed gas cylinder, depending on the type of gas, could ignite and cause an explosion. Leaking gases, under high pressure, can cause burns or frost bite to exposed skin.
- Never drop or roughly handle compressed gas cylinders.
- Keep the cylinder valves protected with proper fitting protectors or caps.
- Store compressed gas cylinders as per the manufacturer's recommendations.

## Class B: Flammable and Combustible Materials

Flammable and combustible materials may ignite or explode, or spontaneously burst into flame. These materials may be in solid, liquid or a gas state. Several safety features for flammable and combustible materials include:

- Flammable materials will ignite readily at normal temperature.
- Combustible materials must be heated before they will ignite.
- There are six divisions of Class B materials:

*1. Flammable Gases:* Compressed gases that are also flammable, (i.e. propane, butane).

*2. Flammable Liquids:* Liquids with a flashpoint less than 100F (38C), (i.e. gasoline).

*3. Combustible Liquids:* Liquids with a flashpoint less than 200F (93C), but more than 100F (38C), (i.e. diesel fuel). *Note, if the flashpoint exceeds 200F (93C), the material is not controlled.*

*4. Flammable Solids:* Solids that burn, caused by friction, retained heat from manufacturing or processing, or materials that readily ignite and burn violently and persistently, (i.e. sulphur).

*5. Flammable Aerosols:* Most aerosols contain flammable type propellants and active ingredients, (i.e. spray paints).

*6. Reactive Flammable Materials:* These materials are spontaneous and combustible in air, or in contact with water, (i.e. metallic sodium).

- Keep flammable materials away from heat and sources of ignition.
- Avoid static discharge or any type of friction or impact that could cause sparking.

## Class C: Oxidizing Material

Oxidizing materials are dangerous because they release oxygen, which promotes combustion. Oxidizing materials contribute to the burning of another material by yielding oxygen or another substance that yields oxygen. Oxidizing materials will support a fire and are highly reactive with other types of materials. Several safety features for oxidizing materials include:

- When a substance burns, it is "oxidized", (chemically reacts with oxygen). Normal air contains only 21% oxygen. By increasing the supply of oxygen, oxidizers:
  - enhance combustion, and
  - may cause substances that would not burn under normal conditions to become spontaneously combustible.

- Keep oxidizing materials away from heat sources and store in cool dry places.
- Keep these materials away from flammable and combustible materials.

*Note: An example of an oxidizing material is sulphuric acid which, when poured onto paper, will cause the paper to burn. Other examples include oxygen gas, hydrogen peroxide, and chlorine and potassium permanganate. These substances are extremely hazardous.*

## Class D: Poisonous & Infectious Materials

A poison is defined as any substance which, when taken into the body by eating, drinking, breathing, or through the skin, is injurious to health. It is excessive quantities or doses which are taken into the human body that result in ill health effects. Poisons of all types are encountered at home and, more commonly, in the workplace. Each Canadian jurisdiction (provincial, territorial and federal) has standards for exposure to poisonous materials in the workplace. These standards are set so that employees will not be harmed if exposure levels are within the acceptable standards. There are three divisions of Class D materials:

 **1. Materials Causing Immediate and Serious Toxic Effects:** These materials are highly poisonous and immediately dangerous. Their effects are nausea, dizziness, breathing difficulties, headaches, and in severe cases, death. Examples include, cyanide, strychnine and hydrogen sulphide.

**2. Materials Causing Other Toxic Effects**: These materials are considered toxic and their effects are serious, but there are no immediate adverse effects to target organs or to the reproductive system. Usually these effects result from repeated exposure to a toxic substance over a period of time.

Immediate, but temporary effects may occur to the skin, eyes and respiratory system. Examples include, asbestos fibers, saccharin, mercury and ammonia.

*3. Biohazardous Infectious Materials:* These materials are organisms that cause disease in people and animals. The materials are germs, such as bacteria, viruses, and fungi. They also include cultures, concentrates, and specimens (i.e. blood, sputum, urine, organ or body tissue) containing or suspected of containing such organisms. Examples include, AIDS, Hepatitis B and salmonella.

*Note: Biohazardous infectious materials are typically found in medical and health care facilities. In these environments there are many exposure risks and workers may not know whether the material they are sampling is contaminated, such as blood samples taken for analysis. For this reason, "universal precautions" are common in the health industry. Workers are trained to assume that every blood or tissue sample is contaminated and handle it accordingly.*

- Always wear suitable personal protective equipment.
- Keep containers tightly closed and sealed.
- Seek immediate medical help if you feel ill after handling these infectious materials.

## Class E: Corrosive Materials

Corrosive materials are capable of destroying human tissue or other substances by chemical action. These materials can cause severe burns to exposed skin, eyes and to the tissues of the respiratory system, if the vapors are inhaled. These chemical burns, internal or external, result in irreversible tissue damage. It is this "irreversibility" property of Class E materials that distinguish corrosives from skin, eye, and lung irritants in Class D - 2.

The effects of irritants are temporary, whereas the effects of Class E corrosives are permanent.    Examples include, sulphuric acid, caustic soda, and many cleaners and disinfectants.

- Avoid any skin or eye contact with corrosive materials.
- Wear appropriate personal protective equipment and use recommended respiratory protective equipment.

## Class F: Dangerously Reactive Material

Dangerously reactive materials which, by chemical reaction with other materials or self- reaction under conditions of shock or increases in pressure or temperature, can pose an extreme hazard.  Some of these materials may even react dangerously with water to produce a poisonous gas.  Class F materials include a wide variety of chemicals that have potentially self-reactive characteristics.

Several safety features include:
- Self-reactive materials may undergo vigorous polymerization, decomposition or condensation.
- These materials may become self-reactive under unstable conditions of pressure and temperature changes, shock, or react vigorously with water to release dangerous poisonous gases.
- If a material is dangerously reactive, the MSDS will indicate that it is "unstable." Examples of Class F materials include epoxy resins, fiberglass repair kits, sodium, acetylene, vinyl acetate, calcium carbide, potassium and magnesium.
- Keep any of these materials away from heat sources.
- Avoid contact with water.
- Avoid shock and friction conditions.
- Wear suitable personal protective equipment and use recommended respiratory protective equipment.

- In case of fire, evacuate the premises, and call the fire department immediately.

*Note: Many chemicals that are not considered self-reactive will nevertheless react vigorously with other chemicals to create a fire or explosion, or release poisonous gas. Any two chemicals that react this way are said to be "incompatible." The MSDS will identify which chemicals the controlled product will react with.*

## Physical States of Chemicals

Chemicals may be found at home or in the workplace in a number of forms, also called "physical states."

- Solid
- Liquid
- Gas
- Vapor
- Aerosol

*Solid:* Is a state in which the substance has a form and retains that form, independent of its container.

*Liquid:* Is a formless fluid that takes on the shape of its container and flows in accordance with the laws of gravity.

*Gas:* Is a formless fluid that expands to fill the space it occupies; it is always in the gaseous form at normal room temperature and pressure.

*Vapor:* Means the gaseous form of a substance that is found in a solid or liquid state at normal atmospheric pressure. Heating a solid to a sufficiently high temperature causes the solid to give off vapors; for example, lead. Evaporation is the way in which a liquid gives off a vapor at room temperature.

*Aerosol:* Consists of airborne solid or liquid particles of fine enough size to remain dispersed in the air long enough to be breathed into the body.

Aerosols include:

- Dusts (solid particles caused by handling, crushing, grinding, impacting, spraying or detonating a solid)
- Mists (liquid particles)
- Smoke (burned carbon particles)
- Fumes (solid particles formed by the condensation of the vapor from a heated solid)

## Entry into the Body

In order to cause ill health effects, also called toxic effects, chemical substances and biological agents have to enter the body. Entry may occur in one of three ways:

- Inhalation (breathed in)
- Ingestion (eat or drink)
- Absorption (enter through the skin)

The effect on the body may result from a single exposure or as a result of many exposures over a long period of time. The effects may be either acute or chronic.

*Acute Effect:* A single exposure to a hazardous material may cause an immediate ill health effect, such as: headaches, dermatitis (skin rash), loss of consciousness, or death.

*Chronic Effect:* Describes the effect on the body resulting from repeated exposure to a hazardous material over time. Chronic effects may include examples such as asbestosis, allergies, bronchitis, emphysema, or cancer.

### Inhalation

Inhalation is the main route by which chemical substances enter the body. Illustration #121 identifies the airway passage to the lungs showing the routes taken by contaminated air.

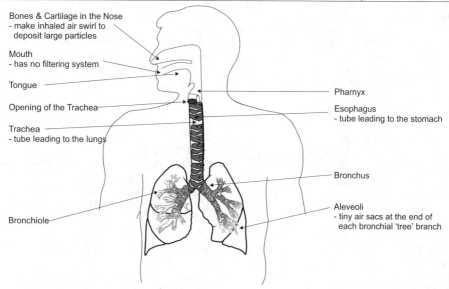

Bones & Cartilage in the Nose
- make inhaled air swirl to
  deposit large particles

Mouth
- has no filtering system

Tongue

Opening of the Trachea

Trachea
- tube leading to the lungs

Bronchiole

Pharnyx

Esophagus
- tube leading to the stomach

Bronchus

Aleveoli
- tiny air sacs at the end of
  each bronchial 'tree' branch

**Illustration #121 - Airway Passage**

Upon inhalation of the chemical substance, and entering into the respiratory system, there may be the following effects:

- Harmful to the tissues in the respiratory system; for example, ammonia may irritate the nose and lungs, and material such as asbestos, may cause scarring in the lung (asbestosis).
- Dissolve in the blood in the same way as oxygen is inhaled and once dissolved, the chemical substance will be transported by the blood to various parts of the body.
- Harmful to the organs which remove chemical substances from the body (liver, kidneys, or bladder).
- Harmful to the organs where chemical substances may be deposited; for example, lead and phosphorous may be deposited in the bones.

### Ingestion

Ingestion is usually the unintentional entry of hazardous materials into the body through the mouth while eating and/or drinking. Illustration #122 identifies the ingestive system and demonstrates how hazardous materials can enter into the blood system. Unintentional entry can be as simple as forgetting to wash hands or leaving food where solid particles or liquid droplets can collect on them.

The harmful effect of ingestion of chemical substances may be the same as inhalation, with the exception of harm to the respiratory system.

## Absorption

The skin is an effective barrier against most hazardous materials. Illustration #123 identifies the layers of skin and shows how hazardous solutions and substances may penetrate the skin and be absorbed into the blood stream.

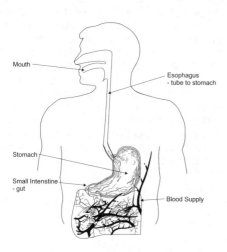

**Illustration #122 - Ingestive System**

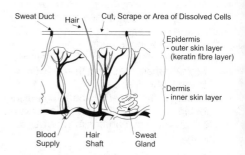

**Illustration #123 - Absorption - Layers of Skin**

Chemicals and biological agents may enter the body where the skin is broken as a result of a cut, sore, rash or puncture. Some types of hazardous chemicals easily pass directly through the skin into the bloodstream; a good example is methanol.

Once a hazardous material has entered the body through the skin, the harmful effect may be the same as inhalation, with the exception of harm to the respiratory system.

## Preventing Entry into the Body

Methods for controlling exposure to hazardous materials may be directed at three different locations:

1. At the source of the hazard.
2. The path between the source and the worker.
3. At the worker.

Control methods directed at the source of the hazard are:

- Substitution of less hazardous materials.
- Change the process to reduce worker exposure; or design and build protective enclosures.

Control methods directed at the path between the source of the hazard and the worker are:

- Proper cleanup, housekeeping practices, and washing hands before eating.
- Proper storage facilities.
- Provide local exhaust extraction at the point of generation of an airborne contaminant.
- Dilute the contaminated air with fresh, clean air.
- Provide adequate ventilation.
- Install protective enclosures or barriers.

Control methods directed at the worker include:

- Education and training programs.
- Provide personal protective equipment.
- Ensure that safe work procedures are being followed.

- Provide reliable monitoring and medical surveillance systems.

## Exposure Limits for Contaminants

Most airborne chemical contaminants in the workplace have an exposure standard or limit. The intent is to set limits below the exposure standard to have no ill health effects. Some substances are extremely toxic, for example, lead and mercury, where even a small dose will result in harm to the body's tissues. Therefore, the exposure limit for these substances will be very low. Some chemicals, such as toluene, solvents and metallic dusts are mildly toxic, thus, the body may be capable of tolerating some higher doses without extreme adverse health effects.

There are three types of exposure limits:
1. Time-Weighted Average Exposure Limits (TWAEL)
2. Short-Term Exposure Limits (STEL)
3. Ceiling Exposure Limit (CEL)

*Note: The values assigned to each type of exposure limit will vary from one jurisdiction to another. However, the recommended guide for such values is the publication called the "Threshold Limit Values and Biological Exposure Indices", published by the American Congress of Governmental Industrial Hygienists. The designation "TLV" (Threshold Limit Value) is a registered trademark of that organization.*

*TWAEL:* The *"Time-Weighted Average Exposure Level"* is the average of the concentration of an airborne contaminant to which a worker may be exposed to daily in an eight hour work day or forty hour work week without harmful health effects.

*STEL:* The *"Short-Term Exposure Limit"* is the maximum concentration of an airborne contaminant to which a worker may be exposed to in any period of up to fifteen minutes.

Only four exposures per work day are permitted at such maximum concentrations. In addition:

- There must be at least sixty minutes interval between such exposures; and
- The TWAEL for the work day cannot be exceeded.

**CEL:** The "Ceiling Exposure Limit" is the maximum concentration of an airborne contaminant to which the worker may be exposed to at any given time.

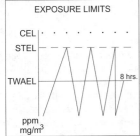

Illustration #124 - Exposure Limits

*Note: The graph shown in illustration #124 represents each of the three exposure values in their order of limits.*

## Units of Measurement

Dusts, fumes, mists and aerosols are measured in milligrams of materials per cubic metre of air ($mg/m^3$). Note, one milligram is 1/1000 of a gram.

Gases, vapors and smoke are measured in parts per million of air (ppm) or in $mg/m^3$.

## Chemical Substances

The following list of chemical substances may be classified by the health effects they have on the human body. These include:

- Irritants
- Allergens
- Asphyxiants
- Poisons
- Mutagens
- Carcinogens
- Teratogens

*Irritants:* Are chemical substances that cause reddening, itching, or pain in the parts of the body exposed to them; for example, skin, eyes or throat.

*Allergens:* Are substances which react with the body's immune system to produce, over some time, an allergic reaction.

*Asphyxiants:* Replace the oxygen in air and, if too much is replaced, normal breathing becomes impossible.

*Poisons:* A poison is any substance that is injurious to health when taken into the body. Almost every substance is a poison if consumed in sufficient quantity.

*Carcinogens:* Chemicals which are considered to cause cancer are called carcinogens; examples include, arsenic, asbestos, benzene, and vinyl chloride.

*Mutagens:* These substances cause genetic mutations. Mutagens cause sudden variations in the makeup of genes so that offspring differ markedly from parents, as opposed to gradual variations from one generation to the next generation.

*Teratogens:* These substances cause the development of deformed fetuses or produce birth defects.

## WHMIS Labels

A WHMIS label is any mark, sign, device, stamp, seal, sticker, tag or wrapper that appears on a hazardous material for the purpose of alerting people to its hazards and provides basic precaution information.

Under WHMIS regulations, all controlled products must be labeled. The purpose of the label is to:

- Identify the product as controlled
- Indicate the nature of the risks associated with the product
- Provide basic safe handling instructions

*Note: The amount of information that the label can provide is limited by its size.*

*The MSDS will always provide more comprehensive safe handling information than the label will.*

There are three types of WHMIS labels:

1. Supplier Labels
2. Workplace Labels
3. Other means of identification

### Supplier Labels

Every controlled product purchased and received for the workplace should display a supplier label, as in the sample label shown in illustration #125.

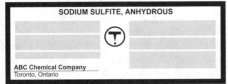

SODIUM SULFITE, ANHYDROUS

ABC Chemical Company
Toronto, Ontario

Illustration #125 - Supplier Label

Supplier labels must contain the following information:

1. Product Identifier

2. Hazard Symbols (appropriate symbols for each class)

3. Risk Phrases (describe the hazard and supplementary information provided by the hazard symbols)

4. Precautionary Measures (recommended safe handling and storage procedures and PPE to use)

5. First Aid Measures (what to do in the event of an accident)

6. Supplier Information (name, address, emergency telephone number of the supplier)

7. Reference to the MSDS (more detailed product information)

*Note: The supplier is responsible for preparing and applying the Supplier Label. If the controlled product does not have a supplier label, the product must not be used until an MSDS and a supplier label have been obtained.*

## Bulk Supplies

The tank or storage bin into which bulk materials are transferred from a delivery vehicle must be labeled with a supplier label or a workplace label.  If the controlled product stored in bulk is subsequently transferred to containers for resale or delivery off the premises, a supplier label must be affixed to each container.  If the controlled product is decanted, as shown in illustration #126, the container must be labeled into which the product is being transferred to.

Illustration #126 - Decanting Procedure

## Workplace Label

Under WHMIS, there should never be a controlled product that is not labeled in the workplace.  As long as the controlled product remains in the original container, with a supplier label on it, no additional labeling is required.  However, there may be times when there is a need to transfer the controlled product into another container for use in the workplace. Now a workplace label must be affixed to the container receiving the transferred product. Workplace labels usually are less detailed than supplier labels. They must contain the following information:

1. Product Identifier.

2. Information for safe handling (hazard symbols, first aid measures, safe handling and storage procedures and PPE).

3. Reference to the MSDS.

4. Other Relevant information.

No prescribed format is enforced by WHMIS for workplace labels. A sample workplace label is shown in illustration #127 for leaded gasoline. The information provided on this sample workplace label meets the minimum requirements of WHMIS. The hazard symbols and PPE methods are optional and may be included at the employer's discretion.

Illustration #127 - Workplace Label - Leaded Gasoline

There are two cases when a workplace label is not required when decanting a controlled product:

1. If it is for immediate use,

2. If the following three conditions are met:

a. it is used only by the worker who filled the portable container

b. it is used during the shift in which the portable container was filled, and

c. the contents of the portable container are identified.

*Note: Company policy may be to label all containers of controlled products with a workplace label. Always check with your supervisor. In general, if a controlled product is transferred from the supplier's container into another container, then the second container must have a workplace label*

## PACE Labels

The PACE label is a special type of workplace label which has been developed for the oil industry. However, it may be used in any workplace label application.

**Illustration #128 - PACE Label**

In addition to the product identifier, safe handling information and reference to MSDS, it displays all eight WHMIS hazard symbols and nine PPE pictorials. A sample PACE label is shown in illustration #128.

With this design of workplace label, simply black out or cover over any of the WHMIS hazard symbols or PPE pictorials that "do not apply."

## NFPA Labels

The National Fire Protection Association (NFPA) is an organization in the United States that provides fire fighting information and develops fire control standards. The NFPA label system has been developed primarily to meet the needs of fire fighters.

NFPA labels are designed to use a combination of colors and numbers to identify the nature and degree of risk posed by the hazardous material. This information may be presented either in a diamond-shaped or color-bar format.

The sample NFPA label shown in illustration #129 uses the color-bar format.

Phenyl ether
Micro-vapor
Emergency Phone #
Phenyl Ether (vapor)

**HEALTH**      **1**

**FLAMMABILITY**      **1**

**REACTIVITY**      **0**

**PERSONAL PROTECTION**      **K**

CAUTION:

Eyes: wash with large amounts of water, get medical attention immediately.

Skin: wash with soap or mild detergent. If skin irritation persists, get medical attention.

Breathing: get fresh air, perform artificial respiration if needed.

**Illustration #129 - NFPA Label**

Colors and numbers represent the following nature and degree of hazards. See table #11 for further details.

| NFPA COLORS/NUMBERS SYSTEM ||
|---|---|
| **Colors** | **Nature of Hazard** |
| Blue | Health |
| Red | Flammability |
| Yellow | Reactivity |
| | |
| **Numbers** | **Degree of Hazard** |
| 0 | Minimal |
| 1 | Slight |
| 2 | Moderate |
| 3 | Serious |
| 4 | Extreme |

**Table #11 - NFPA Colors/Numbers System**

Special symbols are also used to indicate some of the special risks.  See Table #12.

| NFPA SYMBOLS | |
|---|---|
| **Hazard** | **Code** |
| Oxidizer | OXY |
| Acid | ACID |
| Alkali | ALK |
| Corrosive | COR |
| Avoid Water | W̶ |
| Radiation | |

**Table #12 - NFPA Symbols**

*Note: To meet WHMIS workplace labeling requirements, NFPA information must be supplemented with safe handling information and a reference to the MSDS.*

## Combined WHMIS/TDG Labels

Many compressed gases, fire extinguishers, and other types of pressurized cylinders must be periodically sent out by the employer for recharging or testing.  These cylinders are subject to WHMIS labeling requirements while they are in the workplace and to meet the Transportation of Dangerous Goods (TDG) labeling requirements during transport.  Illustration #130 identifies a combination WHMIS/TDG label which meets both requirements.  Many suppliers of controlled products utilize a combined WHMIS/TDG label for larger containers, such as tanks and drums.

Illustration #130 - Combined WHMIS/TDG Label

## Precautionary Pictals

The following pictals, shown in table #13, represent some of the personal protective equipment which should be used when handling specific controlled products. Always discuss with the employer which PPE is best suited for those controlled products being handled.

Wear Rubber Boots

 Wear Splash Goggles

 Wear Lab Coat / Slicker

 Wear Filtered Respirator (Dust and Vapour)

 Wear Required Respirator and Face Mask

 Wear Protective Gloves (Rubber / Leather)

 Wear Dust Mask

 Wear Face Shield

 Wear Self-Contained Breathing Apparatus

 Wear Full Protection Suit

 Wear Rubber / Neoprene Apron

 No Smoking

Table #13 - Precautionary Pictals

## Material Safety Data Sheets (MSDS)

The Material Safety Data Sheet (MSDS) is a document that contains detailed hazard and safe handling information for a controlled product. The MSDS provides much more detailed safety information than is typically found on a supplier or workplace label. The MSDS is prepared by the supplier and provided to the employer as their source for much more comprehensive safe handling and storage information of any controlled product.

In Canada the MSDS must contain information for nine categories. Illustrations #131A-E provides a sample form for an MSDS. The nine categories referred to on the MSDS include:

**1. Product Identifier:** Product identification, product use, supplier name and contact address and telephone number.

**2. Hazardous Ingredients:** Each hazardous ingredient present in significant amounts must be identified and listed in the MSDS, and the percentage and acute toxicity level of each must be shown.

**3. Physical Data:** All significant physical characteristics and data associated with the controlled product are identified on the MSDS. This includes physical characteristics such as appearance, odor, color, freezing and boiling points, volatility, pH, density, etc.

**4. Fire and Explosion Data:** Properties of flammable and combustible materials, such as flash point, autoignition temperature, type of fire extinguisher use, hazardous by-products of combustion and explosion data.

**5. Reactivity Data:** Whether the material is stable or unstable, any conditions of instability, other materials with which the material may be incompatible with.

*6. Toxicological Data:* Toxicological properties of the hazardous material would include: route of entry, toxic effects, exposure limits, irritant characteristics, and any other toxic characteristics.

*7. Preventive Measures:* Would include information on personal protective equipment to be used, safe storage and handling procedures, cleanup recommendations, waste disposal, and special shipping information.

*8. First Aid Measures:* Information about specific first aid measures to be followed in the event of an acute exposure resulting in personal injury or adverse health effect.

*9. Preparation Information:* Information required is usually the supplier name, name of the group or department which prepared the MSDS, telephone number and the date the MSDS was issued.

The MSDS contains a lot of valuable information that can be used to safely handle a controlled product. Do not try to read the full MSDS from beginning to end. Read the MSDS selectively, be concerned with only the information that is most important to you regarding safe handling and storage. The general approach is to:

1. Identify the substance.
2. Know what the hazards are.
3. Understand what the safe handling and storage procedures are.
4. Know what to do in case of an emergency.

**MSDS Points to Consider**

- Verify that the product described on the MSDS is the same as the one in the container or package.
- The product identifier on the supplier label should match the product identifier on the MSDS.

- The supplier name on the supplier label should match the supplier name on the MSDS.
- Check the product appearance and note the odor. The appearance and odor should match the physical data noted on the MSDS.
- Determine the classification of the product.
- Check the hazard symbols on the supplier label.
- Check to make sure that the intended use of the product is the same as that identified for use by the supplier.
- If the product is used in a different manner that is recommended by the manufacturer, the safe handling information provided on the MSDS may not be valid.
- Verify that the product's MSDS is current. The supplier is required to issue a new MSDS every three years, or sooner if updated health hazard information becomes available.
- If the MSDS is more than three years old, it is no longer valid. Contact the supplier and request an updated MSDS, or inform the supervisor immediately.
- The MSDS contains information regarding the material's flammability and combustion properties, including recommended fire extinguishing methods.
- Check for hazardous by-products of combustion information, to know what can happen in the event a fire occurs.
- Check to see whether the material is considered to be stable or unstable.
- Determine what toxicological properties are identified for the material and know the route of entry the substance takes into the body.

- Be sure to understand correct storage and handling procedures and the recommended PPE to be used when exposed to the hazardous material.
- Be familiar with the recommended first aid measures for the hazardous materials if someone becomes exposed to the effects of the material.
- Review the procedures to be used in containing and cleaning up leaks and spills and the methods for best disposing of waste materials.
- Periodically review and discuss WHMIS MSDS information with your supervisor and the company's safety personnel.
- Discuss the specific work procedures required to be followed with all co-workers who may be in contact with the materials and substances being handled.

*Note: The employer is responsible for making sure that the MSDS is readily available to workers. The employer must establish a file system for all MSDSs for controlled products that are handled in the workplace. If there is no MSDS for the controlled product, bring it to the immediate attention of the supervisor and do not handle the controlled product if there is no MSDS for it.*

## MATERIALS SAFETY DATA SHEET

### SECTION I - PRODUCT IDENTIFICATION AND USE

| Product Name/Material Name/Trade Name | | Product Code | |
|---|---|---|---|
| Manufacturer's Name and Address | | Supplier's Name and Address | |
| Business No. | Emergency No. | Business No. | Emergency No. |
| Product Use | | | |

### SECTION II - HAZARDOUS INGREDIENTS

| Hazardous Ingredients | Approximate Concentration % | C.A.S. Number P.I.N. Number | $LD_{50}$ (Specify Species and Route | $LC_{50}$ (Specify Species and Route |
|---|---|---|---|---|
| | | | | |

Illustration #131A - Materials Safety Data Sheet

## SECTION III - PHYSICAL DATA

| Physical State | ☐ Gas | ☐ Liquid | ☐ Solid |
|---|---|---|---|

| | |
|---|---|
| Appearance and Odor | |
| Odor Threshold (ppm) | Specific Gravity |
| Vapor Pressure (mm Hg) | Vapor Density (Air = 1) |
| Evaporation Rate | Boiling Point (°C) |
| Freezing Point/Melting Point (°C) | Solubility in Water (20°C) |
| % Volatile (by volume) | pH |
| | Coefficient of water/oil distribution |

## SECTION IV - FIRE AND EXPLOSION HAZARD DATA

If YES, under which conditions?

**Flammable**    ☐ Yes    ☐ No

| | |
|---|---|
| Extinguishing Media | |
| Flash Point (°C) and Method | Autoignition Temperature (°C) |
| Upper Explosive Limit (% by volume) | Lower Explosive Limit (% by volume) |

Illustration #131B - Materials Safety Data Sheet (cont'd)

| Special Procedures | Hazardous Combustion Products |
|---|---|

| Explosion Data | |
|---|---|
| Sensitivity to Mechanical Impact | Sensitivity to Static Discharge |

## SECTION V - REACTIVITY DATA

| Stable | ☐ Yes   ☐ No | If NO, under which conditions? |
|---|---|---|
| Hazardous Polymerization | ☐ Yes   ☐ No | If YES, under which conditions? |
| Incompatible with Other Substances | ☐ Yes   ☐ No | If YES, which ones? |
| Hazardous Decomposition Products | | |

## SECTION VI - TOXICOLOGICAL PROPERTIES/HEALTH HAZARD DATA

Route of Entry/Exposure
☐ Skin Contact    ☐ Skin Absorption    ☐ Eye Contact    ☐ Inhalation    ☐ Ingestion

**Illustration #131C - Materials Safety Data Sheet (cont'd)**

| Effects of Acute Exposure to Material | | |
|---|---|---|
| Effects of Chronic Exposure to Material | Sensitization to Material | |
| Exposure Limit(s) | Irritancy of Material | Synergistic Materials |
| Carcinogenicity, Reproductive Effects, Teratogenicity, Mutagenicity | | |

## SECTION VII - PREVENTIVE MEASURES

| Personal Protective Equipment | | |
|---|---|---|
| Gloves (Specify) | Respiratory (Specify) | Eye (Specify) |
| Clothing (Specify) | Other (Specify) | Footwear (Specify) |
| Engineering Controls (eg. ventilation, enclosed process) (Specify) | | |
| Leak and Spill Procedure | | |
| Waste Disposal | | |
| Handling Procedures and Equipment | | |
| Storage Requirements | | |
| Special Shipping Information | | |

**Illustration #131D - Materials Safety Data Sheet (cont'd)**

## SECTION VII - FIRST AID MEASURES

Skin

Eyes

Inhalation

Ingestion

Sources Used

Additional Information

## SECTION IX - PREPARATION DATE OF M.S.D.S.

| Prepared by (Group, Department etc.) | Phone Number |
|---|---|
| Date | |

**Illustration #131E - Materials Safety Data Sheet (cont'd)**

# SECTION SEVEN

## HAZARD COMMUNICATION STANDARD (USA)

## Hazard Communication Standard

In the United States the Occupational Health and Safety Administration (OSHA) has developed a Hazard Communication Standard to help identify chemical hazards in order to protect the employees in any workplace.

The OSHA Hazard Communication Standard (1910.1200) focuses on five main areas:

1. Identifying Hazardous Materials
2. Hazardous Product Warning Labels
3. Material Safety Data Sheets (MSDS)
4. A Written Hazard Communication Program
5. Employee Training

## Identifying Hazardous Materials

The Hazard Communication Standard requires that identification of hazardous materials be the full responsibility of the manufacturer and importer of the hazardous materials and each employer who uses the hazardous materials. It is the employer's responsibility to provide accurate hazardous material information to each employee in the workplace who will be working with and handling the hazardous material.

***Manufacturers and Importers:*** The Hazard Communication Standard requires that all chemical and hazardous material manufacturers and importers of these products to:

- Identify all physical and health hazards of any material they produce or import into United States.
- Report both the physical and health hazards by:
  - Attaching a warning label to each container holding the specific chemical.
  - Ensuring that a Material Safety Data Sheet (MSDS) is provided to the company to whom the hazardous material is shipped.

***Note: There are two types of hazards:***

- *Physical Hazards:* These can produce a dangerous situation external to the body. Flammable or explosive substances pose physical hazards.
- *Health Hazards:* Health hazards are generally classified as being internal health problems which can be either acute, where the health hazard affects the body from short-term exposure, or chronic, where the health hazard affects the body slowly through long-term exposure.

***Employers:*** Each employer that uses hazardous materials must act on the hazard identification information provided by the manufacturer or importer.

- The employer must identify all hazardous materials in the workplace.
- The employer must obtain and keep up-to-date Material Safety Data Sheets (MSDS) for each hazardous material.
- The employer must adopt necessary engineering controls, ensure safe work practices are enforced and provide suitable personal protective equipment.
- The employer shall ensure that all workers receive the hazardous material information and required training in order to perform their work safely.

***Individual Workers:*** Each worker in the workplace has the responsibility of using the hazardous material identification information provided by both the manufacturer and the employer.

- The worker must thoroughly read the instructions identified on the hazardous material warning labels and the MSDS provided for the material.
- The worker must be in full compliance with the hazardous material identification instructions provided on the product label and the MSDS.
- The worker must wear the personal protective equipment recommended by the manufacturer and the employer for the hazardous material being handled.

## Product Warning Labels

- The worker is expected to follow the safe work practices and procedures identified for the hazardous materials as taught in the employee training programs.

*Note: For further information on hazardous materials, chemicals, and effects on the body, see Section Six, pages 258 to 272.*

## Hazardous Product Warning Labels

The Hazard Communication Standard stipulates that the hazardous product warning labels must be used to identify the hazards of the product. These warning labels are designed to alert personnel that the material in the container is dangerous. Unfortunately, the warning label may not provide all the information one needs to know about controlling the dangers or for personal protection. Generally, the warning labels should provide the following information:

- The identity or name of the hazardous material in the container.

- The appropriate hazard warnings (physical and health).
- The name and address of the hazardous product manufacturer, importer or other associated organization.

With few exceptions, hazardous product warning labels are required on:

- All containers of hazardous materials found in the workplace.
- All containers of hazardous materials being shipped (transported) from one location to another.

In some cases, hazardous material labels are not necessarily a requirement under the Hazard Communication Standards.

For example:

- Portable containers do not require a label if the product inside was transferred from a labeled container and immediately used by the employee who undertook the actual transfer.

The employee must never leave an unmarked (no label) container of a hazardous material unattended.

- Common to many industries are specific or individual process containers holding a particular hazardous product. These types of containers can be marked with other types of signage, including placards, process sheets, batch stickers or tags, operating procedures, or other forms of written documentation attached to the container, instead of hazardous material warning labels - but only under the following two conditions:
  - The signage, whatever type it may be, must identify which containers the hazardous material warnings refer to.
  - The written method used must contain the same information that would typically be found on the hazardous material warning label, such as the physical and health hazards.

Examples of various types of warning placards common to most workplaces are shown in illustration #132.

**Illustration #132 - Warning Placards**

- Generally, piping is not considered to be a "container". Piping does not require hazardous material warning labels. However, it is always a good idea to identify the product contained in the piping. Never assume that the product inside the pipe is safe just because there is no warning label on it.

When workers are handling hazardous materials, there are several things they should remember when reading and following instructions identified on warning labels:

- The worker must not mix hazardous products together that are not properly labeled.
- The worker should never assume that an unlabeled container contains a harmless product just because it has no warning label.
- No one should remove a warning label from a hazardous material container unless they immediately replace it with another correct label.
- If any of the information changes for the hazardous material, the employer is responsible for making sure that the warning labels are updated.
- Always remember to read the warning label on the container of each hazardous material being handled.
- Check the hazardous material's MSDS if additional information is required in order to be safer when controlling the material's hazards.
- The worker must fully comply with the instructions for handling the hazardous material as identified on the warning label.

*Note: Hazardous material warning labels should clearly provide anyone who must handle the product with the proper handling and safety precautions. Do not ignore the warning labels found on containers in the workplace. See illustration #133.*

Illustration #133 - Product Warning Labels

## NFPA Labeling System

The National Fire Protection Association (NFPA) Labeling System was developed to help identify the hazards associated with hazardous materials.

The NFPA Labeling System is based on a diamond-shaped label which contains colors and number coded sections. See illustration #134.

### Colors:

- *Blue* - Health hazard information such as toxicity or corrosiveness.
- *Red* - The material's flammability.
- *Yellow* - The material's instability.
- *White* - Special hazards.

**Numbers** - indicate the degree of hazard intensity based on the color category:

- Zero - Lowest and safest. For example, zero in the blue area, means the material is non-toxic or non-corrosive.
- Four - Highest and most dangerous. For example, the four in the red area, means the material is highly flammable.

Illustration #134 - NFPA Labeling System

## Material Safety Data Sheets (MSDS)

The OSHA Hazard Communication Standard identifies the need for detailed information for each hazardous material located in the workplace. The warning labels commonly found on containers of hazardous materials identify some of the product hazards and handling procedures, but for detailed information the workers must go to the proper Material Safety Data Sheet (MSDS) which must be readily available. If an MSDS is not available, the employee's supervisor must look into providing one before any further handling is done of the product.

The more the workers know about the hazardous materials they have to work with and handle, the more they are able to protect themselves from the dangers of the product. The MSDS is designed to give detailed information about the product's components, characteristics, dangers and how to safely handle it.

*Note: Be sure to read the product's MSDS before handling or working with the product. This is an accident preventive measure.*

The eight section MSDS Form (174) provided by OSHA for the workplace includes the following:

- Section One: Manufacturer's name, address, contact information and date.
- Section Two: Hazardous ingredients and identity information.
- Section Three: Physical and chemical characteristics.
- Section Four: Fire and explosion hazard data.
- Section Five: Reactivity data.
- Section Six: Health hazard data.
- Section Seven: Precautions for safe handling and use.
- Section Eight: Control measures.

A more detailed MSDS form is required by some regulatory agencies, such as the EPA (Environmental Protection Agency) and DOT (Department of Transport) if the product is to be shipped or there is a spill or leak.

The American National Standards Institute (ANSI) has approved a standardized format developed by the Chemical Manufacturers Association (CMA) that is designed to help make MSDS forms consistently easier to read and understand. (ANSI Z400.1).

This format is used throughout the United States. This ANSI approved MSDS format has been developed and laid out in a logical order with general information about the hazardous material in the first sections and technical information about the product in the latter sections of the MSDS. This MSDS format has sixteen distinctive sections. It is important to become familiar with each section to make it easier to find the information required to safely handle the product.

The following is a summary of each of the sixteen sections:

### Section One: Product and Company Identification

This section of the MSDS form provides information about the product and the manufacturer:

- Product name as documented on the label.
- Any other names by which the product may be known.
- The preparation date or date of last revision.
- The manufacturer's name, address and telephone contact number.
- Any emergency contact telephone numbers.

As shown in illustration #135, use this section of the MSDS to verify that the correct MSDS is available for the product, as shown on the label attached to the actual product being used.

Always be sure that the most recent MSDS is available, since product information may be periodically updated.

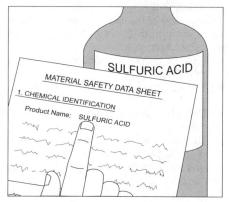

Illustration #135 - MSDS - Verification of Product

### Section Two: Information on the Product's Ingredients

This section of the MSDS form lists the ingredients (components) which make the product potentially dangerous. In some cases, the ingredients may be considered "trade secrets", therefore, they may not be identified on the MSDS. This section of the form also provides exposure limits for hazardous materials which are considered to be health hazards. The various limits identified are time-weighted, meaning they are given as an average over a specific period of time, usually for an eight hour workday. Exposure limits given could include:

- *Threshold Limit Value (TLV):* Cannot be exceeded during any eight hour workday without providing proper personal protection.

- *Permissible Exposure Limit (PEL):* Cannot be exceeded during any eight hour workday without providing proper personal protection.
- *Short-term Exposure Limit (STEL):* Is the acceptable amount of a substance a person can be exposed to over a fifteen minute period.
- *Ceiling Value:* A limit which should never be exceeded during any part of the person's working exposure.

*Note: The TLV and PEL are maximum concentrations of the substance that a person can be safely exposed to, averaged over an eight hour workday.*

**Section Three: Hazards Identification**

This section of the MSDS will identify the material's hazards. Information is designed to give emergency responders, such as firefighters, medical personnel and others who must know quickly what specific hazards are involved with handling a particular dangerous substance.

This section of the MSDS will provide the following types of information about the product's hazards:

- *Characteristics:* The odor, color and other physical characteristics for easy identification.
- *Immediate Potential Hazards:* Indicate whether the material is poisonous, corrosive, explosive, flammable, or what other physical hazards may be present with it.
- *Potential Health Effects:* Indicates how the product enters the body and how it can effect a person's health (symptoms of exposure and immediate health hazards).
- *Long-Term Health Effects:* Provide a warning of the material's potential for causing health problems which may be chronic in nature (cancer, lung disease, heart problems, or reproductive problems).

### Section Four: First-Aid Measures

This section of the MSDS provides basic first-aid information and is primarily written for those who are not necessarily trained in first-aid or emergency response. There are many examples when a few seconds can be very critical in dealing with exposures to potentially dangerous materials. It is important that those personnel who have to work with dangerous products become familiar with the first-aid procedures for that product before any exposure occurs.

In many cases where people have been exposed to hazardous materials, proper first-aid procedures included getting the victim to a doctor as quickly as possible. Never assume that the victim is okay once the immediate symptoms have subsided.

Some of the more common first-aid procedures listed in this section of the MSDS include:

- Flushing the affected area with water for a specific period of time following exposure
- Giving artificial respiration to the victim.
- Relocating the victim to fresh air if a hazardous substance was inhaled.
- Induce vomiting or administering a fluid such as milk to neutralize the substance.

Specifically, this section of the MSDS provides information on:

- First-aid measures.
- Response procedures for spills or leaks.
- Basic fire fighting methods.

### Section Five: Fire Fighting Measures

This section of the MSDS explains why a hazardous material may present a fire or explosion threat under certain types of conditions. In this section there maybe reference to:

- *Flammable Limits of the Material:* Indicates the explosive limits for the product.

- *Lower Explosive Limits (LEL):* Lowest concentration of vapors in the air at which the material will burn when an ignition source is present.
- *Upper Explosive Limit (UEL):* Maximum concentration of vapors in the air that will burn when an ignition source is present.
- *Flash Point:* Minimum temperature at which the hazardous material gives off vapor concentrations that can ignite if an ignition source is present.
- *Autoignition Temperature:* A temperature at which the hazardous material will spontaneously ignite or burn.

*Note: This section of the MSDS may also list any hazardous by-products of the burning material. This is very important information for emergency responders and fire fighters.*

*There is usually reference to basic fire fighting methods and includes safe extinguishing agents such as water, dry chemicals, foam or other extinguishing methods and materials.*

## Section Six: Accidental Release Measures

In this section of the MSDS, information is provided for handling situations where an accidental release of the hazardous material has occurred. An accidental release may be disastrous for people, property and the environment. Even a small release of some hazardous materials can cause severe damage, injury, illness or death.

Much of the information provided in this section of the MSDS is designed for personnel trained in emergency response procedures. Some types of information which may be included:

- Removal of all potential sources of ignition from the vicinity of the released material.
- Alerting the appropriate authorities about the accidental release.
- Preventing unauthorized entry of personnel into the release area.
- Reporting requirements and other information related to the spill.
- Clean-up procedures.
- Recommended personal protective equipment to be worn during clean-up activities.
- Proper disposal methods of waste materials.

**Section Seven:  Handling and Storage**

This section of the MSDS contains useful information for the safe handling and storage of the hazardous material. The requirements are designed to protect against accidental release, spills and ignition, as well as to protect against dangerous chemical reactions with other types of hazardous materials.

Dangers from chemical reactions with certain hazardous materials are an important consideration when storing and handling certain products.   Consider the following points:

- Is the product itself considered stable or unstable?
- Under what conditions and with what other materials is there a risk that a chemical reaction will take place with the material being handled?
- Are there any dangerous substances that can be produced when the hazardous material has reacted with other substances?

*Note: Proper storing and handling of potentially hazardous materials will significantly help in keeping workers safe on any work site.*

**Section Eight: Exposure Control and Personal Protection**

This section of the MSDS contains useful exposure prevention information. Information will be provided that tells the worker and the employer what can be done to prevent exposure and to protect oneself from the effects of the hazardous material. Information which may be included:

- Identify specific engineering controls (ventilation, fire protection, storage, etc.).
- Identify exposure levels and maintaining these levels through proper monitoring and engineering controls. See section two of the MSDS for the exposure limits.
- Identify proper personal protective equipment (PPE) for the safe handling and working with the hazardous material (gloves, respirators, protective suits, boots). See illustration #136.

*Note: Be sure that you are familiar with and know how to use the PPE that is required when working with specific hazardous materials.*

Illustration #136 - Proper Personal Protective Equipment (PPE)

## Section Nine:   Physical and Chemical Properties

In this section of the MSDS information is provided which assists in identification of the physical and chemical properties of the hazardous material.  Information provided may include:

- What is the physical state of the hazardous material (solid, liquid, or gas)?
- What is the physical appearance of the material (color, thickness, odor, taste)?
- Identify other properties such as freezing, melting and boiling points, vapor pressure, specific gravity, and evaporation rate of the material.

*Note: If there is a need to know detailed property specifics about the material being handled, section nine is the best place to examine the various physical properties of the product.*

## Section Ten: Stability and Reactivity

This section of the MSDS is designed to identify which types of materials may be incompatible with the hazardous materials the MSDS has been prepared for.  The information should also include any types of reaction characteristics there are for each material. Some of the reactions identified would include:

- Flammability
- Explosiveness
- Polymerization
- Release of heat
- Release of toxic fumes or gases

Included in this section should be some indication as to how stable or unstable the hazardous material is.   Unstable hazardous materials must always be handled with extra care and caution, since even under "normal" conditions, these materials may become self-reactive, decompose, polymerize or condense.

In the event of decomposition, the material may cause a release of other kinds of dangerous gases or fumes. These too, should be identified in this section of the MSDS.

### Section Eleven: Toxicological Data

Section eleven of the MSDS identifies specialized information related to toxicological data normally in the form of laboratory and test results of the hazardous material. This type of data is extremely useful for physicians. They may be able to determine the effects that a certain hazardous material may have on humans, in particular with respiratory ailments, skin irritation, visual impairment, and stomach and bowel disorders.

### Section Twelve: Environmental Data

This section of the MSDS identifies what effects the hazardous material may have on the environment if there was an accidental release. This information is beneficial to environmental specialists, as the information may help them to better evaluate the effects the hazardous material might have on the soil, water and air near the released substance.

As well, the information provided in this section may be useful for emergency response personnel and those who are in charge of cleaning up the waste materials resulting from the released hazardous materials.

### Section Thirteen: Disposal Information

This is a specialized section of the MSDS, providing information for the proper disposal of hazardous material. This may include information on waste and disposal classification and identification, limitations and specific restrictions for disposing of the hazardous materials.

The information found in this section of the MSDS is particularly useful to those who are in charge of waste disposal in the workplace.

It is important to be familiar with both the local and federal regulations for correct waste disposal of specific hazardous materials.

### Section Fourteen: Shipping/Transportation Information

This section of the MSDS contains useful information for shipping and transporting the hazardous material safely. The information provided would include applicable regulations and the type of shipping information required on the container used to store the hazardous material.

It is always important to know and follow the Transportation of Dangerous Goods regulations and to ensure that the required shipping precautions are being met in any transported hazardous material.

### Section Fifteen: Regulatory Information

This section of the MSDS provides regulatory information at the state, federal and international levels to assist employers with compliance to all safety requirements when handling hazardous materials.

### Section Sixteen: Additional Information

This final section of the MSDS contains any additional information which may not have been included in any of the previous sections of the MSDS. Additional types of information might include:

- Updated information on the hazardous material and any revisions to any section of the MSDS.
- Interpretation of abbreviations or acronyms used in the MSDS.
- Reference information.
- Label text and hazard codes and ratings.

Material Safety Data Sheets (MSDS) are provided to give accurate and complete information on the safe handling of potentially dangerous materials. The MSDS is designed to give practical and understandable information to employees for working safely and effectively with hazardous products.

As shown in illustration #137, it is the employer's responsibility to have the current MSDS forms available and easily found so any worker can access a particular one they need for the material being handled. All the worker should have to do is read it to understand what his or her responsibilities are and what precautions they must take, before they are involved in a dangerous situation.

Illustration #137 - Making the MSDS Available and Accessible

The information on the MSDS can greatly improve safety in the workplace and help reduce the risk of exposure to potentially hazardous materials. It is important to keep the following points in mind:

- Every employee must know where the MSDS for every hazardous material in their work area is located.

- Each employee must be familiar with the most critical and important sections of the MSDS in order to be in control of the potentially dangerous material.
- Employees must remember to check the MSDS whenever they need to know more information about the product they are handling.
- Each employee should be able to locate emergency response information on the MSDS form accurately and quickly. This action could save lives.
- It is important that each employee follow the safe procedures and practices identified in the MSDS for the product he or she will be handling. This action could save lives, including your own.

## Hazard Communication Program

The fourth requirement of the Hazard Communication Standard is for the employer to have a written Hazard Communication Program. This document will describe the various hazardous materials in the workplace and indicate to the employees how they will be told about the dangers each material presents. The written document should include the following types of information:

- A complete list of all the hazardous materials located in the workplace.
- A full description outlining the procedures required for placing warning labels, managing MSDS forms and how employee education and training will be conducted.
- A description of how employees will be notified/informed about the potential hazards related to unlabeled piping in the workplace.

- A description of how the employer's workers will be told the hazards of performing "non-routine" tasks and activities.

*Note: Employers must make this information available to all their employees through the company's written Hazard Communication Program.*

## Employee Training

The fifth requirement of the Hazard Communication Standard is for the employer to provide hazardous material education to each of its employees. Employee education and training is required to ensure that everyone in the workplace who uses or handles hazardous materials knows how to safely work with them.

Employee training must focus on the specific hazards each worker faces with those hazardous materials located in their work area.

The training program should include the following subjects related to the Hazard Communication Standard:

- Identify to each employee the types of potentially hazardous materials they may encounter.
- Review a list of all hazardous materials located in the company's workplace.
- Discuss those hazardous products produced in the workplace and those that are commonly imported by the company and introduced into the workplace.
- Inform the employees of any processes or operations in the workplace where hazardous materials are present.
- Explain to the employees the method used to detect the presence or release of a hazardous substance.
- Inform employees of the correct ways to protect themselves from the hazards of dangerous materials.

- Inform the employees of the safe work practices for handling the hazardous materials in their work areas.
- Inform the employees what the proper emergency procedures are for each of the hazardous materials in their particular work area.
- Inform the employee of the location and availability of the employer's written Hazard Communication Program - including the details of the program, an explanation of the warning label and MSDS system, and how to use this information effectively to ensure safe work practices are carried out to prevent any injuries, illness or deaths.

The employer's training program must be kept current and updated frequently whenever a new material is introduced into the workplace, and whenever any hazard due to a material change is documented and communicated to the employees.

Under the current OSHA regulations, the employer and the employees may be interviewed during an audit or OSHA Safety Inspection. Audits and inspections are used to determine whether the employer is providing adequate training for their employees on the safe handling and use of hazardous materials. The employee must be able to demonstrate to the auditor or inspector that he or she has the basic knowledge and understanding of the potential dangers of the various hazardous materials in their work area.

## Handling Tips for Hazardous Materials

- Know the identity of the material before beginning to work with it.
- Never work with materials that you have no knowledge of.
- Use the proper container for storing and transporting the hazardous material.
- Make sure that all containers are compatible with the hazardous material.
- Make sure that the container is leak proof, sturdy and stable.
- Check to see if the container must be UL-approved with spark arresters and self-closing caps.
- Stack containers carefully and do not block off aisles or emergency exits.
- Do not store incompatible hazardous materials near each other.

- Treat all compressed gases as potential explosives and all containers as potential bombs.
- Store compressed gas cylinders in cool, dry, spark free environments.
- When compressed gas cylinders are empty, cap them and mark them as being empty.
- Always strap or chain upright compressed gas cylinders to prevent them from falling over.
- Never use a compressed gas cylinder which has no identification indicating its contents.
- When carrying a flammable or toxic liquid in a glass bottle, place the bottle into a protective cradle.
- Always keep ignition sources far away from flammable liquids.

- Enforce the "No Smoking" rules.
- Provide proper signage in areas where there are potential hazards from dangerous materials.
- When transferring flammables from container to container, use a static grounding clip to prevent static electricity from igniting the liquid.
- Store flammable liquids in fire proof/explosion proof cabinets or designated storage areas.
- Store hazardous materials which are considered "oxidizers" away from flammables as they can easily promote combustion.
- Try to keep storage areas well ventilated, no matter what type of hazardous material is being stored.
- Always remember to consult the hazardous material's MSDS for handling and storage guidelines.
- Become familiar with the first-aid measures for the commonly handled hazardous materials in the work area.
- Know the emergency response procedures in your work area in the event there is an accidental release of a potentially dangerous substance.
- Always wear the approved personal protective equipment when storing and handling hazardous materials.

# SECTION EIGHT

# ELECTRICAL SAFETY

## Introduction

Electrical safety in the workplace is the personal responsibility of each worker. Electrocution continues to be one of primary causes of workplace fatalities in North America. Wherever there are possible electrical hazards to people, equipment or property, the personal safety of people depends on knowing and practicing safe work practices. There are several basic levels of protection and precautions taken to help people work safely around electricity:

1. Implementing Engineering Controls
2. Having Designated Safe Work Conditions, Procedures and Practices
3. Providing Personal Protective Equipment (PPE)
4. Proper Response to Emergencies

## Engineering Controls

It is the responsibility of the employer to provide adequate engineering controls to eliminate potential shock hazards from electrical systems in the workplace. Engineering controls are designed to safeguard people from electrical shock and by law have to be installed and maintained as primary protection devices. Common engineering controls used to protect workers from electrical shock include:

- Insulation Materials
- Grounding Systems/Bonding Systems
- Machinery Guarding
- Circuit Protection Devices

***Insulation Materials:*** Electrical current can flow easily through some materials and is blocked by other types of materials. Insulation material is commonly used to cover items which are considered to be conductors of electricity.

Illustration #138 shows how copper wires, used as an electrical conductor, are covered by an insulation material. The insulation material on this wire has a very high resistance to the flow of electricity and serves to protect workers, property and equipment from electrical shock. Common insulating materials used include: some types of plastics, rubber, glass, porcelain, wood and mica. Insulating materials not only serve to protect people from electrical shock, but also protect the conductor from moisture, corrosive materials and help keep the conductor protected from rubbing and abrasion.

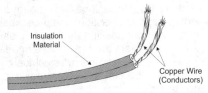

Illustration #138 - Insulation Covering

***Grounding Systems:*** The importance of grounding of electrical systems and electrical distribution equipment cannot be overstated. Under normal conditions, an electrical system can continue to operate even without proper grounding. However, it is not until an abnormal condition has occurred that the importance of safe and proper grounding becomes evident. Grounding may be one of the least understood points in electrical safety.

Grounding is a method of providing a predetermined safe path for stray electrical current. There are six principle reasons for grounding systems:

- To limit the voltage rise on the system due to a lightning strike.
- To limit the voltage rise due to line switching surges.
- To limit the voltage rise as a result of accidental contact with a higher voltage system.

- To stabilize the voltage to ground during normal operating conditions.
- To facilitate the operation of overcurrent devices in the case of a ground fault on a solidly grounded system.
- To alarm and/or trip a protective device on impedance grounded systems.

From an employee safety perspective in the workplace, the primary reason the employer must provide reliable grounding systems is to protect both employees and the public from all exposed surfaces of electrical apparatuses and to insure that those parts of electrical equipment that personnel can be in contact with will not be at a voltage value higher than ground potential.

The most familiar type of grounding system is the lightning rod, as shown in illustration #139. The lightning rod is designed and located to attract high voltage energy from lightning strikes and to conduct the energy harmlessly to the ground.

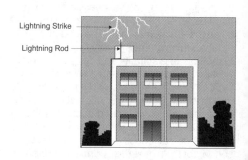

Illustration #139 - Lightning Rod Grounding System

Ground faults occur due to the loss of ground connection. Double casings and properly installed ground connections help to keep stray current from passing through any part of the body. System ground devices protect electrical components within an electrical circuit from damage due to excessive voltage or line surges.

Illustration #140 demonstrates a common ground system inside an electrical control panel.

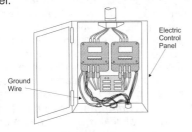

Illustration #140 - Common Ground System

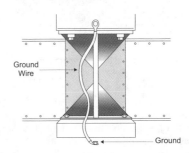

Illustration #141 - Building Structure & Grounding Device

Illustration #141 demonstrates how a grounding device is used to provide a pathway into the earth from a large metal structure within a building. This method allows the electrical charge to dissipate into the earth. The earth is considered to be a zero potential connection of grounded system conductors and electrical equipment to the earth, which would ideally have no resistance.

However, as shown in illustration #142, connections to earth will have some resistance. This could be due to resistance between the electrode and grounding conductors, resistance between the electrode and adjacent earth, and resistance of the surrounding earth.

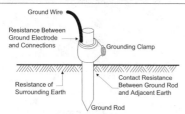

**Illustration #142 - Grounding to Earth**

Bonding is the procedure of electrically connecting two objects so that they are at the same electrical potential. Illustration #143 shows how two containers are connected together by a bonding wire.

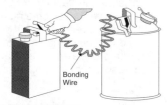

**Illustration #143 - Bonding Wire**

The bonded containers should also be connected to ground, so static charges can be completely dissipated. Always keep the containers closed until after the bonding has been completed and when the job is finished, close the containers before disconnecting the bonding wires. Bonding can also be achieved by direct contact between two objects, as long as the contact is not impeded by surface paint or another type of coating.

*Note: Grounding and bonding systems should be checked at regular intervals with a meter to verify proper continuity.*

*Machinery Guarding:* Another common engineering control used to protect workers in and around electrically driven machinery is machinery guarding. The guard does not necessarily protect the worker from the hazards of electrical shock, but it is in place to protect the worker from being hurt if he happens to come in close contact with the driven (energized) parts of the machine.

It is important for all personnel to follow the employer's machinery lockout procedures while performing any type of maintenance or cleanup work on powered (energized) equipment. The purpose of lockout procedures is to ensure that the machinery is completely de-energized and the workers are protected from accidental start-up of the equipment while they are performing maintenance or cleanup duties on it.

***Circuit Protection Devices:*** Another common engineering control for providing safety in electrical systems are circuit protection devices. These devices are considered an essential electrical component designed to protect against major electrical damage and fire.

Circuit protection devices prevent current overload by melting, tripping, or otherwise disengaging (opening) in order to break the electrical circuit.

There are various types of circuit protection devices available to protect electrical circuits, equipment and personnel from injury under abnormal conditions. As well, there are many types of abnormal conditions, of which some of the more common are listed in table #13.

Circuit protection devices include:
- Fuses
- Circuit Breakers
- Ground-Fault Circuit Interrupters (GFCI)

Overloads and short-circuits will impose excessive heating and mechanical stresses on electrical components. For example, when conductors become overheated they become annealed or softened. This softening condition removes the resilience from the conductor and may cause excessive looseness at the connection points in the circuit.

| Abnormal Circuit Conditions | |
| --- | --- |
| Type | Description |
| Overload | Current exceeds rated values.<br>Overload values are usually no greater than 6 times rated values. |
| Short Circuit | Excessive current at least 6 times above rated values are flowing. |
| Underload | Current or power flow decreases below a predetermined value. |
| Undervoltage | Source voltage drops below a tolerable predetermined value. |
| Overvoltage | Source voltage rises above a tolerable predetermined value. |
| Reverse Phase Rotation | Source phase sequence is reversed from a predetermined order. |
| Phase Unbalance | Polyphase currents (eg. three phase motor) are not equal and balanced. |
| Reverse Current | Currents are flowing out of a circuit instead of into a circuit. |
| Ground Fault | Electrical circuit is unintentionally in contact with ground or earth. |

Table #13 - Abnormal Circuit Conditions

Overloads and short-circuits will bring about increased temperatures within the electrical circuit. Any rise in temperature can increase the rate of oxidation, thus the electrical integrity of a terminal connection.

Copper or aluminum conductors can become weakened and in some cases, enough heat is generated through oxidation to completely destroy the terminal connection.

Overheating can also cause the conductor's insulation to become dry and brittle. In time the insulation may crack, fall off and expose the conductor. A fire could occur if exposed conductors come into contact with each other or other grounded equipment.

Illustration #144A,B,C identify various types of circuit protection devices. Each of these devices must be rated for the capacity of the system into which they are installed. There are published values of minimum and maximum ratings for overcurrent devices.

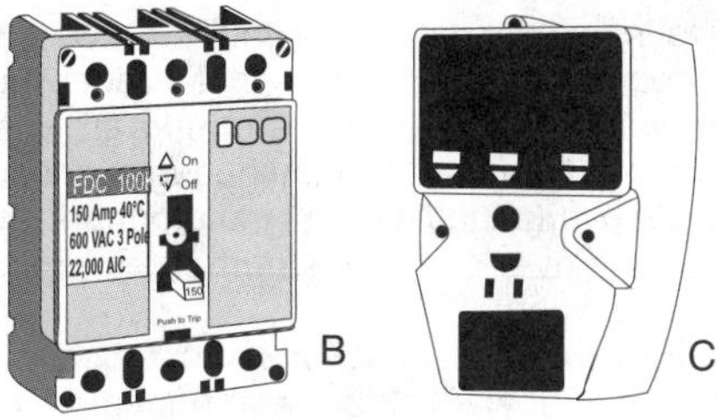

**Illustration #144B,C - Circuit Breaker**
Ground Fault Circuit Indicator (GFCI)

Typically, fuses and circuit breakers must have their ratings clearly marked.

The GFCI, as shown in illustration #144C is an extremely sensitive, quick action power switch that disconnects a circuit as soon as it detects even a small amount of current leaking to the ground.

**Illustration #144A - Fuses**

## Current Overload and Short Circuits

Overloads are low level faults caused by temporary surge currents that occur when motors are started up, transformers are energized, or they may be continuous overloads due to overloaded motors, transformers, etc. Current overload, in summary, may be caused when:

- Equipment malfunctions or overheats.
- Too many electrical components, machines or appliances on the same circuit.
- There is a temporary power surge in the circuit from lightning or other outside voltage leaks.
- When electric motors startup under heavy loads.

Short-circuits refer to electrical current which is out of its normal path. It may be caused by insulation breakdown or due to a faulty connection. During the short-circuit, current bypasses the load and the only limiting factor is the impedance of the distribution system upstream from the fault. If the short-circuit is not cut off within a matter of a few thousandths of a second, then damage and destruction can become very serious.

*Note: Despite the magnitude of electrical overloads being between one to six times the normal current level for electric motors and eight to twelve times for transformers, removal of the overload current within a few seconds will generally prevent equipment damage and maintain a safe condition. Short-circuits are much more serious of a problem because fault currents may be many hundreds of times larger than the normal operating current.*

## Resetting Circuit Protection Devices

When electrical power is interrupted or shut off, consider the following procedures for correctly resetting the circuit protection devices:

- Using proper tools and precautions, remove the blown fuse and replace with the correct fuse, or reset the circuit breaker.
- Wait a few moments to see if the power does in fact stay on once the system is energized.
- Check to see if there is any smoke, heat or unusual smell in and around the electric panels and the electric equipment.
- If you notice anything out of order, de-energize the electric circuit immediately.
- Do not replace the fuse again, or reset the circuit breaker until the problem has been correctly fixed.

## Circuit Protection Safety Tips

- Never overload a typical wall socket, as shown in illustration #145, with an array of power cords.
- Never bypass, bridge or disable any circuit protection device.

- Never insert a metallic object such as a piece of tin foil, washer, nail or copper penny into a fuse socket to replace a blown fuse.
- Always be sure the power is shut off before safely replacing any circuit protection device in an energized or live circuit.
- When replacing a fuse or resetting a circuit breaker in a high voltage system, use caution and wear approved safety glasses for added personal protection.
- Use a proper fuse-puller instead of pliers to remove fuses.
- Always replace a fuse with an exact duplicate.
- The replacement fuse has to have the same rating as the original. A fuse rated for higher voltage will not protect the circuit, while a fuse rated too low could explode and flash back at the worker.
- Be sure that any markings on the new fuse match those shown on the old fuse.

- When re-energizing a circuit protection device, make sure the electrical cabinet door is closed, making for a protective shield in case the circuit breaker explodes. See illustration #146.
- If the circuit breakers in the electrical cabinet have to be exposed for some reason, stand to one side of the device, as shown in illustration #147, and look away while switching the device on or off.

Illustration #146 - Re-energizing

Do Not Overload
Wall Sockets

Illustration #145 - Overloaded Wall Socket

Illustration #147 - Stand To One Side

## Safe Working Conditions, Procedures and Practices

The human body is made up of water and various minerals and chemicals, therefore, it is an excellent conductor of electricity. Because the passage of electric current depends on simultaneous contact between two different amounts of voltage, any part of the body that accidentally bridges the gap can create a new electrical circuit through the body, which happens to be the path of least resistance. When this happens, an electrical shock occurs.

Workers must learn to recognize unsafe conditions associated with electrical circuits and equipment. Several precautions to consider in regards to safe work practices include:

- Do not work around a source of electricity when the surroundings are wet or your clothes and tools are wet.
- Hands should be as dry as possible when working around electrical circuits.
- Use covering protection when working outside in the rain on electrical equipment.
- Make sure that dust particles and flammable vapors are minimal around electrical circuits.
- Ventilate the work area to try and lower the concentration of atmospheric hazards below the danger level around electric circuits.
- Always remember to inspect electric powered tools before beginning the job.
- Insulated grips on electrical tools only offer full protection when they are in good condition, free of cracks, tears and worn spots. Never try to improvise tool insulation.
- Only rely on approved insulation materials when working with electrical equipment. Never assume that insulated tools are safe for every job, especially when working on energized electrical circuits.

- Check power operated tools to see that double-insulated casings and the third wire power cord grounding work properly.
- Check to see that safety shields and guards are properly in place and all switches are secure and power cords are not cut, worn through or frayed.
- Be sure that all power cords are rated for the tool being used.
- Always use a three-wire power cord with a working Ground Fault Circuit Interrupter (GFCI).
- Make sure the plug and wall socket are in good condition and are designed to fit together.
- Do not raise or lower power tools with their flexible power cords, as this stretches and damages the insulation and could loosen the connections.
- Never remove the grounding post from a three prong plug to make it fit into a two plug wall socket.

- Do not use more than one plug adapter for each duplex wall outlet.
- De-energize electrical circuits before connecting test equipment. Energize only to take readings and then de-energize again to disconnect the test equipment.
- Select the correct test equipment for the job and use the recommended test procedures.
- Never exceed the limitations of the test equipment and ensure that the equipment is in safe condition. Check probes and leads for any defects.
- Always use non-conductive, sturdy, fiberglass or wooden ladders when working on electrical equipment. Never use aluminum ladders that conduct electricity.
- Always position ladders so that they are secure, and will not slide or fall.
- Check to see that rubber caps are on the ladder feet. These devices give added anti-slip and shock protection.

- Vehicles and mechanical equipment should maintain a safe distance from energized electrical panels and cabinets, overhead lines and unguarded electrical equipment.
- Workers who are not qualified to work near exposed energized or de-energized overhead lines must stay back a required minimum distance.

## Testing Instruments

Voltage, current, resistance and power measurements are routinely made in electrical circuits. Electrical instruments are used to measure and monitor these circuit values. The most common field instruments used by electricians to test and/or troubleshoot electrical circuits are voltmeters, ammeters, ohmmeters, megohmmeters, and occasionally wattmeters.

Often three instruments are combined into one single instrument known as a VOM, volt-ohm-milliammeter, as shown in illustra-

tion #148. These multimeters are designed to allow the user to choose the type of electrical unit (current, voltage, resistance) to be measured by means of a selector switch. Multimeters (VOM) are available in analog (needle movement) or in digital (DMM-digital multimeter with discreet numbers appearing on a screen) form.

VOM (Volt-Ohm Milliammeter)

DMM (Digital Multimeter)

**Illustration #148 - Multimeters**

In addition to these instruments, there are numerous other measurement devices used to measure, monitor, analyze, and interpret the behavior of electrical circuits.

## Qualified Person

Throughout industry in North America, the designated person most qualified to work on electrical circuits and equipment is an electrician. This specialized trade may vary somewhat in job scope and design in each province or state, but a major part of the electrical trade-training program includes hazard recognition, proper safe work practices and sound knowledge of the work area.

Also, the electrician must be familiar with the construction and operation of the particular electrical equipment they are to be involved with on the job.

Employers and supervisors are responsible for ensuring that only qualified personnel perform work on electrical systems.

*Note: Unsafe work practices are one of the major causes of accidents in industry. Employees and supervisors must work together to implement approved, safe work procedures, in particular when working with and around electrical circuits and equipment. Employees must be alert to the hazards when working with electrical systems, and to always remember to keep themselves protected and safe.*

## Providing Personal Protective Equipment

It is not only the employer's responsibility to ensure that adequate engineering controls and safe work practices are in place for the workers when working with electrical circuits and equipment, but it is also their responsibility to provide proper personal protection equipment (PPE) which meets the approved standards required for effective electrical safety.

As shown in illustration #149, personal protection equipment for the worker who is working in and around electrical equipment would consist of:

- Approved hard hat.
- Approved safety glasses, goggles or face shield.
- Insulated gloves, preferably made of insulating materials like rubber and protective arm coverings (mats).
- Approved safety work boots (safety toe protection with insulated soles and heels).

In addition to the required personal protection equipment, each worker who must perform work in and around electrical circuits and equipment should keep in mind the following clothing and PPE points:

- Do not wear clothing which is too baggy as it may get caught on protrusions or sharp objects, as well, too tight of clothing may limit freedom of movement.

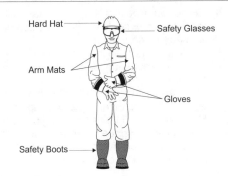

Illustration #149 - Proper Personal Protective Equipment

- Keep shirtsleeves buttoned up, remove neckties and scarves and jewelry such as necklaces, bracelets, rings and wristwatches, as the metal in jewelry and watches is a good electrical conductor.
- In some way, secure long hair away and under the hard hat.

- Do not wear belts with large metal buckles, since they could easily make contact with energized equipment.
- Tradespeople working on electrical circuits and equipment should wear a standard electrician's tool belt. Never let tools hang freely from pockets and belts, as they might drop on energized equipment. Remove the tool belt before beginning to work in tight spaces. Remember that metal parts and rivets on the belt could easily conduct electrical current.

## Proper Response to Emergencies

### Effects of Electrical Shock

The passage of electrical current through the body is known and felt as "shock". Electrical shock has no warning, it happens suddenly and can be deadly. In most cases, electrical shock occurs because of human error.

Sometimes the electrical shock may not cause any direct injury, but the reflex response by the body's muscles may cause sudden moves, falls or slips. Serious injury may then result from the reflex action, not the actual shock.

The extent of injury to the human body from electrical shock will depend on the amount of current that passes through the body and the length of time the current is maintained (length of time the body remains in contact with the power source).

It is important to remember that resistance determines amperage in electrical systems, therefore, low voltage can be just as deadly as high voltage. The human body's resistance to electricity remains dependent upon several critical factors:

- Length of time the person remains in contact with the power source.
- The area of contact on the body with a conductive surface.

- How much moisture is on the skin or clothing.
- The degree of pressure being applied on the contact point of the conductor.
- The amount of current flowing through the body (measured in amperes and determined by voltage and resistance).
- The general health of the person receiving the electrical shock.

*Note: Even low amperage current, or just a short period of contact time will not guarantee safety or no damage done to the body. A crucial factor in electrical shock is the path the electric current takes. Electrical current passing through the human body can affect the nerve system and may even cause the heartbeat to stop and/or breathing to cease. See illustration #150.*

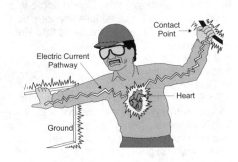

Illustration #150 - Current Passing Through the Body

A severe electrical shock can cause considerable damage to the body. There may be internal bleeding, destruction of tissues, nerves and muscles and, as mentioned previously, shock is often only the beginning as the last injury in sequence may be from a fall.

Any electrical shock, from a mild tingle to a severe jolt, must be considered serious as it could be fatal. Generally, there are three levels of shock:
- Mild shock
- Severe Shock
- Deadly Shock

**Mild Shock:** Is caused by making very brief contact with an electrical current less than 5 milliamperes (mA). The physical effects would include tingling sensation in the affected area, slight discoloration of the skin and a minor burn area on the skin surface. See illustration #151.

If a worker receives any mild electrical shock, take the following first-aid procedures:
- Have the worker sit down and try to calm him or her down.
- Attempt to ensure that their muscle movement is normal.
- Check for loss of feeling or numbness in any part of their body.

- Check their pulse rate and look for signs of breathing irregularities.
- Find out if the person is feeling any severe pain.

Tingling Sensation

Illustration #151 - Mild Shock

**Severe Shock:** Is caused by making much longer contact with an electrical current from 5 mA to 25 mA. The physical effects would include numbness or temporary paralysis of affected body parts, moderate to serious pain, loss of muscle control, muscle spasms, breathing problems and possible loss of consciousness.

Higher current amounts may cause muscle contractions to occur, and these can be so severe that the victim will not be able to let go of the conductor or shock contact point.

***Deadly Shock:*** Happens when a person is "frozen" to an electrical contact point and receives a continuous flow of current greater than 25 mA through their body. See illustration #152.

The physical effects would include paralysis of respiratory muscles and second and third degree burns. In some deadly shock cases, the shock is severe enough to completely destroy nerves, rupture internal organs, shatter bones and teeth and tear muscle tissue.

Illustration #152 - Frozen to Electric Contact Point

Table #14 illustrates how a difference of less than 100 mA exists between an electric current that is barely perceptible and one that can be deadly. Low voltages can be extremely dangerous. The degree of injury is proportional to the length of time the body is in the circuit. Low voltage does not mean low hazard!

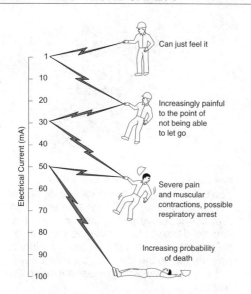

Table #14 - Range of Body Tolerance

### First-Aid Procedures

If a worker sees that a co-worker is in a situation where they are receiving continuous shock, immediately shut off the power. If the power cannot be shut off, the victim must be freed from the power source by using something non-conductive such as a wooden broom handle or chair, a plastic pipe, or a rope. See illustration #153.

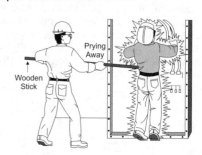

Illustration #153 - Freeing the Frozen Worker

What must be done safely is to:
- Move the victim from the power source.
- Try to pry the victim away from the power source.
- Or safely lift the power source off of the victim.

Never use bare hands to try and free a victim who is "frozen" to a continuous energized power source. The person attempting to free the victim could easily end up as a second victim, frozen helplessly to the same electrical power source. See illustration #154.

Once the victim is free of the power source, take immediate actions to:
- Call for help.
- Send for medical assistance.

While waiting for medical help to arrive:
- Tend to the victim, comfort him as much as possible.
- Check for regular pulse.
- Determine what the victim's breathing is like.

- Look for external bleeding.
- Look for broken bones.

Man Attempts to Free "Frozen" Worker

**Illustration #154 - Never Use Bare Hands**

## Traumatic Shock

Unless the victim's life is in immediate danger from fire and explosion do not attempt to move an injured person. Wait for qualified medical personnel to arrive. Electrical shock and related injuries can cause the victim to go into a state of shock known as "traumatic" shock.

Traumatic shock is a serious condition. It is the body's reaction to severe injury and causes a sharp decrease in the body's vital functions, such as:

- Decreased muscle strength.
- Reduced rate of breathing.
- Reduced heart rate.
- Affects the blood pressure.
- Affects the ability to regulate body heat.

If the victim shows signs of traumatic shock, take the following immediate actions:

- Make sure the victim remains lying down.
- Try to quiet and calm the victim, offer the victim reassurance that they are going to be okay.
- If the victim's skin seems unusually warm, loosen their clothing and try to cool them down.
- If the victim's skin feels cool and clammy, cover the victim with a coat or blanket to maintain normal body temperature.

- Elevate the victim's head if their face appears to be red, keep the victim's feet higher than their head if their face appears pale.
- If there is any reason to believe that the victim has suffered a neck or spinal injury, do not move the victim, except in a life-threatening situation.

## Burns and Other Injuries

A burn is one of the most common shock related injuries.

There are three types, all of which could occur at once, depending on the situation:

- Electrical burns.
- Arc or flash burns.
- Thermal contact burns.

*Electrical Burns* are the result of the electrical current flowing through the tissues or the bone. Tissue damage is caused by the heat generated by the current flow through the body.

*Arc or Flash Burns* result from high temperatures in close proximity to the body and are produced by an electric arc or explosion. Electric arcs can produce temperatures in excess of 5400°F (3000°C), which is more than enough heat required to melt steel.

*Thermal Contact Burns* are those burns normally associated with skin or clothing coming into contact with hot surfaces of overheated electrical conductors or other equipment. Clothing may ignite in an electrical accident resulting in a thermal burn.

*Note: It is important to remember that all burns are serious and must receive immediate medical attention.*

Electricity can quickly create other dangers in the workplace as well. For example:

- Electric arcing and flashes can cause injury or start fires.
- High-energy electric arcs may have the capability to destroy equipment, causing fragmented metal and pieces to fly at high velocity.
- Low energy electric arcs have the possibility of causing violent explosions in atmospheres that contain explosive gases, vapors, or combustible dusts.
- Electric arcs and flashes can also generate very intensive ultra-violet light and cause serious eye injuries, even at great distances.

Remember, electrical fires are Class C fires. These types of fires present special hazards:

- Smoldering or burning conductor insulation can give off noxious or poisonous fumes.
- Any type of smoke should be considered dangerous in tight spaces, which most electrical enclosures are.
- Electrical fires may ignite nearby materials and cause any of the other three classes of fires (Class A, B or D).

- Water or chemical fire extinguishers can be very harmful to electrical circuits and equipment. Water should not be used directly on an electrical fire, as water is a good conductor of electricity, and this could prove to be dangerous to those attempting to extinguish the fire.
- If smoke is seen coming from an electrical panel or from electric equipment, turn the power off immediately.
- If there is an electrical fire, shut off all electric power in the area of the fire, but leave the lighting on if possible.
- Never attempt to open up the door of a smoking electrical cabinet unless an approved Class C fire extinguisher is readily available.
- Remove any materials from around the electrical fire which might help the fire to spread and clear all non-essential personnel from the area.

- Use only approved Class C fire extinguishers, such as carbon dioxide. These are designed to deplete the oxygen in the air around the fire without doing much harm to electrical components.

## Lockout Procedures

It is important for the employer to establish approved equipment lockout procedures in order to prevent accidental startup of equipment and machinery.

Lockout procedures are to be followed by the employees whenever they perform work on powered equipment. This is a required safety procedure for any industry in North America.

Using approved locks and tags, as shown in illustration #155, on electric circuits and equipment has proven to be a safe and effective way of reducing electrical accidents in the workplace.

Detailed lockout and tagout procedures for a variety of energized equipment are given in *Section Thirteen of the handbook*. In summary though, the following procedures for lockout must be implemented:

- As shown in illustration #155, lock the power disconnect in the "off" position and tag it.
- Attach locks onto the lock clip so that the de-energized handle or switch is secure in the "off" position and no accidental removal can take place.
- The tag must identify who it belongs to, and have a statement that prohibits unauthorized removal of the tag.
- Anybody who is performing work on the equipment must install their lock and their tag on the disconnect, and only the owner of the tag and lock can remove them, or if the employer's lockout procedures indicate that a supervisor is allowed to remove them.

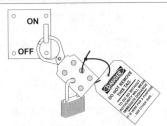

Illustration #155 - Lockout and Tagout

*Note: If the employee has any doubts at all about the lockout procedures for electrical equipment, they are advised to check with their company's safety department or with their immediate supervisor before proceeding any further.*

## Overhead Power Lines

Accidental electrocutions are among the most common accidents with mobile equipment, in particular with cranes, boom trucks and other types of mobile lifting and hoisting equipment.

## Overhead Power Lines

Most electrocutions are caused by the boom or other high point of the mobile equipment contacting or approaching too close to energized overhead power lines. The fatality rate in industry across North America is high, particularly amongst riggers guiding the loads being lifted by cranes. Inexperienced boom truck operators are also the cause of too many fatalities.

The safest procedure, when working around energized power lines with mobile equipment, is to have the local electrical authority cut off the power to the overhead lines. If this is not possible or practical, and it is necessary for the mobile equipment, such as cranes and boom trucks to be under or near "hot" power lines, a recommended safe working distance must be maintained. See table #15 for recommended safe working distances for cranes and mobile equipment having to be located near energized power lines.

| Operating Near High Voltage Power Lines | |
|---|---|
| **Normal Voltage (Phase to Phase)** | **Minimum Required Clearance** |
| to    50 kV | 10 ft.   (3.05 m) |
| Over  50 to  200 kV | 15 ft.   (4.60 m) |
| Over 200 to  350 kV | 20 ft.   (6.10 m) |
| Over 350 to  500 kV | 25 ft.   (7.62 m) |
| Over 500 to  750 kV | 35 ft.   (10.67 m) |
| Over 750 to 1000 kV | 45 ft.   (13.72 m) |

| In Transit With No Load & Boom Lowered | |
|---|---|
| **Normal Voltage (Phase to Phase)** | **Minimum Required Clearance** |
| to    75 kV | 4 ft.   (1.22 m) |
| Over 75  to   50 kV | 6 ft.   (1.83 m) |
| Over 50  to  345 kV | 10 ft.   (3.05 m) |
| Over 345 to  750 kV | 16 ft.   (4.87 m) |
| Over 750 to 1000 kV | 20 ft.   (6.10 m) |

Table #15 - Operating Near Powerlines

Always check with OSHA/OCHS and local authorities to ensure full compliance is maintained.

Every live overhead power line has an area around it called the "limit of approach" (see illustration #156). A crane boom, a load line, or a load being hoisted or lowered cannot operate in this area unless the power is cut off. ***There are no exceptions to this rule.***

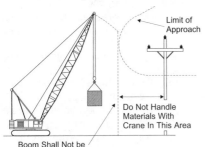

**Illustration #156 - Powerline Limit of Approach**

The absolute limit of approach will vary somewhat with provincial, state, federal or other regulating bodies. However, the guidelines shown in table #15 are similar to the guidelines of most regulating bodies.

## Power Line Approach Guidelines

- Maintain a safe operating distance and always observe the absolute limit of approach.
- A "signalman" must be used when the crane boom or the load can swing within the limit of approach. See illustration #157. The signalman must be positioned to estimate the minimum distance as per the guidelines in table #15, and give warning to the operator as the boom approaches the minimum distance. The person giving the signals must not have any other duties.
- All power lines must be considered "live". Always assume that the power is on.

# Overhead Power Lines

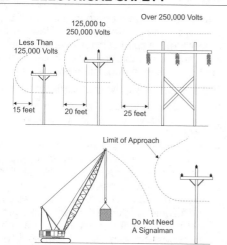

Illustration #157 - Use of Signalman Near Powerline

- Always notify the local electric authority when doing work with mobile equipment around live power lines.

- All personnel, except the operator, must stay well back from the equipment when the equipment is positioned near the limit of approach. No one should contact (touch) the equipment.
- Only use taglines to control the load or to prevent it from spinning. All types of ropes will conduct electricity, although dry polypropylene is less conductive than other rope materials.
- The operator is required to slow down the crane operation while working around power lines.
- Even warning devices and protective insulators are not to be considered "fail safe". They all have limitations.
- The absolute limit of approach should be increased when operating mobile equipment near a long span of overhead power lines, as the span can move outward a great distance in windy conditions.

- Use extreme caution when traveling with a crane or other mobile equipment underneath overhead power lines. Rough ground that the equipment is traveling over may cause lengthy booms or arms to bounce or undulate and make contact with the lines.
- When practical, use synthetic web slings for lifts.
- Always hold a "tailgate" meeting before preparing to work around overhead power lines. Make sure everyone is knowledgeable with the safe work procedures for work around power lines.
- Recent ANSI/ASME B 30.5 code changes may require a pre-lift meeting between the crane company and the utility company. Check with the B 30.5 code and the utility company.

*Note: When operating mobile equipment near overhead power lines, your first line of defense against contact is the distance the equipment is located from the lines. The second line of defense is the proper operation of the equipment by the operator and those designated to provide assistance from the ground.*

- When moving any high loads under power lines, as shown in illustration #158, make sure there is sufficient clearance at all times.

Illustration #158 - Moving High Loads Under Powerline

- Do not attempt to fall trees near an overhead power line, as demonstrated in illustration #159. Contact the local electric authority and seek their advice and assistance.

Illustration #159 -Don't Fall Trees Near Powerlines

- Never build scaffolds close to overhead power lines, as demonstrated in illustration #160.
- The minimum safe distances must be maintained at all times in order to protect the workers. Scaffolds must be positioned in a manner to prevent toppling onto adjacent overhead power lines.

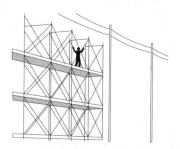

Illustration #160 - Do Not Build Scaffolds Near Powerlines

- Do not work close to unstable utility poles. Ask the local electric authority to support the pole or have them removed and replaced.

## Assurance of Safe Conditions

If inspection of the work site shows that safe clearances cannot be maintained in and around overhead power lines, do not proceed until an assurance in writing has been obtained, which states that the overhead power conductors will be:

- De-energized, or
- Guarded, or
- Displaced or re-routed.

## Power Line Contact

Should the mobile equipment make contact with the energized overhead power line, the operator is safer to remain on the machine until the power has been shut off or disconnected. The electric current will flow from the overhead power line, into the machine, to the ground. If the operator's feet were on the ground and he happened to touch the machine, there is a good chance that a deadly charge of electricity would flow through his body to the ground. If the operator remains on the machine, he would be relatively safe as long as he did not touch or step onto anything, which would provide a path for the electrical current to flow to the ground. All ground personnel must stay well back from the equipment as it remains in contact with the power line. If they make contact with the machine, as shown in illustration #161, they will be in immediate danger.

If the operator is in a safe position, and can move the machine to break the contact, the operator must first warn the people on the ground to stand clear of any part of the machine, its lines, loads or other equipment attachments until the machine is well clear of the lines.

If the machine has made contact with the overhead power line, as shown in illustration #161 and the machine cannot be moved, or there is danger from fire or other imminent hazards, the operator will be forced to abandon the machine in a safe manner.

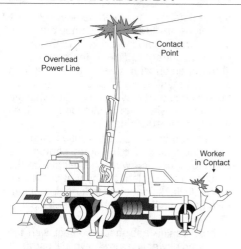

**Illustration #161 - Making Contact with "Live" Machine**

Illustration #162 shows the operator jumping from his machine. He must jump clear with both feet landing on the ground together and

his hands should be clear and free from making any contact on the machine. He cannot touch any part of the machine with his hands.

**Illustration #162 - Jumping Clear After Contact**

Always keep in mind that the machine, and anything in contact with it, will be energized (including the ground for some distance around the unit).

Illustration #163 shows the energized zone around the crane. Wet ground and water pools will extend the danger area and make a safe escape for the operator even more difficult. Therefore, stay with the machine if at all possible.

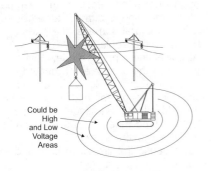

Could be High and Low Voltage Areas

**Illustration #163 - Energized Zone Around Crane**

A safe escape, as shown in illustration #162, can only be made if the operator's feet are kept together and he makes a short jump. The objective is to ensure that the entire body clears the machine and that the landing is solid on the feet, not stumbling and falling over. Keep the feet together and hop on both feet, taking care to remain upright. In addition, keeping the feet together will ensure that the person is not "straddling" two zones having different potentials, and this greatly improves the person's chances of a getting to safety. Continue to hop until you are a good distance away from the energized area. Contact the local electric authority to have the power shut off and warn others to stay well away from the danger zone and the machine.

## After Contact

After contact has occurred with an overhead power line there are several important points for the operator and the ground personnel to consider. These are:

- After contact was made, the operator must not panic and make any hasty moves. If the operator has not been injured or impaired in any way, he must assess the situation the best he can and warn others on the ground to stay away.

- If the machine is still running, and it looks safe to do, gently try to swing the crane away from the lines or move the machine back from the contact zone. If the machine breaks freely from the lines, move it well back from the danger zone. If part of the machine is "welded" to the power line, do not try to break the contact, as any movement could bring the lines down on top of the machine or other machinery or people in the area.

- The operator should remain in the cab of the machine until the utility company arrives and de-energizes the power line. If waiting is not possible, due to a chance that a fire might occur or other dangerous hazards are present, then as a last resort, the operator must jump clear of the machine, as mentioned previously and shown in illustration #162.

- Once the machine has been freed from the overhead power line, it must be thoroughly inspected before reuse. If any part of the machine is burned, arced or suffered structural damage, the parts must be repaired or replaced.

- All power line contacts made, must be reported to the local electric authority, as they are responsible for checking the lines for damage and making any repairs to avoid potential breakage at a later date.

- Rubber tired machines must be parked until the air in the tires cools. The contact could cause the tire air to heat and expand.

## Underground Power Cables

Underground electric wiring is often used for supplying electricity in urban and rural areas.

Care and attention must be given when digging, leveling, drilling or trenching in areas where underground power cables may be located.

There are many instances where people have died because they happened to strike an underground power cable with a shovel blade or with a bucket from an excavator or backhoe. In some cases, the buried power cable is protected from contact by having a length of treated wooden board placed on top of the line. Some of the more recent underground installations may have a bright yellow ribbon of plastic buried about 6 - 12 inches (15 - 30 cm) below the surface as a warning that a cable lies beneath it.

Should someone discover these markings, or suspect that underground cables are present, they must contact the local electricity authority before digging any further. Consider the following safety points:

- Driving metal ground rods or any other length of rod or pipe into the ground in areas of underground power distribution is dangerous unless one is absolutely sure that they are not going to make contact with a power cable. See illustration #164.

**Illustration #164 - Driving Metal Ground Rod**

- A common practice is to drive fence postholes deep into the ground or to drill postholes with a powered auger, as shown in illustration #165. Make sure that there are no underground power lines in the area before beginning to install fence posts.

Illustration #165 - Drilling Fence Post Holes

Illustration #166 - High Voltage Equipment

- Always pay attention to the "Danger- High Voltage" signs located on the sides of high voltage equipment, such as that shown in illustration #166. This equipment houses the various electrical connections for underground electrical cables.

Before beginning any trenching work with a powered machine, as shown in illustration #167, in areas where there are buried power cables, establish exactly the location of the cables.

Illustration #167 - Trenching Work

- When moving from one safe location to another, as shown in illustration #168, a piece of equipment such as a drilling rig may have to pass through a danger area under a power line. Not only does the location of underground power cables remain important to consider, so does the location of the drill mast in relation to overhead power lines.

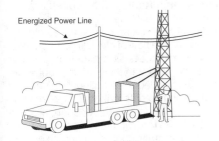

Energized Power Line

**Illustration #168 - Maintain a Safe Distance**

- In this example, the drill mast must be lowered between moves to avoid the overhead hazard.

## Storage Batteries

Storage batteries are common to many industries, as they provide sources of backup electricity for emergency use when there has been a power failure. The batteries may be used as energy sources for starting up stationary engines driving generators, pumps, compressors or other types of equipment. Storage batteries may have a high amount of stored energy and there is a good chance for a person to receive a strong electrical shock from the batteries if accidental contact is made.

Short-circuiting the electrical flow on batteries is common when a worker's ring or wristwatch bracelet makes contact with a battery lead or terminal. The worker may receive severe burns from the contact.

Always keep in mind that the overall voltage of multiple banks of storage batteries, as shown in illustration #169, may be high enough to produce a severe shock.

**Illustration #169 - Multiple Banks of Storage Batteries**

Always use insulated tools while performing work on battery terminals, connections or leads, and while doing any type of connection or disconnection work.

It is very important that the worker wears the appropriate personal protective equipment around storage batteries, because the battery acid and corrosive materials often found around the batteries can be quite irritating to the eyes and breathing system. The fumes coming from the battery acid can also be quite toxic.

## Static Electricity

Another important safety consideration when working with electricity is the serious conditions often created by static electricity. Electricity is the flow of electrons. Each electron is a part of the basic makeup of all matter and matter is everything in the universe. When these electrons buildup in unequal amounts on two different objects, and when the buildup becomes large enough, electricity flows in the form of "static discharge", or a "spark". The static charge on one object can transfer to another object in two ways, either by conduction or induction.

For conduction to occur, the two objects must be touching each other for the charges to transfer. See illustration #170A.

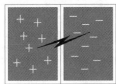

**Illustration #170A - Conduction - Objects Touching**

For induction to occur, as shown in illustration #170B, the objects do not have to be touching each other for the charges to transfer.

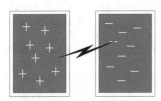

**Illustration #170B - Induction - Objects Not Touching**

A charged object will transfer electrons to a non-charged object until there is a balance of charges on both. This balance is known as "equilibrium". Static charges can buildup on all types of matter, for example:

- Gases and vapors.
- Dust particles.
- Within liquids.
- Inside pipes, vents and other types of lines.
- Inside or alongside moving machine parts and equipment.
- Between people.

Since static electricity is everywhere, and it cannot be totally eliminated, various recommended precautions are advised to be taken to control static discharge.

- In potentially explosive areas, workers should be careful not to rub objects together.

- Workers should wear specially designed clothing, which suppresses electrostatic buildup and discharge.
- Employers can install special equipment to collect dust and minimize static buildup.
- Sensitive work areas, such as computer stations, should have insulating materials such as floor mats, tablemats and air-ionization systems installed to minimize static buildup and discharge.
- Employers may consider installing specialized anti-static floor finishing and coverings and advise their employees to wear footwear made from anti-static materials.
- Ground all conductive parts of equipment such as pipes, rubber belt conveyors, vent lines, funnels, screens, silos and other storage type containers.
- Be extra careful handling powders in the presence of flammable gas or vapor.

## Static Electricity and Explosions

Some very serious explosions have been caused by static electricity. These have caused unnecessary fatalities and have been very costly. Because of the extreme danger presented by a buildup of static electricity, it is important to have approved policies and procedures in place throughout the work area where there are high risk situations due to the type of materials being handled or the way materials are being moved. The following conditions in the work area may cause an explosion to take place:

- The presence of a flammable atmosphere, where gases, vapors or fumes have accumulated and combined with oxygen in the air.
- A source of generated static charges such as when material is moved from one place to another through piping, by conveyors, through filtering systems or by pouring methods.

- A buildup of static charges.

In order to achieve equilibrium, the static electricity must discharge, and this is usually causes a spark.

To prevent explosions caused by static electricity, consider the following points when handling flammable gases and liquids:

- Remove the flammable gases and vapors surrounding the material in which static buildup might occur.
- Control the amount of static charge generated within the material in question.
- Provide adequate bonding or grounding to balance and dissipate the electrostatic discharges.
- Control the speed and rate of material flow through pipes, vents, pumps, filters and other containers and material conveyance systems.
- Transfer liquids slowly from one container to another when using a pouring method.

- Always try to keep the amount of liquid misting, spraying and splashing to a minimum.
- Make sure that pipes, pumps, filters, and containers are clean and free of rust and metal particles.
- Always allow time for the static charges to recombine or go into a state of equilibrium. This is better known as "charge relaxation".

To prevent explosions from static electricity when working with rail cars, tanker truck units and the holds of marine vessels, several precautions can be taken:

- Attach the grounding or bonding cable to clean metal before attempting to open the covers on the top of a tanker unit. Make sure that good metal-to-metal contact is made.
- Consider grounding all personnel working nearby by ensuring they are wearing proper clothing and footwear.

- Perform all operations within a closed system.
- Use inert gases to blanket the materials, if necessary, during loading and unloading operations.
- Reduce excessive splashing, swirling, spraying and misting of liquid products.
- Try to limit the rate of material flow into the tank or container.
- After filling of the tank or container is completed, close off and seal the covers and remove the bonding cable, in that order, before moving the unit.
- The bonding procedure is the first and last step in the operation.

## Review of Electrical Safety

Electricity is a silent, invisible force that can injure or kill without warning if its dangers are either ignored or not controlled properly. Always remember to treat electricity with respect and caution, and be alert to its unique characteristics. Workers should not fear electricity, but they must learn to appreciate how powerful this energy source is.

Safe work conditions, procedures and practices and the worker's own sense of responsibility are some of the best assurances against accidents due to electrical hazards. Keep in mind the following safety points:

- Always be alert when working with electricity.
- When a worker sees something he or she is not sure about with some electrical circuit or equipment, seek immediate assistance from qualified personnel.
- Never proceed with a job concerning electricity if you have any doubt about what you are doing. Seek assistance from someone who is familiar with the job or situation.
- Remember to ask qualified people questions about any electrical concerns you might have. There is no embarrassment in asking questions about electricity.

# SECTION NINE

## SAFE FORKLIFT OPERATION

## Forklift Accidents

Every year there are hundreds of forklift accidents, some are quite minor, but many of these accidents result in serious injuries, causing thousands of lost workdays. Unfortunately there are also several dozen workers who die in forklift related accidents, mostly because of improper safe operating procedures and practices. The Occupational Safety and Health Administration (OSHA) has created a regulation for powered industrial trucks, 29 CFR 1910.178. This OSHA regulation identifies the safety requirements and features for forklifts and provides guidelines for forklift operation and operator training.

Forklifts have an important role as industrial forklifts are used in nearly every type of product oriented business.

Without forklifts many business could not survive because of the volume of materials that must be moved and handled. However, forklift operation often receives very little attention until there is a serious incident or accident. Forklift training has also been neglected. Any worker would simply jump on the forklift and attempt the task at hand. There were very few controls as to who was designated to operate the forklift and in most cases formalized training programs were very limited. Unlike other types of mobile equipment, forklift operators were usually not required to be specially trained and authorized. Like any mobile equipment in the workplace, forklifts require regular scheduled maintenance so there is some assurance of having safe operation and effective functioning.

## Causes of Forklift Accidents

OSHA statistics indicate that the primary cause of forklift accidents is the failure of operators, pedestrians and co-workers to always follow safe work practices. To prevent forklift related accidents and injuries, attention must be focused on several key areas of forklift safety and operation:

- Having full knowledge about the characteristics, operation, and limitations and capacities of the forklift.
- Having full knowledge of the work hazards that are present during forklift operation.
- Having full knowledge of the safety rules and safe work practices associated with competent forklift operation.

Accidents occur as a result of the forklift operator not following safe working practices, including:

- Operator fails to have clear visibility in the direction of travel.
- The operator dismounts the forklift without following the necessary safety precautions.
- Not fully lowering the forks when parking the unit.
- Insufficient operator training and unauthorized operation.
- Operators placing their arms or legs outside the framework of the forklift.
- Jumping on or off the forklift.
- Colliding with another forklift, vehicle or pedestrian.
- Making quick, sharp turns, causing the forklift to tip over.
- Driving the forklift off the edge of a loading dock or ramp-way.
- Accidents arising from improper refueling procedures.
- Accidents resulting from improper battery recharging procedures.
- Using a forklift which is under rated for the lift being attempted.

## Causes of Forklift Accidents

- An unsecured trailer unit moves, causing the forklift to fall.
- Suffocation by carbon monoxide or propane fuel vapors.
- Operator losing control of the vehicle.
- Loads falling from elevated forks.
- Loads being too top heavy, causing the forklift to tip.
- People being struck by falling loads.
- The load is beyond the forklift's center of gravity or outside its area of stability.
- Operating the forklift too fast; not observing speed restrictions and road/surface conditions.
- Malfunctioning brake system and steering mechanism.
- Faulty hydraulic systems, causing cylinders to creep under load.
- Operator not paying attention to the route being traveled; failure to sound horn at intersections.

- Operator not checking behind before traveling in reverse direction.
- Presence of oil, grease or other slippery substances on the floor, causing the forklift to skid.
- Not keeping the forks close to the ground when traveling with a load.
- Not tilting the mast a few degrees back, to the rear of the forklift, to aid in load stability.
- Operator should face the direction of travel; drive in reverse if the load in front obscures vision.
- Failure to keep the load uphill when moving up a grade or down a grade that's more than ten degrees.
- Attempting to make a turn while moving up or down a grade, causing the forklift to tip over.
- The operator allows another person to ride on the forklift; do not do this unless the unit is so designed.

- Failing to allow for adequate space in aisles, or between storage racks.
- Failing to chock the forklift wheels when parking on an incline.

The OSHA regulation for forklift safety and operation requires employers and employees to take specific precautions with forklifts:

Employers must:

- Train employees to operate and maintain forklifts safely.
- Permit only trained, authorized, competent employees to operate forklifts.
- Provide the correct type of forklift for the material handling jobs and work area requirements.
- Ensure that a safe containment area has been designated for re-fueling and/or recharging of forklifts, and the procedures are in place.

Employee responsibilities include:

- Participate in forklift safety and operator training programs.
- Operate forklifts only if fully trained and authorized.
- Have complete understanding of forklift design and load capacities and limitations.
- Compliance to forklift safe operating procedures.
- Maintain the forklift so it functions safely and effectively.
- Follow safety precautions when working around forklifts.

The most important reason for the employer to provide training and the employee to participate in the forklift training programs is for the safety of the operators and their co-workers. Forklift related injuries and accidents are generally caused by the operator being inattentive, distracted, driving at excessive speeds, and having poor driving habits.

Well planned and professionally conducted training will help the forklift operator to:

- Avoid injuries and workplace accidents.
- Be aware of the hazards associated with forklift operation.
- Work safer and more effectively.
- Reduce material and product damage.
- Prevent forklift and other equipment damage.

## Forklift Types and Components

As with most modern machinery, there are many types and models of forklifts and truck carrying/lifting designs. Generally, the most commonly used forklift types are:

- Counterbalance Forklifts
- Narrow-aisle Forklifts
- Industrial Low-lift Trucks

### Counterbalance Forklifts

The counterbalance forklift, as shown in illustration #171, is generally used to handle and move a variety of products and packaged materials. They are common to industries such as shipyards, loading terminals, maintenance shops, assembly plants, warehouse operations, rail yards, trucking depots, heavy construction and military facilities.

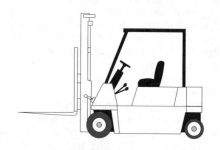

**Illustration #171 - Counterbalance Forklift**

The basic components of the counterbalance forklift are shown in illustrations #172A & B. The mast section includes a set of tracks housing the rollers and chains which provide the drive for moving the carriage section up and down.

The mast tilts the load forward and back during loading and unloading operations. The carriage section is attached to the mast and the load is placed in this section, up against the backrest on the forks. The backrest and forks are attached to the carriage. The primary purpose of the backrest is to support and stabilize the load, preventing the load from tipping or falling backward.

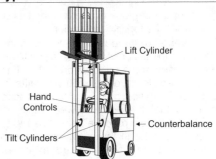

**Illustration #172B - Forklift Protection**

The forklift lifting mechanism is powered by either one or two hydraulic lift cylinders. Lift cylinders are "single acting" cylinders; they only work in one direction. The tilt cylinders are positioned horizontally to enable the operator to safely work the forks under the load for lifting, or to place the load flat when unloading. Tilt cylinders are double-acting and work in two directions for forward tilt and backward tilt.

**Illustration #172A - Basic Components**

For operator safety, never move the tilt controls while the forklift is in motion.

The overhead guard is made like a "cage", designed to deflect falling objects and to give the operator some roll-over protection if the forklift were to tip over. Many forklifts are equipped with seat belts. It is always recommended that the operator wear their seat belt. This safety practice helps to keep the operator secure in the seat and under the protection of the overhead guard. In some jurisdictions it may be a mandatory requirement for forklift operators to wear their seatbelts at all times. See illustration #173.

Illustrations #174A & B show two types of fork designs: half-tapered forks and full-tapered forks. Half-tapered forks are typically used on those forklifts having heavy load capacities.

**Illustration #173 - Forklift Protection**

This fork gradually increases in thickness from the tip to its maximum thickness at a point approximately midway back on the length of the fork. The full-tapered fork is generally used on forklifts having lighter load capacities and for narrow pallets and loads where the operator has to work the fork under the load because of small clearances. This type of fork design gradually increases in thickness from the tip of the fork, back the full length of the fork to its heel.

Half Taper

**Illustration #174A - Half Tapered Forks**

Full Taper

**Illustration #174B - Full Tapered Forks**

The forklift has several other features which the operator must be familiar with. Each unit will have a manufacturer's nameplate or label for identifying the forklift's load capacity, range and other operating limitations. The operator must become familiar with the various mast controls as well as have a good feel for the braking and acceleration/deceleration of the unit. Lights, horn and alarms will be necessary for safe operation in most work areas, as they warn pedestrians of the vehicle's approach. A fire extinguisher is often mounted on the forklift for emergency use, and should be regularly inspected. The operator must be familiar with the forklift's fuel storage system, in particular, the operator must know the safe procedures for refueling the unit. If the forklift is battery operated, as in the case of many smaller units, there has to be correct procedures for connecting and disconnecting the battery recharging system.

*Note: Counterbalance forklifts differ greatly from many other types of mobile equipment. They weigh much more, as the counterweight located in the rear section of the forklift frame counterbalances the loads being lifted and transported. When loaded, and because of their tall and narrow frame design, forklifts can be quite easy to tip over. In addition, they steer with the rear wheels, not the front wheels, which most people are far more accustomed to.*

### Narrow-aisle Forklifts

Narrow-aisle forklifts are very common to an indoor material and package handling environment. Because most of these units operate in an indoor environment, they are usually battery operated. This type of forklift is often used when lifting requirements are not too demanding and in areas where aisle space is limited, such as a warehouse or retail or commercial business.

Illustration #175 identifies a common style of narrow-aisle forklift.

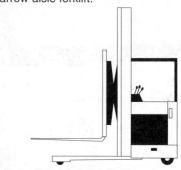

Illustration #175 - Narrow-Aisle Forklift

The narrow-aisle forklift is quite different in design to the counterbalance design of forklift. As shown in illustration #176, the operator is in a standing position, directly behind the mast and carriage assembly. There is very little protection for the operator if a load being handled falls.

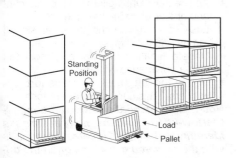

**Illustration #176 - Operating Narrow-Aisle Forklift**

Illustration #176 shows probably one of the best and safest applications for this design of forklift, as the loads are balanced and loaded neatly onto pallets. Each pallet has clearance underneath it, so the forks can slide under without interference.

The load is lifted up level and square to the proper shelving unit and the operator slowly moves forward and sets the loaded pallet in place. He then backs out squarely until the forks are free from the pallet.

At all times, the operator must be in good visual position to observe the position of the load and where the forklift is in relation to shelving, pedestrians and objects in the aisle. Usually these types of forklifts are well equipped with flashing lights, horn and alarms to give warning to people in the area of its presence.

### Industrial Low-Lift Trucks

There is a wide variety of styles of industrial low-lift trucks common to industry and business. In every workplace there are some materials and packages that must be moved by hand. Many companies tend to use industrial hand trucks to make it easier for workers to move products and to avoid injuries from heavy and awkward lifting.

Employers and employees must be aware that both manual and powered hand trucks can themselves cause injury if they are not properly used and maintained. Causes of accidents with industrial low-lift trucks include:

- Inadvertently rolling the wheels off the edges of ramps and loading docks.
- Pinching hands, fingers and feet between the truck and other objects in the work area.
- Not paying attention and running into pedestrians.
- Accidentally running into other equipment and obstacles in the working area.
- Loss of control of the truck on sloped ramps and roadways.
- Underestimating the power associated with a powered low-lift truck.
- Using the lift truck to transport co-workers. This should never be done.

*Note: Both manual and powered industrial low-lift trucks share many of the risks identified. But, the greatest danger is with the powered trucks, as often the operator underestimates the power available in this type of mechanical driven unit.*

There are at least four types of industrial low-lift trucks commonly used. Each has its own unique safety and operational features.

- Two-Wheeled Hand Trucks
- Four-Wheeled Hand Trucks
- Pallet Movers
- Powered Hand Trucks

## Two-Wheeled Hand Truck

Illustration #177 identifies a common design for a two-wheeled hand truck. The load must be well balanced and safe on the flat bottom plate (chisel) and tight up against the back of the truck's frame.

Always make sure that the chisel is all the way under the load and for bulky, fragile or dangerous loads, strap the load to the truck frame to prevent accidental tipping. Always place the larger and heavier objects on the bottom when moving a stack of objects, as shown in illustration #177.

Operating the two-wheeled hand truck safely means that the operator must at all times protect his hands and feet and ensure the load does not fall on him. Try to grip the hand truck at the widest part of the frame. The operator should never try to brake the hand truck by placing his foot on the wheel. When the operator is taking the hand truck down a ramp, as shown in illustration #178, the idea is to keep the truck ahead of themselves in order to be in control and to not endanger themselves or others who happen to be on the ramp.

Load

Chisel

**Illustration #177 - Two-wheeled Hand Truck**

**Illustration #178 - Operating the Hand Truck**

Illustration #178 also shows the best practice for controlling the hand truck, by pulling it behind him, while bringing it up the ramp. At all other times, face the direction you are walking in. Store the hand truck by leaning it up on its chisel, with the handle and frame leaned into and up against a wall.

**Four-Wheeled Hand Trucks**

Illustration #179 identifies a common design for a four-wheeled hand truck. The operator always must be careful to not injure his hands or feet while operating this type of load carrying equipment. A common injury with these trucks is to run the truck up over one's ankle while pulling it. Consider standing to one side if the truck is to be pulled.

Always arrange the cargo so the heavy objects are flat and on the bottom and ensure the load is secured to prevent accidental tipping. The operator must be careful going up and down ramps.

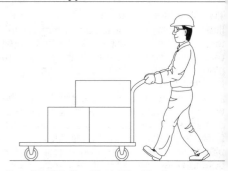

Illustration #179 - Four-Wheeled Hand Truck

Depending on how heavy the load is, the truck may have to be pushed from behind up a ramp and held back while going down a ramp. It can be quite a challenge to control a fully loaded four-wheeled hand truck. Always try to stay within the painted boundary lines on the floors to avoid other equipment and people.

When leaving the truck unattended, consider locking the wheels or placing chocks behind or in front of the wheels to prevent accidental rolling. A heavily loaded, unattended rolling hand truck can create a very dangerous situation for unwary people in the work area. Never carry a co-worker on this type of truck, and the operator should not consider riding on the truck while it is free-wheeling down an incline. Do not carry more than the truck's maximum load capacity and when operating the truck, walk at a normal pace.

## Pallet Movers

Illustration #180 identifies a special type of industrial low-lift truck designed to move materials and objects sitting on pallets. The pallet holds the load, and the pallet mover forks are spaced the required distance to accommodate the size and type of pallet being used.

**Illustration #180 - Pallet Mover**

Illustration #181 identifies a load placed on a pallet. Inspect pallets regularly for damage, and take defective ones out of service. Stack unused pallets flat, on top of each other, in an area where they won't get in the way or become damaged.

In order to safely transport and lift a load on a pallet with a pallet mover, the load must be stable. Consider blocking loads which are circular or round shaped, or have irregular features. It is best to stack regular shaped objects neatly, and interlock boxes on the pallet when possible. Some packages can be shrink-wrapped with plastic or strap the load to keep it secure.

Pallet movers raise the load only a short distance from the ground. This type of industrial low-lift truck is very suitable for safely transporting heavy loads, requiring very little effort from the operator, as the only manual operation required is to either pull or push the truck into position to take on a load or to off-load.

**Illustration #181 - Loaded Pallet**

## Powered Hand Trucks

There are two basic models of powered hand trucks. Each model is powered by a high capacity electric storage battery. The main difference between models is how each is controlled by the operator. The two models of powered hand trucks are:

- Walking Type Powered Hand Truck
- Rider Type Powered Hand Truck

Illustration #182A identifies the walking type powered hand truck. It has similar features to the pallet mover, with the exception of how it is driven and controlled. The operator walks alongside the truck and controls it by hanging on to the control handle. Illustration #182B identifies the riding type powered hand truck. The operator rides this type of truck in a standing position and controls it from the handle.

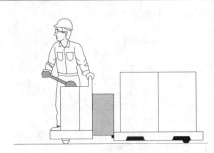

**Illustration #182B - Rider Type Powered Hand Truck**

There are several important safety features found on powered hand trucks. These special features are added to reduce the hazards and to prevent serious injury to the operator. Illustration #183 provides a view of the control handle for a powered hand truck. If the operator were to let go of the handle, whether this is a walking or riding type of truck, the power would be cut off and the unit would stop.

**Illustration #182A - Walking Type Powered Hand Truck**

This special feature is referred to as a "dead-man" control. The illustration shows a special switch called the "belly-button" stop switch. This feature prevents the operator from getting caught between the handle and some type of stationary object, as the handle would push up against the operator's mid section, make contact against the switch, thus cutting off the power to the truck. The truck brakes are applied by moving the steering handle up or down.

It always best for the operator to take some time to become familiar with the controls and operation of a powered hand truck. In particular, it is important to know how to change directions, from forward to reverse, and to practice braking, lifting and lowering loads. Often with electric powered trucks, the actions are quick, with no cushion effect at all.

Another important aspect of learning how to control and operate a powered hand truck is to practice its maneuverability and judge clearances between the truck and the various objects in the work area. These trucks are heavy and take up considerable space.

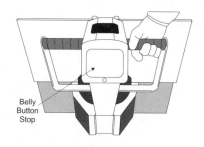

Belly
Button
Stop

**Illustration #183 - Control Handle**

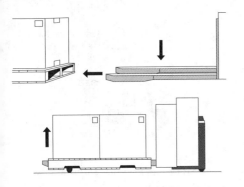

**Illustration #184 - Loading Procedures**

As shown in illustration #184, there are several guidelines for operating a powered hand truck, whether it be a walker or rider:

- Always approach the pallet with the truck's forks square to the load.
- Keep the forks low and in alignment with the pallet's openings.
- Ensure that the forks are evenly spaced and are centered in order to have a balanced load.
- Make sure the forks are positioned all the way under the loaded pallet.
- Try not to strike the vertical uprights of the pallet or its deckboards.
- Raise the load a short distance above the ground for traveling.
- Note, if the powered hand truck is running, but has no power to lift the load, this is usually a sign that the battery is low. It will require re-charging.
- The operator should face in the direction they intend on going, and travel with the forks in a raised position.
- Normal operation of a powered hand truck is having the operator in a pulling position, rather than a pushing position.

- The operator must stand to one side of the control handle, as shown in illustration #185, not directly in front of the truck.
- The operator must be careful to keep his feet clear from being run over.
- Do not operate the truck by leading the truck's forks into a blind area, such as around a corner or when exiting a doorway.
- It is recommended to go with the load first into freight elevators and into other tight spaces - this prevents the operator from getting crushed against the wall as they enter, and it prevents the operator from having to exit blindly.
- Do not attempt to ride on a walking type powered hand truck and never give co-workers a ride.
- Do not jump off a riding powered hand truck until it comes to a complete stop.

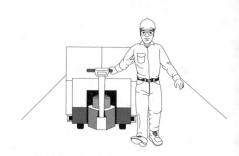

Illustration #185 - Operator Standing to One Side

## Forklift Inspection

Every forklift, no matter its age or design, must always be in safe working order. OSHA regulations require that forklifts be inspected before each day's use, and before each shift for forklifts used in 24 hour a day operations. The physical operating condition of a forklift may change throughout the day and shift by shift.

A "pre-start" inspection identifies potential hazards which can greatly increase safety risks for the operator and to those in the immediate work area. The competent forklift operator will make these inspections part of their daily routine before beginning their work day.

***Note: Never use a forklift that is damaged or has an operating problem. Report any problems to the supervisor and remove the forklift from service until the problem has been corrected.***

The following check list identifies several key forklift pre-start inspections:

- ☐ Gauges and Control Lights and Dials
- ☐ Tire Condition
- ☐ Hydraulic System Fluid Levels
- ☐ Power Steering Fluid Level
- ☐ Brake Fluid Level
- ☐ Engine Coolant Level
- ☐ Engine Oil Level
- ☐ Air Filter/Cleaner Condition
- ☐ Condition of Coolant Lines, Hoses, Fluid Tanks
- ☐ Bends, Cracks and Welds On Forks, Mast, Backrest and Overhead Guard
- ☐ Condition of Mast Rollers, Tracks, Chain and Pulleys (Wear, Looseness, Alignment, Lubrication)
- ☐ Hydraulic Cylinder Leaks, Hose Condition and Mount Securement
- ☐ Fuel Tank Condition and Securement (Gasoline, Diesel, Propane)
- ☐ Fuel Lines, Hoses, Valves, Switches and Connections
- ☐ Battery Electrolyte Level
- ☐ Battery Connections, Cable/Wiring Condition and Vent Caps
- ☐ Engine Exhaust System Condition
- ☐ Engine Coolant Hoses and Radiator Conditions
- ☐ Engine Belts and Pulley Conditions
- ☐ Clutch Operation
- ☐ Brake System Condition and Operation

❑ Lights, Mirrors, Horns, Alarms and Other Warning Systems

❑ Operator Foot Pedals and Hand Controls

❑ Operator Seat Cushion and Back Rest/Arm Rest Condition

❑ Safety Belt Securement and Operation

❑ Fire Extinguisher Placement and Service

*Note: Anytime the forklift operator has to handle a propane tank (cylinder), it is recommended that this be done outside, away from the building and other workers. Smoking, open flames and hotwork, such as electric arc welding and oxy-acetylene cutting and welding are never to be done around propane tanks. A fully charged fire extinguisher should be nearby, mounted close to the operator's seat.*

## Forklift Lifting Principles

As shown in illustrations #186A & B, forklifts use a "fulcrum and lever" principle for lifting heavy loads. Both the counterbalance and narrow aisle forklifts, have a fulcrum point located at a point where the load being lifted by the forklift is balanced. Illustrations #186A and B refer to the fulcrum point as the "pivot point." On the counterbalance type, the pivot point is located at the drive wheels. The pivot point on the narrow-aisle forklift is located under the front load wheels.

The rated load capacity of a forklift is directly related to the amount of weight the forklift is designed to lift, its load center and leverage. Where the load sits on the forks, in relationship to the rest of the machine is a major factor in how much weight can be safely lifted.

The closer the load is to the backrest of the machine, the heavier the load can be.

Do not attempt to lift any heavy load from just the fork tips, as there will be almost no leverage at this point.

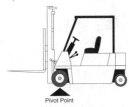

Illustration #186A - Counter Balance Forklift - Pivot Point

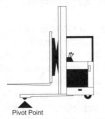

Illustration #186B - Narrow-Aisle Forklift - Pivot Point

As shown in illustrations #187A & B, the nearer the load is to the back rest, the safer the operation. If the load is some distance from the backrest, the forklift loses some portion of its rated load capacity and it may become unstable and create a serious safety problem. In fact, in a situation as shown in illustration #187B, the operator would be unable to properly steer and control the forklift if it was loaded this way.

*Note: It is always important to know how much the load weighs before ever attempting to lift it. If the weight of the load is not clearly marked or made readily available, the forklift operator can try a simple test to determine if it is safe to lift it. First, get the forks directly under the load and up against the backrest as firmly as possible. Now, try to lift the load only an inch or two.*

*The knowledgeable operator should sense that the forklift feels stable and notes that the rear wheels are in firm contact with the floor. If everything seems to be acceptable to the operator and the steering seems normal, the load can be moved. But, if the operator feels that the forklift is not behaving normally, set the load down and do some further investigation to determine the load weight. A forklift with a higher rated load capacity may be required.*

Illustration #187B - Poorly Placed Load

- Never exceed the rated load capacity of the forklift.
- Make sure the load is stable and no part of it will shift when traveling.
- Spread the forks to the widest possible distance in order to provide for maximum load stability. See illustration #188.
- Forklifts should not be used to push or pull loads or vehicles. They are meant to lift and transfer loads.

Illustration #187A - Properly Loaded Forklift

- The operator must not exceed the posted speed limit in the working area.
- Extra caution must be taken while braking. Slamming the brakes on hard will most certainly cause the machine to go into a skid, resulting in a loss of control and stability for the machine and the load.

Illustration #188 - Positioning Forks

## Handling and Moving Loads

### Loading the Forklift

Before the forklift operator starts to pick up a load, some consideration should be given to planning and preparing for the lift.

- Check the travel route.
- Make sure the route is free of obstructions and other potential hazards.
- Check the floor or roadway surface for slippery, bumpy or uneven sections.
- Check the load itself to be sure it is within the rated load capacity of the forklift.
- The load should be centered and stable, not top heavy.

To pick up the load, consider the following procedures (refer to illustration #189):

- The forklift must be in a position so it is square up to the load.
- Approach the load slowly and with the forks in a low traveling position.
- The forks should be spread as wide as possible and be level.
- Stop the forklift when the fork tips are just one foot (.3 m) away from the load.
- Level the forks out and slowly drive forward until the load is up against the backrest.
- Raise the load an inch or two (2 - 5 cm) to make sure it feels stable and the forklift's rear wheels remain on the floor.
- Raise the load level and high enough to have good ground clearance.
- Carefully tilt the mast back to stabilize the load.
- Make sure it is all clear behind the forklift and back out slowly when so required.
- Drive in reverse if there is poor or no visibility over the load.
- Slow down to go up or down a slope.
- Keep the load "uphill" if traveling up a slope.
- Drive in reverse going downhill, keeping the load uphill.

*Note: Do not overload the forklift. Do not raise or lower the load while traveling. Do not tilt the load forward except while unloading. Do not carry anything on the side or on the overhead rack of the forklift and refrain from striking objects and bumping into walls, stacks of boxes and packages, and keep in mind height clearances when working in low overhead areas around overhead sprinklers, pipelines and electrical trays.*

1. Stop One Foot From Load Area, Check for Alignment, Proceed Slowly Under the Load.

2. Lift the Load Level, Only a Short Distance From the Ground.

3. Look Over Both Shoulders.

4. Tilt the Load Back.

**Illustration #189 - Picking Up A Load**

## Unloading the Forklift

The forklift operator must consider the following procedures before beginning to unload the forklift.

- Get the forklift slowly into the right position where the load is to be placed.
- Make sure that there are no pedestrians close to the unloading location.
- Give a warning that the forklift is in the work area by sounding the horn or alarm.

To unload the forklift, consider the following procedures (refer to illustration #190):

- Drive slowly to about one foot (.3 m) from the spot the load is to be located.
- Drive halfway over the location and level out the load.

- Drive in the remaining way and position the load directly over the destination.
- Keep the mast vertical so the load remains level.
- Slowly lower the load on the spot where it is required.
- Place the load so it is straight and square.
- Check that no pedestrians or objects are directly behind of the forklift.
- Before beginning to backup, sound the horn or alarm. Back away slowly, with the forks just above the floor.
- To make sure the forks won't hook the load when backing out from under it, tilt the forks slightly forward.

1. Stop One Foot From Load Area, Make Sure the Way is Clear.

2. Drive Halfway Over Location, Tilt Forks Forward.

3. Position Load - Lower Load

4. Back Away Slowly With Forks Forward Slightly, Make Sure the Way is Clear.

**Illustration #190 - Unloading The Forklift**

## Stacking and Unstacking Loads

There are many examples where loads must be stacked to increase the facility's storage capacity. The forklift operator must always keep in mind that the higher the load is positioned the less stable the forklift becomes. As shown in illustration #191, lifting a load from a stack of boxes on pallets for example, is quite similar to lifting a load directly off the floor.

- Approach the load slowly and be sure the forks are square to the load and in a traveling position.
- Stop about one foot (.3 m) from the load and raise the mast so the forks are located at the correct height.
- Level the forks out and slowly drive forward, ensuring that the forks are free to slide under the load.

- Keep going forward until the load is firmly up against the backrest.
- Raise the load slowly, just enough to clear what it was resting on.
- The operator must check over both shoulders to make sure it is clear behind him.
- Sound the horn or alarm to give notice that a forklift is in the work area and it is backing up.
- Back out slowly, keeping the forklift straight.
- Once the forklift has backed out far enough so the load is cleared from the top of the stack, stop and lower the mast to the traveling position.
- Tilt the forks back slightly, and begin to drive in reverse to the destination where the load is intended to go.

1. Stop, Raise Mast

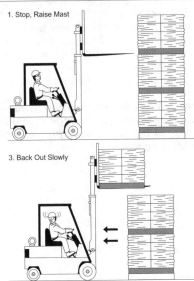

2. Level Forks, Pull Forward

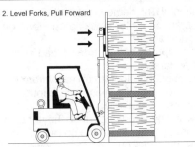

3. Back Out Slowly

4. Lower Mast

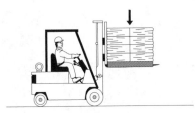

**Illustration #191 - Lifting a Load From a Stack**

## Stacking Loads

Illustration #192 demonstrates the correct forklift procedures for stacking one load on top of another load.

- Again, approach the stacked load slowly and squarely.
- Stop about one foot (.3 m) away from the load and raise the mast high enough to clear the top of the stack.
- Slowly drive forward until the load is square over the top of the stack.
- Level the forks out and slowly lower the mast until the load is no longer supported by the forks.

- The operator must check over both shoulders to make sure it is clear behind him.
- Sound the horn or alarm to give notice that a forklift is in the work area and it is backing up.
- Back out slowly, keeping the forklift straight.

*Note: Unloading and loading loads supported by a rack type storage assembly is similar to the procedures just described for stacked loads.*

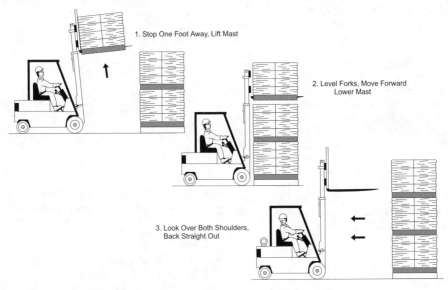

1. Stop One Foot Away, Lift Mast

2. Level Forks, Move Forward
   Lower Mast

3. Look Over Both Shoulders,
   Back Straight Out

**Illustration #192 - Stacking a Load Properly**

## Forklifts on Loading Docks

Many industrial facilities have areas where loading and unloading docks are situated for receiving and shipping goods and products. In these areas, forklifts are commonly used to transport and carry heavy loads, in all shapes and sizes and to and from various types of mobile transportation vehicles. Loading docks are designed so large truck-trailer units can back up to a dock and make safe access for forklifts. Illustration #193 identifies how a trailer has been backed up to a loading dock and accessed by the forklift.

To unload or load this trailer, or if it were a rail car, there are several procedures that must be followed in order to prevent any serious accidents.

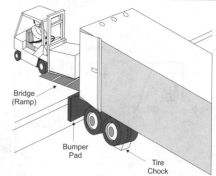

Illustration #193 - Loading Dock

- The forklift operator or the loading dock worker must be sure that the truck, trailer or rail car brakes are set so no accidental movement can occur.
- If the trailer unit is parked at the loading dock, unattached from the truck, the trailer must be supported and positioned by its fixed jacks to keep it stable.

- Use wheel blocks (chocks) to prevent movement. Some installations may have a feature called a dock lock to secure the trailer.
- Properly position the bridge or dock plate so the forklift can safely enter and leave the trailer or rail car. See illustration #194.
- Check to make sure the bridge or dock plate is secure and can hold the weight of a fully loaded forklift.
- When driving into the trailer or rail car, always drive straight on the bridge plates and never accelerate at this point.
- Drive at a steady controlled speed to prevent skidding.
- Before beginning to do too much work inside the trailer or rail car, it is best to check the condition of the floor. Check for loose boards, holes, large splinters and cracks.
- Use additional trailer jacks to support the weight of a loaded forklift if it is deemed to be too heavy for the trailer.

- Always keep in mind the height of the trailer or rail car doorway entrance/exit before driving in for the first time.
- Always double check to ensure the trailer is backed up and square to the loading dock before starting the forklift work.
- Use either or both dock lighting and the forklift's headlights if working in dark trailers or rail cars.
- Check that it is clear when backing out of the trailer or rail car. Sound a warning, and back out slowly.

Illustration #194 - Properly Positioned Bridge

# Entering Elevators

There may be times when it is required to take a forklift from one floor to another in a large industrial complex. Heavy duty industrial elevators are rated for large load weights, often carrying freight, machine parts and other packages and objects. To safely enter an elevator with a forklift it is important to know the rated load capacity of the elevator. Make sure the elevator can handle the combined weight of the forklift and the load it is carrying. There are several other points to consider when entering elevators with forklifts:

- Before driving the forklift onto an elevator, stop at least 6 feet (2 m) before the elevator doorway.

- The forklift operator must ensure that the elevator is ready and positioned to receive the forklift.
- Drive the forklift in very slowly.
- Once fully inside the elevator, set the forklift brakes, put the controls into neutral position, and turn off the start key/button.
- The operator should climb off the forklift and stand next to the elevator controls to access the control panel.
- Once the elevator transports the forklift to the desired floor location, the operator must ensure that the elevator is positioned properly and the doorway is fully opened and secure.
- The operator can start up the forklift, disengage the brakes, and slowly back the forklift out of the elevator.

## Parking a Forklift

Under OSHA regulations it is a violation to leave a forklift unattended while it is running. According to OSHA, an "unattended" forklift is one which the operator is more than 25 feet (8 m) away from, or the forklift is out of the operator's view.   Before leaving a forklift parked, take the following safety precautions:

- Park away from a high traffic area. Park on flat even surface.
- Do not block aisles, stairs, doors, exits, emergency showers, fires extinguishers or electrical control panels.
- Lower the forks to the floor and tilt them forward so they are flat on the floor.
- Put the controls in neutral and turn off the start switch or key.
- Set the brakes to prevent the forklift from rolling.   If parked on a slope, set the brakes and block the wheels.
- Remove the ignition/power key.

## Preventing Forklift Tipovers

Illustration #195 identifies one of the most common tipover situations for forklifts. When a forklift is tipped over on its side it is referred to as "lateral" tipover.  It is usually caused by:

- Making sharp turns at excessive speed.
- Maneuvering with a load too high.
- Driving over uneven surfaces, bumps or debris.

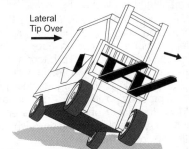

Lateral Tip Over

**Illustration #195 - Lateral Tipover**

If a lateral tipover happens, it is best for the operator to try and stay with the forklift, under the protection of the overhead guard. The operator has to hold on tight to the steering wheel, and push hard with his feet to remain in the seat. If the forklift is equipped with a safety belt, the operator must wear it. It could help prevent the operator from becoming seriously injured in tipovers. The mast will prevent the forklift from rolling over all the way and crushing the overhead guard.

Another very serious forklift tipover is shown in illustration #196. In this situation, the forklift fell between the loading dock and the trailer unit. This may have happened because the wheels on the trailer were not chocked properly, or the bridge or dock plate was not properly positioned. Another cause could be the driver of the truck-trailer unit pulling away from the loading dock while the forklift was inside the trailer.

Illustration #196 - Falling Off a Loading Dock

*Note: As the forklift backs out of a trailer, the rear wheels can catch on the end of the bridge that is not flat against the floor of the trailer. The front drive wheels can push an unsecured trailer away from the loading dock and out from under the forklift resulting in the forklift falling between the trailer and dock.*

Consider the following points with this type of tipover:

- The operator may consider jumping clear from the forklift in the type of tipover shown in illustration #196. Always check with the company's safety policy and procedures to know what is best to do in these serious circumstances.
- It is best if the forklift operator checks the bridge periodically for proper positioning and to ensure that the trailer wheels are properly chocked.
- Dock locks can be installed to prevent the trailer from moving.

## Forklift Steering

Steering a forklift is different than steering many other vehicles because a forklift's rear wheels do the steering. Because of this, the forklift handles quite differently from other vehicles. Unless the operator takes special care when turning, the rear end could swing around quickly, causing several risks:

- Potential for the forklift to tipover.
- The load could shift and fall.
- The rear end will swing into racks, walls, and other objects or hit pedestrians.

The drive wheels of the forklift act as a pivot point. When the operator makes a turn, the back of the forklift makes a circle around the front. See illustration #197. Always slow down for turns. Take turns wide and slow. When turning into an aisle, the operator must stay wide.

## Forklift Steering

This keeps the load clear from the sides of the aisles and gives the operator a chance to square up with the direction and location where they are going (see illustration #198A).

When the operator backs out of the aisle, as shown in illustration #198B, allow enough room for the forks to clear the sides before beginning to make the turn.

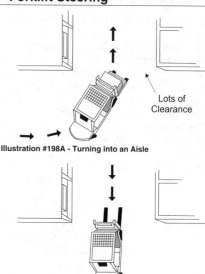

Lots of Clearance

**Illustration #198A - Turning into an Aisle**

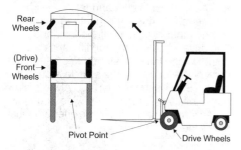

Rear Wheels

(Drive) Front Wheels

Pivot Point

Drive Wheels

**Illustration #197 - Drive Wheels Act as Pivot Point**

**Illustration #198B - Backing Out of an Aisle Safely**

## Driving Over Rail Tracks

It is not uncommon to see forklifts driving over rail tracks in large industrial complexes and in warehouse and storage facilities.

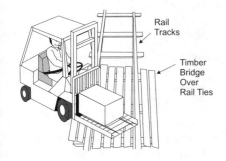

Rail Tracks

Timber Bridge Over Rail Ties

**Illustration #199 - Crossing Rail Tracks Diagonally**

It is very important that the forklift operator consider the following precautions before crossing a rail track:

- Before crossing the rail track, stop, look, and listen.
- If the way is clear, try to cross the tracks diagonally, as shown in illustration #199.
- Never park the forklift close to the rail track.
- Cross at designated rail crossings only.

## Power Sources

Forklifts may be powered by fuels, such as diesel, gasoline, propane, or by electric batteries. Any power source can create hazards if it is exposed to situations and conditions that could create a fire or explosion. Forklift operators require specialized training to refuel a forklift, or to recharge or replace a battery.

OSHA regulations require that a designated area be assigned for refueling or re-charging forklifts. According to OSHA rules, these areas must:

- Permit no smoking.
- Be well ventilated.
- Be furnished with suitable fire extinguishers.
- Have no flames, sparks or anything in the area that could cause a fire or explosion.

To refuel with diesel, gasoline or propane:

- Turn off the forklift and set the brakes.
- Put on any personal protective clothing, such as gloves, glasses, etc.
- Follow the refueling procedures as recommended by the forklift manufacturer's operating manual and the employer's safety procedures.
- Keep spills to a minimum. If any fuel does spill, keep the spill cleanup equipment accessible so cleanup operations can take place quickly.
- Once the fuel tank is full, replace the cap and tighten.

To change or charge a battery:

- Wear suitable protective equipment designed to protect against corrosives.
- Use acid resistant equipment to handle the battery. Do not use bare hands.
- Check the battery for cracks, acid leaks, frayed wiring and loose connections.
- When filling a new battery for the first time, pour acid into the water. Pouring water into acid could cause overheating and splattering.
- Do not let any metal come into contact with the battery terminals.
- When setting up to recharge the forklift battery, follow the company's procedures for safe charging.

# SECTION TEN

## SAFE WORKING SURFACES

## Introduction

Many workers in all types of industries and businesses are injured each year from slips, trips and falls. These types of accidents occur daily in offices, shop floors, and in a variety of both high and low-risk work environments. Many workers are probably more likely to be injured on the job by slipping or falling than by job-related hazards. Walking is such a natural function, that people usually don't pay much attention when walking. They are often not fully aware of their surroundings or of the conditions around them, and sooner or later they slip on something, or trip over an object and fall.

Sometimes people move or work in such a way that they actually create a fall hazard. Avoiding slips, trips and falls is very often a matter of common sense and good judgment:

- Don't move faster than conditions will allow.
- Don't create hazards.
- Use proper tools and equipment correctly.

## Slips and Trips

A slip occurs whenever there is minimum friction or traction between the person's foot and the surface upon which they are walking or standing on. Several common causes of slips in the workplace include:

- Loose or wet material spills on floors.
- Constantly having wet or damp floor or ground surfaces.
- Icy conditions on floors or ground surfaces during cold, freezing weather.
- Mud and/or loose rock, sand or gravel.
- Loose rugs or floor mats.
- Moving across a change in floor surfaces.

Workers can minimize the risk of slipping on wet surfaces by keeping a shorter stride in their walk and maintaining their center of balance under them.

Walking with your feet pointed slightly outward, creates a larger and more stable base. When walking around corners where the surface is wet, try to take a wider turn to avoid short sharp foot placement which may cause a loss of balance and poor stability. Wet floors should be clearly marked, especially in high traffic areas. See illustrations #200A, B, C, and D. Clean up spills, pick up items dropped on the floor, and do not leave "booby-traps" lying around. Wear shaded glasses when outdoors or when walking on ice and snow to help identify possible slippery hazards.

*Note:    Be careful of wet shoes on dry floors. They can be just as slippery as dry shoes on a wet floor.*

Illustration #200B - Pick Up Objects

Illustration #200C - Do Not Leave "Booby Traps"

Illustration #200A - Clean Up Spills

**Illustration #200D - Wet Floor Warning**

Trips can occur whenever your foot strikes an object and your forward or backward momentum causes you to be thrown off balance. Trips most commonly happen when:

- The person's view is obstructed.
- When a person decides to take a shortcut instead of using the appropriate path or walkway.
- When there is clutter and debris carelessly left on or near paths and walkways.

Poor lighting can impair vision and create dangerous situations where a person could easily trip over an object lying in the pathway.

Also, when a person comes into a building from outside where the sun is bright, the eye's ability to adjust to the darker room will take some time and it is easy to trip over something because of impaired vision. Always use a flashlight if you are entering dark areas where there is no available light source. Walk slower than usual when there is not enough light to see clearly. Don't carry large objects that will block your vision, especially on stairways.

Always slow down in situations where you may not see a hazard in time to avoid it. Never rush around a corner or through a doorway where there could be pedestrian or other traffic approaching that you cannot see. When a solid door opens away from you, open it slowly to avoid bumping someone on the other side. When it opens toward you, approach with caution so it will not bump into you.

Carelessly leaving clutter and debris around paths and walkways increases the chances of tripping. All paths and walkways must be kept free of objects and clutter. See illustration #201. Always remember to close cabinet doors and shut pull-out cabinet drawers. Carpets and floor mats that resist lying flat on the floor should be secured to the floor with tape, glue or tacks.

Cables and wires that cross walkways should be covered to reduce possible tripping hazards. Take care to notice any floor thresholds when you step from one room to another or from doorway to a walkway. Thresholds are not always even with the floor. Be careful entering or exiting an elevator, as the elevator floor and the building floor may not match up, thereby creating an uneven section which could easily cause a trip.

Illustration #201 - Do Not Block Passages

*Note: Learn to recognize tripping hazards in the workplace and take time to correct them. Take your time and pay close attention to where you're going.*

*Note: Most people do not pick their feet up very high when they walk. That is why it is so easy for even a small obstacle to catch the forward foot and cause a person to trip.*

## Traction and Balance

Keeping good traction and balance will help reduce the risks of slips and falls on slippery surfaces. Traction is related to friction. The more friction one has between the bottom of their footwear and the floor or ground surface, the less chance there will be for slips and falls. It is easy to lose foot traction when surfaces are covered with grease, oil, soaps, waxes or other types of slippery materials. Workers should wear slip-resistant footwear appropriate for the working conditions. There are a large variety of sole patterns and tread designs specifically designed for slippery work surfaces. Abrasive strips applied to slippery floor surfaces and appropriate footwear, as shown in illustration #202, serve to improve traction very well. It is important to clean up spills when you see them. If that is not possible, draw attention to the spill so others will avoid the slippery area and go around it.

Report the slippery area to the appropriate supervision so they can have someone clean it up fairly quickly.

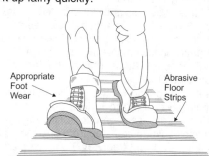

Appropriate Foot Wear

Abrasive Floor Strips

Illustration #202 - Abrasive Floor Strips

Balance is what keeps a person upright and stable in a variety of positions. It is easy to lose your balance if your weight is not well centered over your feet or if the surface is uneven or shifting.

To help maintain your balance, spread your feet apart, and if possible, lower your center of gravity by sitting or crouching, rather than standing. When working in elevated areas, maintain a hand hold, and take extra caution so as to not lean out too far when reaching, as it is easy to lose balance and fall. Do not practice what the worker in illustration #203 is doing. This is very dangerous. Wear appropriate fall protection equipment when working on elevated structures such as scaffolds and ladders.

**Illustration #203 - Leaning Out Too Far**

## Falls

Falls occur when a surface is not strong enough to support the weight of an object, or when there is no support at all. People fall, for example, when they step onto a weakened section of a roof, flooring or other type of working platform or scaffold, or when they step off the edge of a loading dock or stand on something which is unstable and rolls or tips out from under them.

Falls also occur when people lose their balance and cannot recover. Because of the shape of the human body, this can happen fairly easily. As shown in illustration #204A, when standing with the feet together, humans are shaped like an inverted pyramid. Most of the body weight is concentrated above the waist, therefore, the center of gravity is high. The pyramid shape tapers down to the feet, a relatively small base support.

Center
of
Gravity

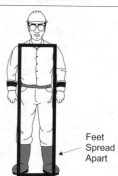

Feet
Spread
Apart

**Illustration #204A - Center of Gravity**
Shaped like this, it is easy for a person's center of gravity to get outside the base of support at the feet. Standing with the feet apart, as shown in illustration #204B, provides for better balance because this position creates a broader base of support.

**Illustration #204B - Good Balance**
Often, when people start to lose their balance, they recover by adjusting their body position or by grabbing onto something with their hands. This reaction can sometimes result in a strained muscle or pulled tendon in the hand, arm, shoulder or back. The injury is more serious, however, when they cannot recover – when they lose their balance and fall.

Whenever people lean over too far and get their center of gravity outside their base of support, unless they can do something to stop themselves, they will ultimately fall over.

The best walking or working surface is flat, level, dry and stable. The surface has no obstacles or holes and offers plenty of room to move around freely. If any of these conditions change, the risks increase for falls to occur. See illustration #204C & D.

Illustration #204D - Inattention

Illustration #204C - Falls Hurt - Be Careful

Illustration #204E identifies a common hazard in a workplace. Never create a hazard by opening a hatch, manhole or drain cover without posting the warnings or barriers necessary to keep people safely away. When the job is finished, put the covers back on securely. Make sure it won't move when someone steps on it.

Obviously, falls from elevated surfaces, such as ladders and scaffolds, are more dangerous than falls from much lower levels. But it is important to recognize that serious injuries can result from falls occurring from short distances.

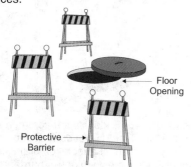

**Illustration #204E - Floor Openings**

When a person is moving, they probably have a much better chance of stopping themselves from falling if they can control their momentum, the forward force of the person's motion. Of course, the faster the person is moving, the more momentum they will have, and the harder it becomes to stop or to change direction of motion. Thus, it is harder to prevent a slip or a trip from becoming a fall.

*Note: Keep your base of support wide and your momentum under control.*

## Portable Ladder Safety

One of the more common causes of falls in workplaces occur when workers are using ladders (or makeshift ladders). It is important that the worker takes time to get the proper ladder for the job and make sure it is used correctly. Ladders must be secure and stable before climbing on them. Always check the rungs to make sure they are solid and not broken or cracked. Check the condition of the ladder feet. Use a stepladder tall enough to avoid having to use the top two rungs, as the ladder will become unstable.

The first step in ladder safety the worker must consider is selecting the correct portable ladder for the job. Ladders are classified by how much weight they can safely support.

- Type 1A: Extra-heavy industrial ladder, 300 lbs. (136 kg) load.
- Type 1: Heavy-duty industrial ladder, 250 lbs. (113 kg) load.
- Type 2: Medium-duty commercial ladder, 225 lbs. (102 kg) load.
- Type 3: Light-duty household ladder, 200 lbs. (91 kg) load.

Remember, when selecting a ladder for the job, it has to hold the person's weight plus the additional weight of any tools and materials placed on it. Ladder safety involves understanding what the ladder is designed for and how it is correctly used.

### *Stepladders:*

One of the more common portable ladders used in the workplace is the stepladder. See illustration #205.

**Note: OHSA regulations require that stepladders must be less than 20 ft (6 m) and shall have a locking device.**

Illustration #205 - Stepladder

- Stepladders remain standing by themselves.
- Stepladders are not adjustable in height or length.
- Stepladders provide the worker with flat wide steps which are 6 to 12 inches apart (15 - 30 cm).
- Stepladders have a wide work surface area at the top.
- Stepladders are hinged and open at least one inch (2.54 cm) for each foot (30 cm) of the ladder's length.

*Note: As shown in illustration #205, make sure the stepladder is fully open and the spreaders are locked in place. All four legs must be level and sitting on a solid surface. Never climb, stand or sit on the top two rungs of the stepladder. This makes the ladder very unstable.*

*Extension Ladders:*

Another common type of portable ladder used in the workplace is the extension ladder. Extension ladders, as shown in illustration #206, are lightweight, durable, and have adjustable length features. Extension ladders are designed with two or more sections, which travel in guides or tracks. Extension ladders are at least 12 inches in width (30 cm) and are no longer than 24 feet per section (7.3 m).

Extension ladders are designed with positive stops to ensure safe overlap of the extension sections. The required overlap will depend on the total length of all the sections measured along the side rails.

**Note: Single ladders or ladder extensions must be less than 30 ft (9 m).**

Illustration #206 - Extension Ladder

The following guidelines can be used to determine the amount needed for safe extension overlap:

- Extension ladders up to 32 feet (9.7 m) require a three foot (0.9 m) overlap.
- Extension ladders from 32 to 36 feet (9.7 to 11 m) require a four foot (1.2 m) overlap.
- Extension ladders from 36 to 48 feet (11 to 14.6 m) require a five foot (1.5 m) overlap.

- Extension ladders, because of their height, have the potential for causing a serious fall if not used correctly. To prevent a fall from an extension ladder, consider the following guidelines:
- Have a co-worker help you to raise and lower the extension ladder sections.
- Make sure the pull rope used to extend or lower the extension sections is free and unobstructed.
- Be sure to secure the ladder feet before attempting to extend it. See illustration #207. The worker is using his feet to secure the ladder before beginning to extend it.
- Follow the "1 to 4" rule. Set the base of the ladder 1 foot (30 cm) out from the wall for every 4 feet (1.2 m) of ladder height. See illustration #208 for an example of the "1 to 4" rule for extension ladders.

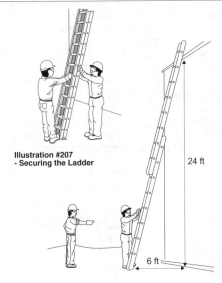

**Illustration #207 - Securing the Ladder**

24 ft

6 ft

**Illustration #208 - "1 To 4" Rule for Extension Ladders**

- Set up the ladder with approximately three feet (0.9 m) extending above the working surface.
- Never use the top three rungs of the ladder.
- To keep the ladder from slipping, have someone hold the base, or tie off the ladder securely.
- When climbing down a ladder, do not skip the bottom rung or step. Climb all the way down, and do not jump to the ground.

**Illustration #209 - Tie Off the Ladder**

## Portable Ladder Safety Rules

- Make sure the ladder feet are positioned on a flat firm surface.
- Try not to set up a ladder in a passageway. If you must, use cones or barricades to warn passers-by.
- Do not place a ladder on an unstable base to gain additional height.
- Use both hands for climbing.
- Hoist tools and equipment (carrying them does not permit you to use both hands while climbing).
- Do not stretch out in order to reach something some distance from the ladder.
- Tie off the ladder at chest height, to prevent movement, as shown in illustration #209. On longer ladders, tie off the top part of the ladder also.
- Use wooden of fiberglass ladders for electrical work or in areas where it is possible to make contact with electrical circuits.

- Whenever hoses or cords are nearby, be careful to position the ladder feet well away from these objects.
- If the ladder must be positioned in front of a door, either lock it shut, or prop it open.
- Look for broken or missing steps or rungs.
- Look for broken or split side rails or other ladder defects.
- Never use a ladder for anything other than a ladder.

## Permanent Ladder Safety

Ladders are often permanently attached to sides of buildings, smokestacks, process towers, or other physical structures. Some permanent ladders have individual rungs attached to the structure, while others, like the one in illustration #210, is designed with its rungs attached to the side rail. The ladder shown in this illustration is dangerous as it has no cage to protect the worker while climbing.

If a fixed ladder is longer than 24 feet (7.3m), it must have a protective cage or well, as shown in illustration #211, to protect falling workers.

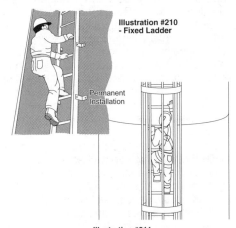

Illustration #210
- Fixed Ladder

Permanent
Installation

Illustration #211
- Fixed Ladder with Protective Cage

Permanent ladders must be able to withstand rigging, impact loads, and adverse weather conditions. The rungs should be parallel and well secured, as well as being uniformly spaced. Rungs should not be more than 12 inches (30cm) apart, nor more than 16 inches (40cm) long. The people who must climb lengthy permanent ladders should be physically fit and accustomed to heights and exposed working conditions. The worker may climb the ladder without fall protection, but once he is at the top, or has reached the work area, proper fall protection equipment must be used.

On permanent ladders, it is important to consider the following safety checks:

- Look for broken, loose or missing rungs.
- Look for loose mounting brackets and damaged side rails and cage parts.
- Check for rust and corrosion, or weak areas in the rungs, side rails and mounting brackets.

- Make sure the connections between the rungs and side rails haven't come loose.
- Notify the area supervisor if faults or problems are found on any type of permanent ladder.

## Stairways

A stairway is defined as being a series of steps and landings that has four or more risers, as shown in illustration #212. Stairways provide access from one level to another level of a structure. They can lead out to platforms, walkways, machinery, or crossovers. As shown in illustration #213, stairways can spiral around tanks, but are usually not permitted in that many industrial applications.

It is quite common to have accidents on stairways in workplaces. Slips and trips lead to serious falls. There are many reasons why accidents occur on stairways, but if workers follow and practice several simple rules, many of these accidents would be eliminated.

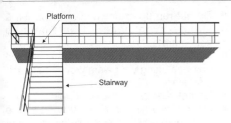

**Illustration #212 - Stairway Leading To A Platform**

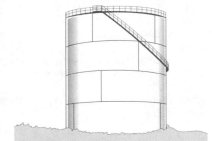

**Illustration #213 - Spiral Stairway**

Some common causes of stairway accidents are:

- Slippery, wet or greasy steps.
- Poor housekeeping conditions. (See illustration #214)
- Poor lighting or glare in stairway areas.
- Poorly designed stairs, uneven placement of steps and risers.
- Not concentrating enough, while going up or down the steps.

**Illustration #214 - Do Not Leave Items on Stairs**

Several simple work practices are provided for climbing stairways safely:

- Workers must pay attention as they climb up and down stairways. On the way down, they should look at the leading edge of each step.
- On poorly lit stairways, workers must be extra careful and take their time going up or down. Use the handrails as a guide and safety precaution. Always use railings and handrails.
- Clean up spilled materials, loose objects or other objects and debris from stairways.
- Do not carry too much going up or down stairs, as fatigue and tiredness sets in, and this is when accidents occur.
- Take periodic rest breaks when going up or down long sets of stairways.

- Do not run up or down stairways, use a steady even pace. Remember to concentrate.
- Make sure that your foot is firmly planted before shifting your weight onto it at each stair step.
- Do not slide down the handrails.
- Do not take two or more steps at a time while going up or down, use each step of the stairway. Do not skip steps or jump from one level to another when going down.

There are certain requirements for safe stairways:

- A fixed stairway should be strong enough to carry at least five times its maximum intended load.
- All stairway treads must be slip resistant and durable.

- Handrails are required on all open sides of stairways and should conform to local size and height regulations. A handrail helps to prevent a person from losing their balance, and if they do trip or slip, they might be able to use the rail to catch themselves and keep from falling. See illustration #215A.

- As shown in illustration #215B, a stairway should be designed to provide a safe working platform for doing everyday operations or maintenance work.

Illustration #215B - Safe Working Platform

Illustration #215A - Using A Handrail

- On open stairs, as shown in illustration #215C, an object on the stairway is a real safety hazard. Not only is it a hazard to the person on the stairs, it is a hazard to anyone below who could be hit if it falls off the step.

Illustration #215C - Do Not Leave Objects on Open Stairways

*Note: Always make sure your foot is firmly planted on the next step before you commit to that step.*

## Ramp Safety

A ramp can be an inclined or level surface designed to link between two different spaces or levels, as shown in illustration #216. The ramp allows people or machinery to safely move from one level to another. The ramp in illustration #216 should not have an incline greater than 30 degrees from the horizontal. If the ramp is steeper than 20 degrees, or if there is a fall hazard of more than four feet (1.2 m), the ramp should be equipped with handrails.

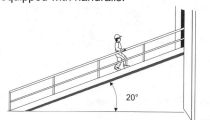

Illustration #216 - Inclined Ramp

The ramp shown in illustration #217 is commonly used in the trucking and material movement industry. These ramps are portable or have at least one end that can change height position. This type of ramp design should never be steeper than 30 degrees. Caution must be used when using this type of ramp with truck-trailer units. Trailer wheels should be chocked to prevent movement and the ramp secured so it won't move. If the ramp can't be secured, make sure it is positioned to overlap the supporting surfaces by at least several inches.

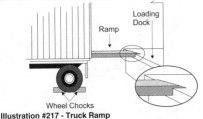

Wheel Chocks
**Illustration #217 - Truck Ramp**

Workers having to use ramps in their daily work should follow several safety rules:

- When walking on an inclined ramp, either up or down, your center of balance may shift.
- The ramp's surface may have a different finish on it to that of the floor or road. Be careful of this possible hazard.
- A ramp may be made in one piece, or it can be made up of separate planking or other joined materials. Be sure the pieces are held firmly together and no tripping hazards are present.
- Use handrails on any ramp equipped with them.
- Never operate machines or vehicles on a ramp that has not been designed to support these types of loads.
- It is important to paint or mark ramps to keep people and machinery at a safe distance apart.

## Scaffolds

Scaffolds are elevated platforms, which provide safe sturdy work surfaces and a means of access to elevated structures and equipment.  Scaffolds may be quite portable so they can be moved to various locations, or the scaffold may be designed as a fixed structure, where it is permanently located until the job is completed.  There are many types of scaffold designs, each having its own unique safety features and safe working practices. Falls from scaffolds continue to be responsible for more injuries and deaths in the workplace than from any other type of walking or working surface.  Supervisors should stress scaffold safety and workers must take extra care and caution whenever they find themselves having to work on scaffold platforms.

One of the most common types of scaffold systems is the suspension scaffold, where the platform is suspended by ropes or wire cable from some type of overhead fixture. Illustration #218 shows a single-point suspension scaffold, often referred to as a boatswain's chair, which is capable of supporting one person. A safety rope is used to tie to the worker's fall protection device.

Illustration #218 - Single Point Suspension Scaffold

Illustration #219 identifies a double-point suspension scaffold. Again, each worker's fall protection device is safely attached to the safety ropes.

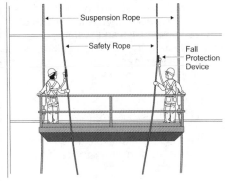

**Illustration #219 - Double Point Suspension Scaffold**

The following safety rules should be followed when using suspension scaffolds:

- Inspect the scaffold parts thoroughly before each use.
- Check the platform for holes, breaks, cracks or any weak spots.
- Check all suspension ropes and wire cable for broken strands, loose or poor fitting connections, fraying and kinking.
- Never try to repair defective ropes or wire cable. Replace defect rope or wire cable immediately.
- If the scaffold platform or any part of the system has been dropped or exposed to anything that might weaken it, inspect it carefully for damage or potential failure.
- Always make sure that the scaffold is capable of supporting the weight which will be placed on it. The platform, ropes, wire cable and all connections must be capable of supporting the intended load, calculated with a recommended safety factor.

- Always take extra caution when winds are excessive, as the suspension scaffold may become unstable and unsafe to be on. It may be necessary, depending on conditions and location, to make the suspension scaffold secure so it can handle high wind loads.
- Before raising or lowering a suspension scaffold, secure all tools and equipment on the platform.
- Make sure the platform is level before raising it or lowering it.
- If two people are on a double-point scaffold, as shown in illustration #219, each worker should stand on opposite ends of the platform, balancing it, and working at the same time to raise or lower each end evenly.

- Always position the scaffold as close as possible to the surface where the work will be taking place. Use guardrails, safety nets and personal fall protection systems.
- When working on any type of suspension scaffold always keep a safe distance from electrical circuits and power lines. Always seek assistance when working near energized power lines and systems.
- Try to keep the working platform of the scaffold free from loose tools, equipment or liquids. Anything that falls off the platform could cause a serious injury to people below.
- It is recommended workers do not cross over from one scaffold platform to another, unless the scaffold has been designed to accommodate for safe crossovers.

- If it is absolutely necessary to cross over to another scaffold, be very careful not to get caught up in ropes or lines.
- The two platforms must be at the same level and properly joined. The worker in illustration #220 should not be attempting to cross over to the scaffold on his right. This is an unsafe act.
- Never use a ladder as a scaffold platform.

**Illustration #220 - Never Attempt A Crossover**

Illustration #221A identifies a mobile scaffold system, which sits on the ground and may be supported by wheels. The following safety rules should be applied:

- Set the brakes or chock the wheels to prevent the scaffold from moving while workers are on it.
- The scaffold will be less stable with people on it, as its center of gravity is higher.
- Never place the scaffold on boxes or other support objects.
- Keep the scaffold well away from energized electrical sources.
- Consider adding approved outriggers to increase the base width and improve the scaffold's stability, especially for higher scaffolds.
- When moving the scaffold, use extra care to prevent tipping it over.
- Make sure the pathway is clear when moving the scaffold.

- Push the scaffold as close to the bottom of the frame as possible.
- Workers are not allowed to ride on the scaffold while it is being moved.
- Give notice to workers on the scaffold when it is being prepared for a move.
- Alert people on the ground that the scaffold is going to be moved.
- Workers should use suitable personal fall protection on high mobile scaffolds.

The supporting surface for a tower type scaffold should be firm and level. Screw jacks may be used to level the scaffold, but only use them if recommended by the scaffold manufacturer. Never use blocks, bricks or barrels to support one or more legs of a tower scaffold. See illustration #221B.

If there is too much slope where the tower scaffold is to be located, it may be wiser to use a suspended scaffold instead of a tower.

Set Brakes on Wheels

**Illustration #221A - Mobile Scaffold**

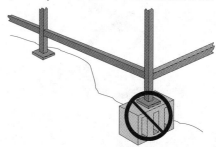

**Illustration #221B - Do Not Use Blocks Under Scaffold Legs**

If a tower scaffold has to be set up on soft ground, the legs of the tower should be supported by a base plate and secured to a "mud sill." See illustration #222. The size and configuration of the mud sills are determined by various factors, including soil composition, wetness, and should be specified by an engineer or the scaffold supplier.

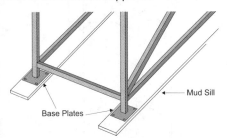

Base Plates

Mud Sill

**Illustration #222 - Base Plate And Mud Sill**

***Note: If there is a possibility of forklifts or any other vehicles driving near the scaffold, locate a warning barricade around it.***

During assembly of scaffolds, it is always recommended to follow the manufacturer's instructions exactly. If the connections do not seem to fit properly or smoothly, do not force the assembly. Check to be sure the scaffold frame is level and square, and that connection parts are not bent, misaligned or missing. All connections must be secure, with locking pins to ensure safe pin placement. Platforms have to be secure on the scaffold frame so there is no chance for slippage. If the platform cannot be fastened in place, it should have cleats at each end, on the underside (see illustration #223), to keep the platform (scaffold plank) from slipping.

Aluminum and fiberglass platforms can both be damaged by strong chemicals and other acidic materials. Before any scaffold platform or plank is used, check to make sure it is not damaged, and find out from the manufacturer if any protective measures are required.

It may be better in some installations to use wooden scaffold planks.

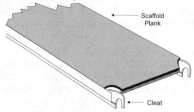

**Illustration #223 - Scaffold Plank Cleat**

Because of the scaffold's high center of gravity, do not build it too tall for its base to adequately support it. Determine what the manufacturer recommends and what the OSHA/OCHS regulations are for safe scaffold height. In some locations the height-to-base ratio for scaffold is only 3 to 1. This means that the scaffold can only be three times higher than the shortest side of the base. In any case, it is best to not exceed the height-to-base ratio more than 4 to 1.

For example, if a 4 to 1 ratio is permitted, and the base of the scaffold is three feet wide (1 m) and five feet long (1.5 m), the scaffold should not be any higher than 12 feet (3.6 m). For this example, see illustration #224A.

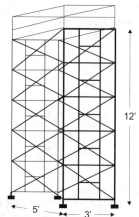

**Illustration #224A - Maintaining 4 to 1 Ratio**

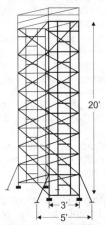

**Illustration #224B - Maintaining 4 to 1 Ratio**

If the same scaffold has one foot (30 cm) outriggers, as shown in illustration #224B, to make the scaffold base five feet (1.5 m) on each end, then the scaffold height could be up to 20 feet (6 m).

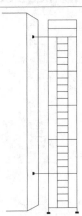

**Illustration #224C - Tall Scaffold Tied Off To Building**

If the scaffold has to be higher than the allowed height, it must be secured to a building, beams, or other anchors to prevent it from tipping or collapsing. Illustration #224C demonstrates how a tall scaffold has been secured to the side of a building to stabilize it.

Guy lines are attached to the scaffold and anchored to the ground.

These guy lines should be installed as the scaffold is erected, and are not to be removed until the scaffold is dismantled to that height. It is best to place the guy lines as close to the scaffold's horizontal bars as possible, with the bottom guy lines no higher than the scaffold's allowed free standing height.

Multiple scaffolds can be connected and stabilized with cross bracing. This, in effect, increases the minimum base dimension of the scaffold, however OSHA/OCHS regulations should be checked before using this method to increase height. See illustration #224E Never build a scaffold taller than the allowed height unless it is secured or braced.

*Note: Tower scaffolds are very top heavy. Never climb up a tower scaffold unless it has total ground support and it is plumb, level and rigid.*

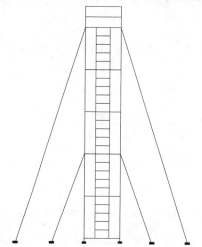

**Illustration #224D - Guy Line Scaffold Support**

Illustration #224D demonstrates how a tall scaffold can be safely supported if there is no structural support nearby.

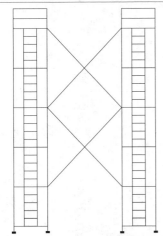

**Illustration #224E - Multiple Scaffold Connection**

Many scaffolds are designed with an internal ladder for access. For others, the worker may have to use a portable ladder set up against one of the narrower ends of the scaffold.

Access is always on the narrower end in order to have the least effect on the scaffold's stability. Never climb any diagonal cross braces on a scaffold. Always climb the horizontal bars of the scaffold.

## Elevated Work Platforms

There are several common designs of elevated work platforms used in industry. Each has its own special operating features designed to provide a convenient way of reaching elevated or high work places quickly. Special care is needed to use them safely. See illustrations #225A and B for two types of elevated platforms.

- OSHA requires trained personnel to operate an aerial lift.
- Set the brakes or chock the wheels to prevent unintended movement.
- Never overload the platform. Know the rated load capacity of the platform.
- Always keep the platform free of loose parts and tools which might fall.

- If the worker needs more height, raise the platform. Never stand on ladders, railings or other objects placed on the platform's working surface.
- Always lower the platform to its base position before moving the platform to the next location it is required at.
- All workers must be off the platform before it is to be moved.
- Make sure the area to which the platform is being moved has firm footing and is free of loose objects and clear of dangerous obstacles.
- Be sure to alert all workers in the area that the platform is about to be moved.
- The platform must be kept clear of energized power sources.
- Rope off the area around the elevated platform to keep pedestrian or other type of traffic well clear.

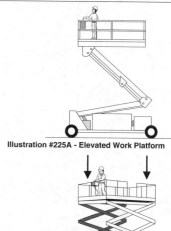

**Illustration #225A - Elevated Work Platform**

**Illustration #225B - Scissor Lift**

When using any type of elevated work platform, extra caution must be taken when working near electrical hazards. Electrical hazards are among the easiest to overlook because they are often out of the worker's normal field of vision. Always watch where the elevated platform is going to be positioned or where it reaches.

Special care must be taken around power lines, as the line voltage is usually very high, and because most power lines are not insulated, their electrical fields may extend several feet from the line.

**Note: It is possible to be electrocuted without contacting the source of electricity. Electrical hazards are one of the leading causes of fatalities on elevated platforms.**

Unless workers are trained and authorized to work around live electrical sources, there has to be a minimum safe distance maintained between the electrical energy source and the worker on the elevated platform, as shown in illustration #226.

Before planning to position an elevated platform anywhere near power lines or other electrical energy sources, check with the local authorities to determine how close the regulations allow the platform to be positioned. The safe working distance will be affected by the amount of voltage at the energy source.

Maintain Recommended Safe Distance

**Illustration #226 - Maintaining Minimum Safe Distance**

Aerial lifts generally are used for one person jobs that usually do not take too long to complete. The aerial lift shown in illustration #227 has the advantage of being quite easy to position and operate. It has a stable base of support, and does not require a lot of set up time.

This design has an articulating and telescoping boom, which permits a horizontal extension in combination with a vertical lift.

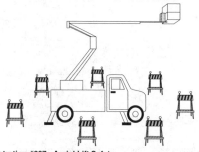

**Illustration #227 - Aerial Lift Safety**

Most aerial lifts have a leveling mechanism to compensate for uneven ground and to increase stability. However, it is always best to try to set up on a level, or nearly level, surface and if the unit comes with outriggers, use them. They will greatly increase the machine's stability.

- If the working platform is on a boom to provide horizontal reach, put up a barricade or use an adequate warning system to keep people and vehicles out from under the boom, as is demonstrated in illustration #227.

- Every platform is rated for a maximum load, and it is important to know the load limit for the platform being used. Be sure the combined weight of the worker, tools and materials does not exceed this load limit. Never overload the platform.

It is important to remember that all aerial lifts and elevated platforms are not operated in the same way.

In addition to differences in load capacity, they may differ in:

- Leveling mechanism
- Controls for raising, lowering and braking
- Method used to lock the wheels
- Operation and design of the outriggers
- Order of boarding the platform, either before or after it is elevated.

*Note: Be sure to understand and follow the recommended operating and safety procedures for the particular elevated platform or aerial lift being used. If fall protection equipment is required, use it. When on the elevated platform, keep both feet on the platform floor. If you can't reach your work, then you must reposition the platform, or use a lift that provides more elevation. Never stand on a guardrail, a ladder, or anything else to try to increase your working height on an elevated platform.*

## Floor and Wall Openings and Roofs

Wall openings, large floor openings and platforms, as shown in illustration #228, are typically made safe with guardrails. Smaller floor openings may be protected by a removable cover, one that is held secure in the floor and will not slip when it is stepped on. Never step onto a removable cover in the floor unless you are sure that it is secure. If you can, avoid stepping on it altogether. If you remove a covering from an opening in the floor, be sure to secure it properly when you put it back in place.

Illustration #228 - Wall and Floor Openings

Never walk on a roof unless you are certain it will bear your weight. Most roofs are designed to support the weight of snow and rain, but not necessarily the concentrated loads and forces of someone walking on them and the placement of equipment and machinery. Always check to find out which parts of the roof are safe to work on and where it is best to walk.

Always be careful when working near the edge of a roof as not only can you lose your balance and fall, but there is also a danger of the roof breaking away from under your weight. Many roofs are designed with an overhang and may not be that well supported from underneath. As shown in illustration #229, a guardrail has been installed near the roof's edge to prevent people from getting too close to the edge and standing on the overhang.

Sometimes skylights are located in roof tops. Skylights are responsible for a number of fatalities each year. Flat mounted skylights can be hidden traps, as they may be covered with snow or are stepped on to get around things on the roof. Raised skylights may seem like convenient resting places because they are at sitting height. Many people have fallen to their death because they used a skylight as a place to rest or as a stepping surface. Skylights should have guardrails around them, or a secure mesh or screen covering that will prevent people from falling through. Never step or sit on a skylight.

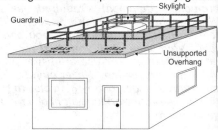

Illustration #229 - Roof Top Safety

# SECTION ELEVEN

# FALL PROTECTION SYSTEMS

## Guardrails and Safety Nets

Falls from high places frequently cause serious injuries or deaths for many workers each year. Personal fall protection equipment can prevent these falls. Personal fall protection devices are covered under current OSHA regulations 29 CFR 1926.500 through 29 CFR 1926.502. In these regulations, three protection systems are referenced, each designed to protect workers from falling and require the use of the systems in those work activities where the risk of falling exists. The three mentioned systems, of the four systems commonly found in industry are:

- Guardrails
- Safety Nets
- Personal Fall Protection Systems

*Note: The fourth system not directly referenced in these OSHA regulations is the fall restraint device. This section of the book will primarily discuss personal fall protection systems.*

Guardrails typically consist of a top rail that is about 3.5 feet (1 m) high, as well as a middle rail, and toeboard or kick plate. The toeboard is usually required where there is a fall hazard of 10 feet (3 m) or more. The toeboard is usually about 4 inches high (10 cm) and serves to prevent tools and other materials from falling

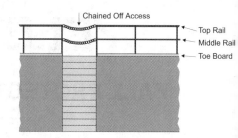

Illustration #230 - Guard Rail

If a guardrail has a gate or chain for access, as shown in illustration #230, make sure the gate is closed or the chain is in place at all times when access is not required.

*Note: Guardrails, under current OSHA regulations, are required on all mobile aerial work platforms and must be in place during all operations.*

Safety nets are often used at construction sites where it is not practical to install guardrails or to use personal fall protection devices. The safety net must meet standards and offer full protection, therefore, it must be in good condition, it has to be free of debris, and must be properly located and supported under the workers who are working at heights above.

Regular inspection of safety nets is extremely important. They should be inspected for mildew, tears, or excessive wear.

At the beginning of each work shift check to see that nothing has fallen onto the netting.

If something drops into a net while workers are above, it should be removed as soon as possible.

It is very easy to develop a false sense of security when workers are protected by a safety net. Always ensure that you are working within the safety boundaries of the net, because if you don't, you will be working without any protection at all. Each year there are reported workplace fatalities where workers have fallen and missed the safety net below because they were outside of the safety net boundaries.

*Note: Safety nets may exist at a work site but due to the mobile nature of aerial platform work, safety nets will be ineffective safety protection for the workers above.*

## Personal Fall Protection Systems

The requirements for a personal fall protection system according to OSHA are very specific. Personal fall protection refers to an entire system of protection on an unprotected edge where workers can fall more than six feet (2 m). This system must have:

- A harness.
- A lanyard or other connecting device.
- A fall arrest device, such as a lifeline; an energy absorber or decelerator (like a clutch device or sewn-loop lanyard).
- An anchorage connector and an adequate anchorage point.

*Note: The typical anchorage points are above the worker because the objective of the personal fall protection system is to prevent a worker from falling more than six feet (2 m). Machines are not anchors for personal fall protection systems.*

The ANSI Standard that addresses personal fall protection is Z359.1-1992 and requires that:

- The personal fall protection system be inspected prior to each use by the user and annually by a competent person.
- The equipment be inspected prior to storage.
- The user calculate their fully equipped weight and assure it is within the capacity range of 130 to 310 lbs (60 to 140 kg).
- The user check the personal fall protection equipment markings to be sure the equipment complies with ANSI standards.
- The user be trained by a competent person on specific personal fall protection topics.
- A single anchorage connector can only be used for one fall arrest system unless the anchorage connector is certified for multiples of the 5000 lb (2270 kg) rating.

There are three major types of personal fall protection systems. These include personal fall arrest systems, positioning devices, and protection systems for climbing activities. The most common system is the personal fall arrest system which is designed to hold workers after they have fallen, as demonstrated in illustration #231.

Equipment used in conjunction with this system includes:
- An anchorage.
- Body harness.
- Lifelines.
- Lanyards.
- Deceleration devices.

## Positioning Devices

Positioning devices help prevent falls by supporting the worker while maintaining a working position, as shown in illustration #232.

**Illustration #231 - Personal Fall Protection System**

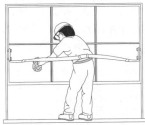

**Illustration #232 - Positioning Device**

Positioning devices are not rated as strong as a personal fall protection device because they are not designed to catch and hold a falling worker. The intent of a positioning device is to hold the worker in a safe position while undertaking an activity where there is some exposure to heights or other dangerous conditions.

Examples of jobs where positioning devices would be used include lineman's belt and pole straps, window cleaner's positioning system and restraint lines used by construction workers and trades personnel.

## Personal Fall Protection for Climbing

Illustration #233 demonstrates how a worker is using another type of fall protection system while climbing up a ladder. In this example, the worker is using a ladder safety device which offers fall protection while ascending or descending the ladder.

**Illustration #233 - Personal Fall Protection On Permanent Ladders**

These devices are very useful when climbing ladders attached to tall buildings or stacks where there is little or no fall protection provided.

## Anchorages/Deceleration

OSHA defines anchorage as a secure point for lifelines, lanyards or deceleration devices.

Lifelines, lanyards, and deceleration devices will not be safe unless there is a secure anchorage system in place to stop the worker who is falling. The farther one falls, the more strength is required to stop the fall. For example, an anchorage supporting a 190 lb (86 kg) person falling ten feet (3 m) has 1900 pounds (263 kg) of force suddenly applied to it. An anchorage system must be able to support the person's weight and hold secure when it stops the fall.

OSHA requires anchorages to hold 5,000 lbs (2272 kg) per employee attached. Or, if the anchorage is part of a personal fall arrest system designed, installed and used under the supervision of a qualified person, the anchorage must be able to hold, at a minimum, twice the possible load intended.

Several methods recommended for decreasing the strain on the anchorage include:

- Using less than six feet (2 m) of free-fall line.
- Advising the employee to attach the lifeline above, instead of in front.
- Not attaching the lifeline below the place the employee is working.

Another common method for reducing the strain on the anchorage system is through the use of a specialized fall protection system called a "deceleration device." A normal or typical lifeline stops the person's fall abruptly and puts extra strain, as mentioned earlier, on the anchorage device. The deceleration device, as shown in illustration #234, helps to slow the fall before the person comes to a full stop. There are several unique varieties of deceleration devices, each utilizes a design which slowly allows a release of energy and absorbs the shock.

Illustration #234 - Deceleration Device

The device may be spring design, elastic or stretch type material or other type of synthetic flexible material. Several important points to consider regarding deceleration devices include:

- If there is less strain placed on the anchorage system when a worker falls, there then should be less impact to the worker's body.
- The deceleration device could permit the worker to fall an additional distance before coming to a full stop. Ensure that there are no pipes, beams, or even the floor or ground to hit after the deceleration device opens.
- The deceleration device must be able to hold a minimum of 5000 lbs (2272 kg) per worker, which includes a safety factor of at least 2000 lbs (909 kg).
- Always check with the local occupational health and safety authority, company safety officers and the manufacturers who make deceleration devices to ensure the device meets the necessary load and safety requirements.

## During a Fall

Even though a worker is securely fastened to an anchorage with some type of approved fall protection system, a fall may still occur. During the fall, several things happen and it is best to know beforehand what to expect during the fall.

- At the beginning of the fall, before the fall arrest equipment begins to work, the worker will be in a period of free-fall. See illustration #235.

- After a certain distance of free-fall, the fall arrest equipment activates.
- It then takes additional distance, referred to as the deceleration distance, to bring the worker to a full stop.
- Force is required to stop a fall and the worker will feel the impact of the force.

The fall arrest force hits the body through the straps of the worker's safety belt or body harness. Illustration #236 shows the force being applied to the straps of the full body harness the worker is wearing. The force is applied to the straps at the shoulders and upper body as well as to the leg straps.

**Illustration #235 - Free-Fall**

**Illustration #236 - Fall-Force**

A deceleration device can help to absorb some of the force to the body, and the full body harness distributes the force to areas of the body, which are protected by the bones.

Always keep in mind the free-fall path below. When selecting the anchor, allow for free-fall distance, the deceleration distance of the equipment and any additional distance the lifeline may stretch. The manufacturer's labels or instructions may indicate the amount of stretch in a lifeline and how much deceleration distance is required.

*Note: The farther your attachment to the lifeline is from the line's anchorage point, the more the line will stretch.*

Another consideration when working where the risks of taking a fall are higher than usual is the affects of taking a "swing" type of fall.

Illustration #237 shows how a worker incorrectly attached his fall arrest equipment and when he took the fall, he swung under the platform and the momentum and swing carried him into the vertical column. Even though the worker's fall was stopped, additional fall forces are included in the swing.

Illustration #237 - Swinging Fall

Workers can be seriously injured as a result of a swing fall. Take extra care to survey the area beside the anchorage point and try to stay clear of pipes, beams and other obstacles if there is any chance of a swing type of fall. To prevent a swing fall:

- Make sure the lanyard or life line hangs straight down from the anchorage point, as shown in illustration #238, and have the anchorage point directly in front of the worker's body.

**Illustration #238 - Lanyard Hanging Straight Down**

- Always change the anchorage position when moving to a new place of work along the high work area. Working even a short distance to the side of the anchorage point can be very dangerous if a fall were to occur.
- Do not position or locate fall arrest connectors on the outside edges of beams or other extending objects.

If a fall occurs, any employee hanging from the fall arrest system must be rescued safely and quickly. The employer should have a rescue plan for carrying out the rescue. Methods often considered for rescuing fallen workers who are hanging include:

- Equipment and systems which allow the hanging worker to rescue him or herself.
- A system for carrying out the rescue using trained and qualified workers and/or safety personnel.
- A method in place for calling in a qualified rescue team.

All good rescue systems will require advance planning and decision making. Workers should know beforehand what the company's rescue plan involves. Determine what rescue equipment is available and know where it is located and stored. Training must be provided by the employer so the employees are knowledgeable, skilled and suitably competent to perform self rescues and help in the rescue of others.

Keep in mind that there are several things to be done during the actual rescue of the hanging worker:

- If possible provide further fall protection for the hanging worker and ensure that the rescuers have the equipment they need to protect themselves from taking a fall.
- Communicate to the hanging worker and monitor constantly.

## During A Fall/Fall Arrest

- Call for additional help. It may be necessary to call in the local fire department, emergency response team and medical services.

### Fall Arrest Equipment

An area where the employee is working may be safe and clear for anchorage, but may not provide adequate places for attaching fall protection devices. There are several types of anchorage devices which can be used to connect the fall arrest device to the anchorage point. Illustration #239 demonstrates how connectors can be attached to a beam or other structural members and then used as part of the fall protection system. A carabiner device is inserted through a hole in the beam and locked in place to provide a secure anchor point for the fall protection equipment. Approved carabiners, brackets, beam clamps, rings and eyebolts can be located to make hooking up fall arrest equipment faster, easier and securely.

Hole in Beam
Carabiner

**Illustration #239 - Anchorage Connector**

These connectors help to avoid such hazards as sharp edges and unsafe or questionable anchorage points.

The equipment supplied by the employer must meet the safety and strength standards set out by OSHA/OCHS or other regulatory agencies. Fall protection equipment must be designed to stop falls quickly and without causing too much force on the body.

- Always make sure that approved equipment is available for the job.
- Follow the equipment manufacturer's instructions on how each item is to be used.
- Use the proper deceleration device with the correct body harness or belt.
- Do not use a chest harness if there is any chance of taking a free-fall.
- Make sure that snap hooks are designed to be used with the hardware they are being attached to.
- All the various parts of the fall protection system must fit and work properly with each other. Do not substitute any items unless it's been approved by the manufacturer or by knowledgeable safety personnel.
- Fall protection equipment must not be used for other types of jobs, such as rigging or lifting. It is only to be used for worker fall protection.

## Hooking Up

### *Lifelines:*

Lifelines can be positioned horizontal or vertical. Horizontal lifelines must be designed, installed and used under the supervision of a qualified person. The more workers tied off to a single horizontal line, the stronger the line and anchorages must be. Vertical lifelines should never have more than one person per line. Terminate or tie-off a vertical lifeline in a way that prevents the worker from moving past the free end of the line, or make sure the line reaches to the ground or to the next working level below.

### *Tying Off:*

Tying off refers to connecting the worker's belt or harness directly or indirectly to a secure anchor point. Illustration #240 shows the worker tying off his lanyard to the end of the vertical lifeline.

Always tie-off before getting into a position where a fall might occur. Follow the manufacturer's instructions on the best tie-off methods for the type and design of fall protection equipment being used.

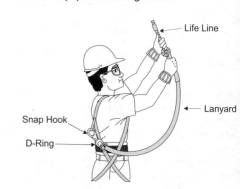

Illustration #240 - Tying Off

There are poor ways of tying off. For example, lifelines and tie-offs are weakened if knots are used. Knots are usually weaker than any other methods of attachment. A knot tied incorrectly can easily come loose, or the knot itself can reduce the lifeline strength up to 50%. See illustration #241. If possible, use a strong lanyard and always try to reduce the free-fall distance.

Tying off around H-beams or I-beams can weaken the line because of the cutting action of the beam's edges. Use a webbing type lanyard with padding around the beam, as in illustration #242. Wire rope slings can also be used.

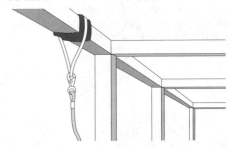

Illustration #242 - Webbing Lanyard and Padded Protector

Illustration #241 - Do Not Use Knots To Tie-Off

## Hooking Up

### Snap Hooks:

There are two basic types of snap hooks commonly used with fall protection equipment. They are the locking and non-locking, as shown in illustration #243. The locking snap hook helps prevent "roll-out" when the snap hook opens accidentally. Therefore it is preferable to use this type of snap hook, as it is safer for all applications.

To avoid "roll-out", consider the following points:

- Do not attach the snap hook to anything that could press it open.
- Do not attach two snap hooks together. See illustration #244.

**Note: OHSA stipulates that only the locking type snap hooks must be used in the USA.**

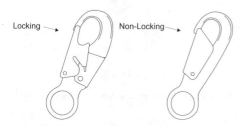

Locking →    Non-Locking →

Illustration #243 - Snap Hooks

Illustration #244 - Avoid Snapping Two Hooks Together

Avoid attaching a hook in any of the following ways unless the locking snap hooks are so designed:

- Directly into a horizontal lifeline, as shown in illustration #245A.
- Directly to webbing, rope or wire rope.
- Back onto its own lanyard, as shown in illustration #245B.
- To a "D-ring" that has another snap hook or other connector attached to it, as shown in illustration #245C.
- To any object whose size or shape would permit it to press or release the snap hook's latch.

The "D-ring" shown in illustration #245D should be large compared to the snap hook so that the ring will reach beyond the hook's latch, rather than press against it. After attaching any snap hook, ensure that it is tightly closed, secure and "roll-out" is impossible.

Illustration #245A - Avoid Attaching Directly Into a Horizontal Lifeline

Illustration #245B - Avoid Attaching Snap Hook Back Onto A Lanyard

Illustration #245C - Avoid Attaching Two Snap Hooks To A D-Ring

Illustration #245D - D-Ring Large Enough To Accommodate Snap Hook

### *Hookup Hazards:*

There are several hazards associated with safe anchorage points for fall protection equipment. Selecting a safe place to hook up calls for close inspection of the working area.

Two obvious hazards to avoid are:

- Electrical components, such as loose wires, open insulators, transformer boxes, circuit boxes and conduit lines. Any of these could break or cause the connection to break.  Always be extra careful when working around any electrical systems, as the hazards from high voltage electricity are extremely dangerous.  Never attach a lanyard onto electrical conduit for example, as shown in illustration #246.  Conduit lines are commonly found running along beams and columns, but they are not strong enough nor are they meant to be used as any type of anchor point for fall protection or rigging and hoisting equipment.

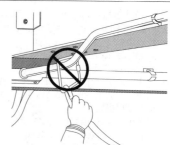

Illustration #246 - Avoid Attaching a Lanyard to an Electrical Conduit Line

- Another hazard commonly found in work areas where fall protection equipment is used is grinding sparks and hot welding and/or cutting splatters, which can easily burn through webbed lanyards, rope or other synthetic or non-metallic fall protection equipment.  See illustration #247.  It may be best to cover the lanyard to minimize burning.

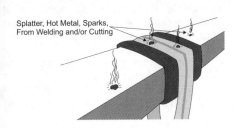

Splatter, Hot Metal, Sparks, From Welding and/or Cutting

Illustration #247 - Avoid This Type of Exposure

*Note: Small sized pipes, antenna, electrical conduit, projections, exposed bolts, and lips of H-beams and I-beams are not adequate anchor points for fall protection equipment.*

*Body Belts and Harnesses:*

Illustration #248A identifies a full body harness with the safety line attachment located at the back of the harness, either in the center of the back at shoulder level or above the chest.

This type of attachment positioning minimizes the forces to the body when a fall occurs. Illustration #248B identifies a body belt which fits snugly onto the person's body. The attachment must be in the center of the back, on or behind the hips. The force felt in the body will probably be greater to the worker who chooses to wear the body belt.

Illustration #248A
- Full Body Harness

Illustration #248B
- Body Belt

*Note: OSHA stipulates that a full body harness must be used in the United States.*

## Fall Protection and Confined Spaces

Fall protection systems must be considered in work conditions where a worker is confined. Even if the worker survives the fall, they can be trapped in the confined space. The fall arrest system the worker is wearing serves as a means of pulling the worker out in a case of an emergency. It is important to take into consideration what type of fall protection equipment will be best for working in confined spaces and if a rescue has to be performed. Consider the following rescue points regarding confined spaces and fall protection systems:

- It is much easier to reach a fallen worker in a confined space if he or she is attached to a lifeline.
- If there is a lack of oxygen or chance of asphyxiation, the worker may have passed out inside the confined space.
- Suitable fall protection equipment may be the only safe means rescuers can use to pull the fallen worker out of the confined space.
- In some types of confined spaces, the worker may be covered in dirt, grain or other type of material. The lifeline could serve as the only safe way to be pulled out.

*Note: It is quite possible to have an excellent fall arrest system for any work situation, but the system is useless without safe and secure anchorage. Anchorage is the most critical element of any fall arrest system.*

## Care And Inspection of Equipment

- Inspect all personal fall protection equipment before each use.
- Keep the equipment in good working order and well maintained, stored and clean.
- Any defective equipment must be identified and replaced at once.
- Consider developing a regular schedule for inspecting the equipment.
- Check all equipment for wear, burns, rot, mildew, or distortion and breakage.
- Make sure no straps are cut, broken, frayed, torn or scraped.
- Check for damage from fire, acid or other corrosives.
- Hardware should be free of cracks, sharp edges, worn areas or burrs.
- Snap hooks should close and lock tightly.
- Buckles and snaps should work properly.
- Check ropes for wear, broken fibers, pulled stitches, frays and discoloration.

- Make sure that all anchors and mountings are solid and not damaged or loose.
- If any item of the fall protection system is defective or damaged, immediately remove it from service. It should be either destroyed or marked as unusable.

## Aerial Work Platforms and Fall Protection

OSHA regulations 29 CFR 1926.500 through 29 CFR 1926.502 cover fall protection in construction activities. When working with aerial work platforms several regulations are required concerning fall protection systems for workers:

*Guardrails* are found on all aerial work platforms and must be in place during all operations.

*Safety Nets* may exist at a job site but due to the mobile nature of the aerial work platform will most likely make for an ineffective fall protection system.

*Personal Fall Arrest Systems* are usually not required on an aerial work platform. The purpose of personal fall arrest systems is to prevent the worker from falling down. Personal fall arrest systems are used only when other permanent means of fall protection cannot be provided.

Guardrails are the permanent means of fall protection on aerial platforms, and make personal fall arrest systems unnecessary.

*Fall Restraint Devices* are not required on boom type aerial work platforms where guardrails protect the worker. They can, however, be catapulted from boom type aerial work platforms, therefore a safety belt or harness is recommended. The attachment is meant to restrain the worker so they do not fall if they are projected upward and out by the boom movement.

OSHA/OCHS and ANSI standards do not require safety belts or harnesses to be used with scissor lift aerial work platforms. Always check and follow the local regulatory requirements as they may be more stringent than the minimums established by OSHA/OCHS.

All standards for aerial platforms do require that users be in compliance to the equipment manufacturer's instructions. The basic safety precautions for scissor lifts include:

- Belts, harnesses and lanyards are usually not required on scissor lifts, but are recommended.
- All guardrails must be completely installed and proper gates fastened and secured.
- No one is ever to climb or stand on the toeboard or guardrails on the lift's platform.
- No one is to hang outside the platform's guardrails.

# SECTION TWELVE

## BACK CARE

## Back Injuries

Back injuries continue to be the number one occupational health and safety problem in North America. Many back injuries are extremely painful and can result in long term discomfort, pain and lead to permanent disabilities. Workers having back injuries suffer serious consequences such as lost time from work, lost income, and long term pain and suffering. Employers who have workers experiencing frequent back injuries are seeing their health care and compensation costs rising. The long term medical costs will only increase unless back injuries are reduced or prevented in the workplace. Fortunately, the number of back injuries can be reduced through well planned prevention programs.

## Back Anatomy

The moving parts and anatomy of the back are intricate. Each part is designed to work as an integral and smooth unit. Illustration #249A identifies the moving parts of the spine. There are 24 bones with flexible joints called vertebrae in the spine. They support the body and protect the nerves of the spinal cord. The spinal discs protect the nervous system and serve as shock absorbers between the vertebrae. The leg muscles provide much of the lifting power in the human body. Therefore, it is important to know how to use the legs for lifting in order to protect the back from overloads resulting from heavy lifts and strenuous or awkward movements and positions.

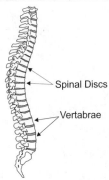

**Illustration #249A - Moving Parts of the Spine**

Spinal Discs

Vertabrae

Illustration #249B shows the anatomy of the spinal cord. The spinal disc absorbs shock and keeps the vertebrae from grinding together and breaking up. Too much bending, twisting and heavy or awkward lifting can wear away at the discs and this can lead to serious and extensive injury and pain.

Muscles, ligaments and nerves connect to the spine. Anytime these are over stretched or over stressed, muscles in particular, may not return to their original shape. When this happens, ligaments, tendons, nerves and spinal discs have to take up the slack, and this usually leads to persistent back, neck, and sometimes arm and leg soreness and pain.

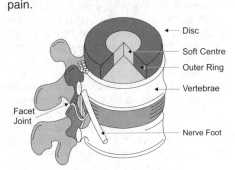

Disc

Soft Centre

Outer Ring

Vertebrae

Facet Joint

Nerve Foot

**Illustration #249B - Anatomy of the Spinal Cord**

## Neutral Position

To prevent back injury, use a neutral posture position as much as possible. Try to keep your spine relaxed and allow the spine's "S" curve to distribute the body's weight evenly. When the back is out of the neutral position, there will be additional stress put onto the back. By standing with your back up against a doorjamb for example, you should be able to feel the neutral position. Touch the doorjamb with your upper back and buttocks and keep your heels flat and a few inches from the jamb. See the side view demonstration in illustration #250. Once in this position, slide your hand between your lower back and the doorjamb. It should slide in easily, but your hand should also touch both your back and the doorjamb. Illustration #250 shows how the person's neck, shoulders, hips and the front part of their ankles are all in one line.

Illustration #250 - The Neutral Position

## Preparing for a Lift

t is very important to check the entire work area and walkways before starting to lift or carry anything. Make sure good solid footing s maintained and there will be no chance for tripping, slipping or stumbling on something. The shoes worn by the worker must provide good traction, support and balance.

- Clear any moveable obstacles out of the way and make sure it is known where large unmovable objects are laying before beginning to carry a heavy or awkward object.
- Survey the route which must be taken and know where you are going to avoid having to move the load twice.
- Use caution when uncertain of the object's weight. Carefully try to heft it and try to determine its weight and center of gravity. If it feels too heavy, do not proceed any further, get help or use the proper

lifting apparatus to make the job easier and safer.

- Do not just bend over and grab the object and lift it up. The worker in illustration #251 did not prepare himself for the lift and no doubt he will suffer some discomfort and pain as a result of his poor lifting practices.

Illustration #251 - Poor Lifting Practice

## Performing a Lift

Performing a lift is when most back injuries occur on-the-job. Consider the following tips for performing a safe lift:

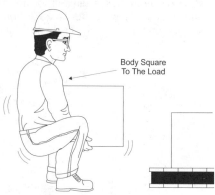

Illustration #252A - Properly Preparing for a Lift

As shown in illustration #252A, the worker i properly facing the object he is going to lif His body is square to the object and his bod is up close to it.

- This worker is properly balancing himsel as he has his feet slightly apart and his po sition is solid to the ground.
- He is in a squatting position; his knees ar bent and back arched.
- His grip is firmly under and to the sides o the object. He takes a deep breath an holds it.
- He tightens his abdomen and then begin the lift by using his legs to bring him up to standing position, keeping his bac arched, as demonstrated in illustratio #252B.
- This worker is making a smooth lift and i demonstrating full control of the lift.

Again he tightens his abdomen muscles, bends his knees and lowers himself slowly. If the load is extra heavy and doesn't have to be stored on the floor, consider setting it elevated off the floor on a stable bench or rack which is capable of supporting the weight.

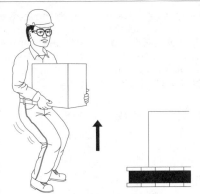

Illustration #252B - Rising Up To Proper Standing Position

The worker in illustration #252C is demonstrating how to carry and lower the load. While carrying a load it is important to maintain a firm grip and hold the load closely to the body as possible. To begin lowering the load, the worker must arch his back slightly.

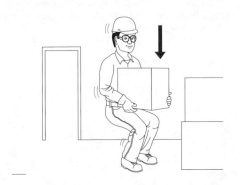

Illustration #252C - Properly Carrying And Lowering The Load

Another safe method for lifting a load is shown in illustration #253. Again, as in the previous illustrations, the worker is up close to the load, but in this example he has dropped to one knee. He will lift the load up and balance it on the other knee, pause to adjust his grip and slowly rise to a standing position, while holding the load as close as he can to his body.

Often workers are required to move heav[y] loads such as cement bags, as shown in il[l]ustration #254. To safely lift and carry thi[s] type of load it is best to stand the load on en[d], flex the knees, bend at the hips and grip th[e] load closely to your body.

**Illustration #253 - Dropping To One Knee To Lift A Load Safely**

**Illustration #254 - Standing The Load On End**

If you have to turn while carrying a heavy load, aim one foot toward the direction you intend on going. Use your feet, not your waist, to pivot or walk out the turn. Never try to lift heavy loads above your waist. If the load is bulky, position the center between your waist and shoulders.

## Carrying Heavy or Awkward Loads

Consider the following safety points:

- Carrying an object that is too large to see over is a hazard because it prevents the person from being able to see where they are walking.
- Carrying a heavy load places extra pressure on the person's lower back. Even if the person doesn't feel any strain while they are carrying the object, there can be long-term damage to the back that can show up later.
- A heavy load being carried by a worker will shift the center of gravity forward, making it difficult to keep in balance.

- The longer a person carries a heavy load, the more likely they will become fatigued. Their awareness of conditions around them decreases, and they are probably less likely to notice an obstacle or other hazard in their path.
- If a worker has to carry a large or heavy awkward object, they should get some help and follow proper lifting and carrying procedures.
- Have a secure grip on the heavy object. If another person is helping to carry the load and you drop your end, you or your partner could fall, maybe underneath the object.
- Before beginning the lift, turn your leading foot in the direction you intend on going. This helps you start off without having to adjust your balance for a change in direction.

- Try to keep the object level so its weight is distributed evenly between both workers carrying a shared load.
- Both workers should move slowly enough to keep the momentum of the shared load under control.
- Both workers should maintain good communications so that both know what to expect.

*Note: For difficult lifting tasks, keep two options in mind: ask a co-worker for help; or use a pushcart or other appropriate material handling/lifting device.*

## Activities Related to Back Injuries

Besides lifting and carrying, there are several other possible activities related to back injuries which can be detrimental to the worker if proper precautions are not taken. Activities to be considered include:

- Shoveling
- Pushing or pulling a load
- Reaching out and balancing
- Standing or sitting
- Twisting

*Shoveling:* Similar guidelines apply to shoveling as discussed with proper lifting and carrying activities. As shown in illustration #255A, make sure you have a good firm grip on the shovel handle and you are positioned solidly to the ground.

**Illustration #255A - Firm Grip On Shovel Handle**

Keep the shovel close to the body, bend the knees, not the back and use the strength of the thigh muscles to bring the body back up to an upright position, as demonstrated in illustration #255B. You can increase your leverage by keeping your bottom hand low and toward the shovel blade. This practice permits the use of the strength in the arms and shoulders to take the load, instead of the back.

***Pushing or pulling a load:*** Pushing a load, as shown in illustration #256, is easier on the worker's back than pulling. When pushing the load, use the technique that keeps your back neutral. Stay close to the load, don't lean too far forward, use both the arms and shoulders and keep your stomach muscles tight.

Illustration #255B - Proper Upright Position

Illustration #256 - Pushing A Load

If you have to pull a heavy load, face the object squarely, with one foot at least one foot (30.5 cm) in front of the other as demonstrated in illustration #257. Keep the back straight, bend the knees slightly and pull with one smooth motion, shifting your weight from one leg to the other as you take each backward step. Be extra careful to know where you are going and make sure the path is clear.

***Reaching out and balancing:*** Illustration #258 demonstrates a safe practice for reaching out to pick something up off the step or the ground. Many back injuries result from this type of movement. It is best to reach out with one hand and grip a solid object for balance. Balance can be obtained by gripping a handrail or placing your hand up against a wall or door. Raise one leg as you bend forward, use the other hand to pick up the load and return to the standing position. By practicing this technique you maintain your balance. This is safe only when lifting light or quite small loads or objects. It is not intended for picking up heavy loads.

Illustration #257 - Pulling A Load

has to be maintained for a long time, keep your weight unevenly distributed and rest each leg in turn. Use a footrest to slightly elevate one leg while standing, and shift one leg, then the other, to the footrest.

Illustration #258 - Reaching To Pick Something Up

**Standing:** There is a proper standing position. Avoid slouching and/or trying to keep an unnaturally stiff posture. As discussed earlier, and demonstrated in illustration #259, keep your abdomen, buttocks and chin tucked in. Hold your shoulders slightly back and your head high. If a standing position

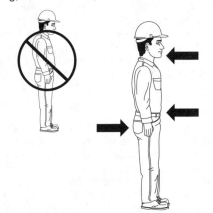

Illustration #259 - Avoid Slouching, Maintain Good Posture

*Sitting:* Sitting can be just as hard on the back as standing and for some people sitting for prolonged periods of time is more harmful than standing. Sitting requires good support for the body. The seat must be firm and wide enough to support the lower torso and the backrest high and wide enough to support the upper back. The seat's length should be correct to ensure that the back of the knees are supported and not squeezed in too much. It is best to get up from the sitting position periodically and stretch the legs, arms and back. Footrests are also important to use when sitting.

Driving for long periods of time can be very bad for the back, as the sitting position is often far too long. Take frequent rest breaks, switch drivers if possible, use a pillow or the lumbar control on the seat to support the lower back and keep the seat far enough forward to comfortably reach the instruments and pedals.

*Twisting:* One of the greatest dangers to a person's back is twisting. Instead of twisting, try to use your feet to pivot the turn. This action turns the whole body and will not twist the back.

Whenever possible, it is advised to use specialized lifting and carrying machines and devices, as well as approved equipment for those hard to reach locations.

- Use dollies, trolleys, wagons or other material handling devices to carry loads.
- Use tilt bins or bins with collapsible sides rather than lifting or placing loads.
- Build platforms, ramps or shelves to minimize bending.
- Consider using conveyors to move materials.
- Use ladders and scaffolds for overhead, awkward locations.

## Repetitive Stress

When a person has to do something repeatedly for a period of time without much interruption, the repetition of this causes wear and tear on the muscles, tendons, ligaments and nerves. There are a variety of repetitive stress or strain injuries common in those workplaces where repetitive tasks are undertaken. Some of the more common injuries are carpal tunnel syndrome, bursitis, tennis elbow, and tendonitis.

Consider the following tips for handling those repetitive jobs:

- When a job requires repetition of one main movement, stop at least once every hour and rest, or at the least, do a different task, which requires another type of movement.
- If the job requires plenty of forward bending, periodically straighten up and bend backwards for a few seconds.

- If the job requires lots of upward reaching, gently bend forward and grab a solid object to support and balance yourself.
- Take a break, walk around, and relax those over used muscles.
- Shift the job tasks regularly so different muscles are used.

## Back Exercise Program

Many back injuries in the workplace result from weak, tight muscles. To protect the spine, the various muscles which support the back must be strong, flexible and in good shape. A good exercise program and a balanced diet are two things which can help workers keep their back strong and healthy by giving those key muscle groups flexibility and strength. Consider the following points:

- Consult with your doctor before beginning any back exercise program.

- Warm up thoroughly before starting any vigorous exercise and take time to cool down properly once the exercises have been completed.
- Try to do stretching exercises before beginning a job which is quite demanding physically.
- Maintain good posture and positioning while doing the various exercises in your workout routine.
- Consider exercising with a co-worker, friend or your spouse, as this may keep you motivated to keep up the exercise routine.
- If the exercise causes discomfort or pain, stop doing it. It's important to "listen" to your body.
- Do not over exert yourself while exercising, start slow; don't get into a strenuous program too quickly.

A few pre-shift stretches and bends can help a worker prepare him or herself to be job ready and flexible for the physical job demands. Eating properly and maintaining a balanced diet is key to good back health as well. That extra weight, usually around the worker's mid-section, is not good for anybody's back.

Sports and recreational activities are probably, for most people, the most enjoyable way of maintaining an exercise program for healthy muscles in the back.

Activities that are usually recommended for the back include:
- Brisk walking
- Cycling
- Cross country skiing
- Swimming

Injury to the spine can be caused by sports that require numerous sudden twists and turns.

These twists and turns jar the spine and put extra strains and pulls on those key muscle groups of the back. Always take extra care when playing these types of sports, in particular, squash, racquetball, handball, tennis, basketball, soccer, ice hockey, golf and weight lifting. Several simple exercises that can be used to prevent back problems or to recover from them are identified next, but, if you've had a recent back injury, check with your doctor before beginning these or any other type of exercises.

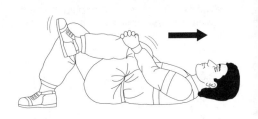

Illustration #260 - Knee-Raise Exercise

*Knee-Raise Exercise* (see illustration #260)
- Lie on your back, with knees bent.
- Slowly begin to bring one knee to your chest and hold it in this position for 20 - 30 seconds.
- Lower your foot back to the floor, and repeat the exercise with the opposite leg.
- Consider repeating this simple stretching exercise 5 - 10 times; always go slow if you are just starting.

*Partial Sit-Up Exercise* (See illustration #261)
- Lie on your back, with your legs bent at the knees and your feet flat on the floor.
- Rise slowly up, with your arms reaching between your legs until your shoulders are about 4 - 6 inches (10 - 15 cm) off the floor.
- Return to the start position and repeat.

- Remember, this is not a full sit-up, it is only a partial sit-up, and it should be done slowly, not fast or jerky.

Illustration #261 - Partial Sit-Up Exercise

### Semi-Squat Exercise *(See illustration #262)*

- Begin this exercise from a standing position.
- Hold onto a sturdy support, about chest height.
- Begin to bend your legs to a 45 degree angle, do this slowly.

- Tighten up the buttock muscles as you do each squat, as this protects your lower back from strain.
- Hold the squat position for several seconds, then return slowly to the standing position.
- Repeat several times, maintain this routine several times, doing it slow and steady.

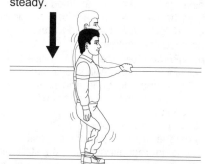

Illustration #262 - Semi-Squat Exercise

*Hip-Stretch Exercise* (See illustration #263)

- Begin by kneeling on one knee, with the other foot out in front.
- Tighten up the stomach muscles.
- Slowly move your upper body forward, shifting the weight onto your front foot, hold that position for a few seconds.
- Switch legs and repeat the exercise 5 - 10 times, do it slow and steady.

*Side-Stretch Exercise* (See illustration #264)

- Begin this stretching exercise by placing one arm on your head and the other to your side.
- Slowly bend to the side opposite your raised arm until you can feel the muscles stretching.
- Breathe at a steady comfortable rate and hold the stretch position for 15 – 30 seconds.
- Repeat this exercise 5 – 10 times: alternating sides.

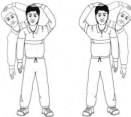

Illustration #264 - Side-Stretch Exercise

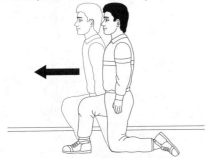

Illustration #263 - Hip-Stretch Exercise

# SECTION THIRTEEN

## EQUIPMENT LOCKOUT AND TAGOUT

## Introduction

Many industrial accidents are caused by the uncontrollable release of hazardous energy. The unexpected activation of machinery or process equipment during regular maintenance and servicing operations can have tragic results. That's why the first step in any lockout or tagout procedure is to be aware of the types of energy sources and hazards which need to be controlled.

Provincial, State, and Federal governments in Canada and United States have comprehensive standards for the control of hazardous energy sources for industry. The information used to write the standards has been gathered from industry, along with governmental regulatory agencies, including occupational health and safety groups, workers compensation boards, the National Institute of Occupational Health and Safety (NIOSH), and the American National Standards Institute (ANSI).

Standards for lockout and tagout are designed to protect employees involved in service and maintenance activities against an unexpected start-up of machines or equipment, or the release of stored energy that could cause injuries. The laws concerning lockout and tagout are generally flexible enough to allow each employer to develop a suitable lockout and tagout program with procedures designed to meet specific needs for the type of machinery and equipment being serviced and maintained by the employees.

## Lockout and Tagout

*Lockout:* This is a method of keeping equipment from being set in motion and endangering employees. Lockout is the use of locks to positively secure the control device(s) used to control the hazardous energy. In lockout a disconnect switch, valve, or other energy isolating mechanism is put in the safe or off position.

A lock is attached so that the equipment cannot be energized as shown in illustration #265.

Illustration #265 - Typical Lockout

*Tagout:* In tagout, the energy isolating device(s) is placed in the safe or off position. An approved tag with "Danger" clearly written on it and "Do Not Remove This Tag", and other specific warnings, is attached to it. Illustration #266 shows an example of a tag attached to a lockout device.

Illustration #266 - Typical Lockout and Tagout

*Note: It is common practice, and in many cases law, that all lockout and tagout materials and devices be supplied by the employer.*

Each device must be: durable; withstand wear; substantial, so it won't come off easily; and recognizable, so the person who applied it can be identified. Many companies issue each employee authorization to apply their own locks and tags.

An "assigned lock" is a lock that the employee is personally responsible and accountable for. They control the key.

### Application of Lockout or Tagout

Procedures for lockout and tagout are necessary whenever performing service and maintenance to any machinery or equipment where there could be injury from:

- Unexpected start-up of the machine or equipment, and/or
- A sudden release of stored or restrained energy.

Two common situations tradespeople and operators are most likely required to have lockout and tagout procedures are:

1. When any part of a person's body could be caught by moving machinery parts.

2. When any equipment guard or safety device must be removed from a machine or piece of equipment.

Some common jobs and activities for which lockout and tagout are used include:

- Repairing or testing electrical circuits.
- Cleaning or lubricating machinery where there are moving parts.
- Inspecting or testing machine parts.
- Clearing debris or product from the machine or process equipment.
- Freeing up jammed parts or mechanisms

## Hazardous Energy Sources

Energy of some sort is always present in any type of powered machinery or equipment. There is always a chance that something can move, by being released suddenly or slowly.

Energy can come from many sources, but is always one of two classifications:

- Kinetic Energy: the force caused by the motion of the object or part.
- Potential Energy: the force stored in an object or part that remains inactive, but can be either slowly or suddenly released

**Electrical Energy:** There are two types of electrical energy sources: generated electric power and static electricity.

*Generated electric power* is found at the main source of electricity to the machine, as well as within the various circuitry of the machinery and equipment. Generated electric power is the energy required to perform work or to produce an action.

*Note: Generated electric power can also be stored energy, such as in batteries or capacitors.*

*Static electricity* is an energy source that is fixed on the surface of an object. An example of this can be found in an electrostatic precipitator. These are commonly used for dust collection in various industrial processes and environmental management installations.

*Mechanical Energy:* Mechanical energy is usually expressed as either transitional (linear) or rotational motion.

*Transitional motion* is usually a linear movement from one fixed point to another. Examples of this would include gates which swing or slide, doors on hinges, and conveyor belts and rollers.

*Rotational motion* is a common form of mechanical energy when working in and around rotating equipment. Rotational energy refers to objects/parts which revolve, such as flywheels, pulleys, gears, shafts, couplings, and rollers.

There can be tremendous amounts of stored energy waiting to be released as rotating energy in any one of these examples. It is imperative that proper blocking and securing procedures are followed in order to protect against rotating energy sources.

*Thermal Energy:* This is one type of energy few people consider when working in and around machinery and equipment.

Typically, thermal energy cannot be just turned off or eliminated; one can usually only control it or cause it to dissipate slowly. Several examples include: the heat from a furnace in a foundry; the heat around the kiln in a cement plant; and the frost and cold in large industrial freezers and coolers.

The power sources to these can be turned off, but the thermal energy remains, and there is a waiting period before the thermal energy dissipates.

*Note: Heat is considered as being an energy source. Cold is an absence of heat and not considered an energy source*

In addition to thermal energy generated by process equipment and certain machinery, certain amounts of thermal energy can be created by chemical reactions.

Chemical reactions can be either exothermic or endothermic. *Exothermic* reactions raise temperatures and *endothermic* reactions lower temperatures. Controlling thermal energy from chemical reactions can be as dangerous, or more dangerous, than either electrical or mechanical energy hazards. Chemical reactions can be quite complex to identify and control. The methods for isolating and controlling the thermal effects of chemical energy must be written specifically

for those chemical processes specific to that location and work area.

*Note: Exposure limits are: 110 degrees F (43 degrees C) maximum and 34 degrees F (1 degree C) minimum. At either of these extremes tissue damage begins. Proper personal protective equipment must be worn when working in conditions beyond these temperatures.*

Whether the thermal energy comes from a furnace, kiln, freezer or cooler, it has to be dissipated. In addition, if the thermal energy source is from a chemical reaction, either eliminate the chemical(s) to prevent any reaction or control the reaction to where the thermal energy created can be safely tolerated.

*Potential Energy:* Potential energy sources, like thermal energy sources, can be difficult to simply turn off, therefore, one may have to dissipate the potential energy source or control it somehow.

Types of potential energy sources within machines and process equipment include: pressurized fluids and gases; springs and linkages, and gravity.

Several common types of pressure sources are used extensively around machinery and equipment. These are: hydraulic fluids, compressed gases, and vacuums.

*Hydraulic pressure* refers to forces being applied to a contained fluid and as the forces on the fluid increase so does the fluid's pressure. The fluid pressure within the container will be equal in all directions and if the pressurized fluid were to be suddenly released, the energy transmitted would be sudden and have tremendous force which could cause severe injury to people or damage to equipment. Hydraulic energy sources are not limited to hydraulic systems, but to any system where fluids are either stored or transmitted under pressure.

*Compressed gases* are at pressures high enough to be safely stored in tanks or cylinders and are commonly transmitted in piping systems or held in lines by valves. There are many types of compressed gases common to industrial and process equipment and machinery: compressed air, nitrogen, oxygen, carbon dioxide, freon, acetylene, hydrogen and helium are only a small sample of the more common ones.

Similar to hydraulic energy sources, compressed gases remain stable when stored under constant pressure within an appropriate confined space or container. If there is any chance that the gases are released from the confined area, the release can be uncontrolled and sudden. The seriousness of this can never be stated strongly enough. Always dissipate or control pressurized gases first from any type of machine or process equipment before any type of maintenance or service work is to be undertaken.

*Note: Be sure to know what compressed gases are in the system before dissipating them into the atmosphere, as the gases could be toxic and/or lethal. Always check first and wear the required protective equipment.*

**Vacuum** sources of energy are another form of pressure, only it is a pressure that is below atmospheric pressure.

There are several industrial examples where extreme caution must be taken to prevent injury from vacuum sources. Vacuum systems are used in special presses for vacuum forming, in certain packaging applications in both manufacturing and food processing, and in other services such as intake ducts and exhaust systems where fans or blowers remove gases and solids with vacuum. Some compressor and pump applications have high vacuum regions on their intake and suction piping and valves as well.

The real danger with most vacuum energy sources is not only with being drawn into a duct or pipe, but lies in machines or equipment which use vacuum as an energy source to activate something on the machine or within the process. Never forget to lockout or tagout a vacuum control energy source.

**Springs** are another source of potential energy. The energy potential of springs varies with their size and application.

Many serious mishaps have been documented which demonstrate how springs have caused serious injury and damage. Springs, when not in any form of tension, either in a stretched or compressed position, pose no real danger. If the spring is stretched or compressed, depending on its design, and held in that position, stored energy is present and if released there is a chance that serious injury and/or damage would result.

Springs and the mechanisms they're attached to can be found throughout many industrial applications. Coil and leaf springs are the most common springs. When working on or near springs always relieve and control the tension first. Ensure that the tension cannot return because of something done on the machine or at another part on an associated machine.

*Gravity* is another source of potential energy. For any machine or piece of equipment being worked on, whether it is operated by electrics, hydraulics, with pneumatics, or even by hand, and with the energy source under control, certain parts or devices may still have to "come to rest", and it is gravity that causes this to happen. It may be that by removing one of the operating energy sources, the weight of some part shifts and due to gravity there is a subsequent reaction or movement of another part.

"What goes up must come down", if there is nothing in place to secure it.

Examples of gravity energy sources which have to be controlled include: counterweights, eccentric drives, camshafts, gates, hydraulic and pneumatic cylinder rods, and conveyors such as bucket elevators and vertical and sloped chain conveyors.

In any one of these examples there is a chance that something can reverse or come down suddenly if there is nothing in place to secure it. Normally there are devices such as brakes and anti-rotation devices (backstops) used to prevent coasting or reversing. Blocks, wedges, dogs, and pins are used to secure or prop a unit or part from moving when there is a chance that gravitational forces are possible.

## Unintentional Operation

In many industries throughout Canada and United States the frequency and severity of on-the-job accidents and injuries have been increasing despite the more comprehensive and stricter occupational health and safety controls and regulations. This may be partly due to an increase in both the complexity and advancement in technology of machinery, equipment and associated processes.

Accidents and injuries may also be partly attributed to pressure to speed up a job and take shortcuts while performing service and maintenance work. None of these factors should ever cause one to overlook using some common sense before starting the job. Lockout and tagout procedures are there to be used by everyone and never should be overlooked. It takes a little extra time to go through the procedures, but there is no time so well spent as the time one takes to properly lockout and tagout the energy sources of the machinery and equipment that will be worked on.

Most organizations have policies and procedures in place to protect workers from accidents caused by unintentional start-up of equipment. Safe lockout and tagout practices provide a system for rendering a piece of equipment inoperable and powerless so that authorized personnel can perform the required work safely.

Several common ways workers can be injured on machines and equipment which is unintentionally started up include:

- Entanglement in belts, chains, ropes or conveyors.
- Crushing, cuts, or amputations when working on presses, shears or in cylinders or crankcases of engines, pumps or compressors.
- Burns from hot materials and fires and explosions.

- Scalding from steam/vapors, hot fluids, solids and fines.
- Falls and immersion into tanks, vessels, and other containers which hold fluids, slurries or semi-solids.
- Asphyxiation in vessels, bins, silos, tanks or other types of confined spaces.

Unintentionally operated equipment can also cause severe and costly damage to equipment. Often there is a "chain effect" when one piece of equipment unintentionally moves and subsequent equipment is either impacted by the first or it shifts in position and presents another problem.

Another reason for lockout and tagout procedures is to prevent injury to users of the equipment. A tradesperson may be required to adjust or repair a machine and sometimes when spare parts are unavailable, etc., the equipment is not repaired for a prolonged period of time.

In that interim period, should the equipment be used inadvertently by the operator, serious damage and injury could occur. This is one more reason why locks and tags have to be used.

A typical equipment lockout program should consist of at least the following components:

- Safety Lockout Policy
- Lockout Procedures
- Lockout Equipment and Resources
- Methods for Enforcing the Procedures
- Employee Training
- Updating and Follow-up Procedures

The equipment lockout policy is usually a series of short statements which clearly state the following:

- Why equipment lockout is necessary?
- When is equipment lockout required?
- Who is responsible?
- What are the consequences for non-compliance?

- What training is required prior to doing the job?

The equipment lockout procedures should clearly describe the approved methods and practices employees must follow prior to beginning work on any machine or piece of equipment. Typical lockout procedures would be similar to these:

- Guarding equipment against mechanical movement.
- Identifying all energy sources to the machine.
- Elimination of stored energy.
- Identifying valves, switches, and controls.
- Determine approved methods for locking out each device.
- Shutdown practices for specific machines and equipment.
- Closing off auxiliary lines, controls, and support equipment.
- Tagging procedures for valves, switches and controls.

- Application of approved equipment lockout devices.
- Using locks and tags.
- Describe color scheme for tags.
- Reporting procedures prior to starting the job.
- Attempt start-up prior to starting the job, after lockout is done.
- Checking that all tools, equipment and parts are accounted for prior to official start-up.
- Ensuring that all work related personnel are accounted for prior to official start-up.
- Carrying out approved lock and tag removal procedures prior to official start-up.

*Note: Equipment lockout policies and procedures must be complied with whenever conducting maintenance, repair, installation and service activities. Failure to comply can put the employee(s) in danger because of the potential hazards associated with the energy sources at or near the machinery and equipment.*

*Note: Performing maintenance or testing on an operating machine, process equipment, or within the system is not permitted when there is danger to the health and safety of any employee.*

In those special cases where it is necessary that the machine, process equipment or part of the system must remain in operation during maintenance and testing work, it is general practice that written safe work permits/procedures be developed in each of these instances.

As a general rule, equipment lockout is the preferred method in most companies for ensuring that machinery and process equipment is properly secured against any unintentional start-up while people are performing maintenance and service functions. Equipment lockout procedures have certain advantages over tagout procedures according to the following:

- Locks are difficult to bypass, as it would require a major effort to compromise a quality lock. Tags can be easily removed.
- Tags can be easily damaged by environmental or physical conditions.
- Tags only serve as a warning and are not to be considered a "safety device", whereas locks are.
- Locks, once applied to a switch, control or valve speak everyone's language.

Locks cannot be easily misunderstood, whereas tags can be if people are speaking a different language or cannot read well. There is no question what a lock means when it is installed on a power switch for example.

Lockout is the preferred method when the energy isolation device is capable of being locked out, but there are certain situations where tagout systems are acceptable on their own.

## Unintentional Operation

For example:

- When the equipment cannot be physically locked out. Some types of machines or equipment may not be easily locked out without significant modification or redesign, therefore, they are considered to be incapable of being locked out.
- There are instances when tagout systems are used very effectively and safely and are considered to be an approved alternative to lockout.

Some machinery or process equipment in complex systems that are controlled through a series of computer systems may be difficult or not even feasible to employ a total lockout system. Appropriate tagout procedures are developed and employed instead.

When tagout is selected over lockout, it must provide the employees with the same level of safety and protection an approved lockout procedure would.

If possible, consider implementing additional measures such as:

- Isolating a portion of a circuit.
- Disconnecting a switch.
- Removing or covering a valve handwheel.
- Taking an electrical plug apart.
- Doing that something extra that gives an edge in personnel safety.

Once the company has determined what procedures are to be used for equipment lockout and tagout, there has to be assurance that the locks and tags meet specific standards in order to be in compliance with the regulations and policy. There are several basic performance requirements for selecting approved lockout equipment:

1. Must be identifiable. The lock and/or tag should be recognized as being the standard type used throughout the organization. No one should be confused by a mixed assortment of locks, tags, and lockout device clips.

2. Locks and tags must never be used for purposes which are not associated with lockout and tagout procedures and functions.

3. Locks and tags must be durable enough to withstand the harsh physical and environmental exposures they are often placed in. Types of exposures considered are: chemicals, extreme temperatures, weather conditions, wet, dusty and abrasive environments. Tags must remain legible throughout their exposure to these types of conditions. A soggy, illegible tag is like having no tag at all.

4. Locks and tags must be substantial. This means that the locks and tags are secure enough to prevent unauthorized removal through the inadvertent or accidental actions of fellow workers.

5. Locks and tags must be standardized in color, shape, and size. These standards must be adhered to by all employees, departments and outside contractors who are working on site.

6. Locks and tags must be easily recognized by any employee. They should easily recognize, the lock, tag or both, and know who is working on the machine or equipment. If a lock and tag is in place, and that person is not around, co-workers will know who to look for when the job is complete, or, if work is still in progress, confirm that the worker is safe.

7. By identifying the people who own the locks and tags the supervisor and safety officer can determine who is and is not in compliance with the equipment lockout and tagout procedures. Action on any non-compliance should be undertaken immediately.

8. The individual is responsible and accountable for the lock and tag. Locks and tags should have the owner's name on them, and in some cases, the owner's photograph may be required. Remember, each individual is responsible for the correct application of his locks and tags and ensuring full compliance with the company's equipment lockout and tagout procedures.

## Applying Energy Controls

Energy isolation and lockout/tagout procedures are to be applied only by trained and authorized employees. While certain procedures will vary because of the diversity of machinery, equipment, and processes, there are basic rules and requirements that are common to most organizations.

When applying energy controls consideration should be given to the following points:

*Purpose:* Convey the message why there are procedures for ensuring lockout and tagout of energy isolating devices for machinery and equipment and why these must be followed whenever maintenance or servicing is performed. It must be clear that full compliance by everyone is mandatory and any violation with these procedures is neither permissible or acceptable.

*Preparation For Shutdown:* Before any machinery or equipment is shut off to lock or tag it out, the following must be known:

- What type(s) of energy sources are present?
- What amount of energy is present?
- What hazards do the energy sources present?
- What method(s) are used to control the energy source(s)?

*Equipment Shutdown:* The equipment must be shutdown using the appropriate operating and process controls. There must be an orderly procedure in place for preparing the machine or equipment for the application of locks and/or tags. When preparing to shutdown any equipment consider the following:

- Notification must be given to all personnel affected by the shutdown and that lockout and/or tagout procedures will be applied. One cannot simply shutdown a piece of equipment or any part of the process when it could effect other parts of the system.

A sudden shutdown could jeopardize someone's safety.

- Shutdown the equipment using normal procedures for each specific piece of equipment so that nobody gets injured during the shutdown.
- Isolation involves the activation of all energy isolation devices from the equipment so there is complete isolation from all energy sources.

***Application of Lockout and Tagout:*** The lockout and tagout devices are applied only by authorized personnel who are doing the work. Only standard lockout and tagout devices supplied by the employer are to be used. A lockout device clip should be used if the lock(s) cannot be placed directly on the energy control. Every employee performing work on the equipment must attach their own personal lock and/or tag. Always remember to provide all the necessary information as requested by the tag.

***Control of Stored Energy:*** Consider the following points when guarding against the possibility of stored energy located within the machinery or process equipment:

- Inspect the system to make sure all parts have stopped moving.
- If required, install ground wires.
- Release any tension on springs or linkages and block/restrain the movement of spring loaded parts.
- Attach warning tags to the pins and clamps of any spring mechanisms and linkages and restrict the release or access to only those personnel who are authorized to do so.
- Block or brace parts that could fall because of gravity.
- Block parts in hydraulic and pneumatic systems that could move because of a loss in pressure.
- Bleed hydraulic and pneumatic lines and leave vents or drains open.

- Drain process piping systems and close valves to prevent the flow of hazardous materials.
- If a line must be blocked where there is no valve, use a blank flange.
- Purge lines, tanks, piping cylinders and casings with proper purging gases or fluids.
- Dissipate extreme cold or heat and wear approved personal protective equipment when working in hazardous material areas.
- If any stored energy can accumulate, monitor for this in order to keep it below hazardous levels.

*Equipment Isolation Verification:* This is the last step taken before actual maintenance or service work begins. There are several ways to verify isolation:

- Attempt start-up, but first ensure that all personnel are clear. Press all start buttons and other activation controls.

## Energy Controls/Disconnecting

- Use test equipment, such as a voltmeter, to determine if there is any electrical energy source at the machine. Other types of test equipment should be made available in order to verify the presence of other energy sources.
- Visually inspect the machine to ensure that any other activation controls and switches are off and that locks and tags are securely in place in all the proper locations.

### Disconnecting Energy Controls

Once the maintenance and servicing work has been completed proper procedures must be taken to disconnect the energy controls before start-up commences. Several steps to consider include:

- Remove all tools from the work area.
- Ensure that the machine and equipment is fully assembled.

- Do a head count to make sure everyone is accounted for and clear of the machinery and equipment.
- Notify everyone who works in the area that lockout/tagout is being removed and start-up is to commence shortly.
- Remove the lockout and tagout devices. Except in emergencies, each device must be removed by the person who put it on.
- In some workplaces the last person to remove their lock is responsible for removing the lockout device clip, taking the tag off and signing it before turning it in to the control room or giving it to a supervisor.
- In some companies, the supervisor removes their lock last.
- Follow a checklist of required steps and procedures to re-energize the machinery or process equipment. In some companies only a qualified electrician can re-energize the electric energy sources.

## Testing/Positioning During Lockout

There are times when the machinery or process equipment must be either tested or re-positioned before any further service or maintenance work is undertaken. In order to safely do this, consider the following steps:

- Make sure that all non-essential equipment, tools, parts, and test instruments are removed from the work area.
- Make sure that equipment guards, safety restraints, blocking, rigging, and parts have been either removed or adequately secured.
- Make sure that non-essential personnel are clear of the machine or equipment.
- Remove the lockout and tagout devices, remembering that only the workers who applied them should remove them.
- Re-energize the equipment and proceed to start the machinery or process equipment which is required in order to perform either the tests or re-positioning.

- De-energize and reapply the energy control devices in accordance with the standard lockout and tagout procedures.

*Note: When maintenance and servicing work lasts more than one work shift, the lockout and tagout protection must not be interrupted.*

At many workplaces employees who are leaving work at the end of their shift do not remove their locks or tags until the job is completed. The job may last several days or weeks. In some cases, an employee cannot remove their lock or tag until people arriving for the next shift are ready to put their locks and tags on in the appropriate locations.

## Outside Contractors

When contractors or other outside personnel are performing maintenance or service on machinery and process equipment they too must comply with the company's lockout and tagout policy and procedures. It is imperative that the outside contractor be completely informed about how the lockout and tagout procedures work. The contractor's employees who are on site are required to fully comply with the rules and procedures as stated by the company's energy control program.

## Lockout and Tagout Training

Without training, the employee might not properly perform equipment lockout and tagout. They may work on the equipment in an unsafe manner. In order to have an effective and safe lockout and tagout system, training (and occasional refresher) programs should be prepared and presented to the company's employees.

The training program should include:

- Purpose of the lockout and tagout policy and procedures.
- Hazardous energy recognition.
- Identify different types of energy sources.
- Locate points of energy control.
- Application of locks and tags.
- Wearing personal protective equipment.
- Re-energizing procedures.
- Enforcement and discipline.

The training program must ensure that personnel are familiar with all procedures and know where to obtain further information regarding the company's equipment lockout and tagout policy and procedures.

Refresher training should be repeated semi-annually and complete training must be provided for all new employees and contractors.

## Enforcement and Discipline

The company should include the means for enforcing full compliance to their equipment lockout and tagout policy and procedures. The company should take disciplinary action when there is non-compliance to the policy and procedures.

Periodic inspection of lockout and tagout procedures should be undertaken by someone qualified to do so. The purpose of the inspection is to locate any non-compliance, and to make appropriate corrections before any further work is completed.

# SECTION
# FOURTEEN

## ACCIDENT INVESTIGATION

## Accident Causes

Accidents and incidents in the workplace occur far too often. Many workers have seen someone experience an accident, or an incident where there were no injuries, but which could have been worse, except for luck. Often, after an accident or an incident has been examined, it is not difficult to see how it could have been prevented.

*Accidents are not so accidental*. A thorough analysis of an accident will conclude that it had one or more causes. Many of the causes are basic. Basic causes could be either job or personal factors, such as engineering, lack of knowledge or skill, improper tools or equipment, or poor work practices from which substandard acts and/or substandard conditions originate. Basic causes may also be referred to as underlying, root or real causes, system defects or contributing causes.

Basic causes are most frequently the result of an inadequate safety system, inadequate system standards, and/or inadequate compliance with standards.

## Accident Prevention

In order to excel at accident prevention in the workplace, workers must be completely safety conscious.

How do workers become safety conscious? To begin with, workers must have a definite understanding as to whether or not they are safety conscious. Many workers think they are. But are they really? Being safety conscious is having a specific state of mind towards safety and accident prevention. Workers cannot put safety on and off like a coat, as the occasion demands. Safety and accident prevention must be part of a person at all times - it is a "feeling".

How is this "feeling", this automatic awareness of the possibility of accidents or injury acquired? Consider the following four factors for achieving this "feeling".

- Development of common sense
- Hard work and constant effort
- Constant vigilance
- Development and use of a system for accident prevention and safe work practices

## Sources of Workplace Accidents

There are many causes of workplace accidents. A rather long list of causes could be developed, but typically there are three sources of accidents common to most workplaces. These include:

- Improper *conditions* or circumstances.
- The *attitudes* of people.
- Improper *methods* or ways of doing work.

The second point, the attitudes of people, is worth additional discussion.

Attitude refers to the person's thinking and beliefs toward safety consciousness and accident prevention. Attitude means:

- The way a person looks at things.
- What the person is thinking about while performing work.
- The person's approach to work.
- How the person receives orders, directions and/or suggestions from supervisors and co-workers.
- The person's ability to "figure out the odds" of an accident occurring.
- The person's work habits and traits.

In order to achieve successful accident prevention, people must attain a high level of safety consciousness and it is this unique state of mind which prevents accidents from occurring. People have to work persistently at acquiring this state of mind. It is difficult to change one's outlook, or way of thinking, in one day.

This change does not occur overnight. It takes time and effort. Make an honest effort to acquire this special state of mind for accident prevention in the workplace.

There are several steps often referred to, and, if carried out, will lead to that desired safety consciousness discussed earlier. The points which make up this system are known as the *Five Point Safety Production System*.

1. Have I checked the entrance to my place of work?

Concentrate on what you see as you travel to your place of work. Keep your mind on what is required, and see that it is done promptly.

2. Is my working place and equipment in good working order?

As in the first point, the person now has to focus their mind on one thing; this time, the place where they are working.

3. Am I working properly?

4. Have I done an act of safety today?

An "*Act of Safety*" refers to the following safety slogan:

*A - ASK* someone about safety
*C - CHECK* someone about safety
*T - TALK* to someone about safety

5. Can and will I continue to work properly?

## Accident/Incident Investigation

Accident/incident investigation is defined as the systematic search and inquiry for factual information on the extent and nature of a specific loss, the related events, the substandard practices and conditions which influenced the events, the basic causes and the management action to prevent or control future occurrences.

### Why Accidents Are Investigated

"Prevention of future accidents is the purpose of an investigation."

An effective accident investigation can:
- Determine what actually happened.

- Find the causes.
- Help identify practical corrective actions.
- Demonstrate commitment of management and the workers to accident prevention and workplace safety.

Effective accident and incident investigations assess responsibility but not blame. Investigations should not be "finger pointing exercises", where management is out to directly blame someone. Information from the investigation should be documented, recorded, and analyzed, but not used to discipline. This type of policy should encourage workers to report accidents, incidents and any near misses they were involved in. As well, this approach to accident investigation should encourage witnesses to accidents to openly tell investigators everything they know about the accident.

**What Accidents Should Be Investigated?**

Many organizations only investigate accidents which result in "time lost" claims filed with worker's compensation. However, "time lost" claims are only a fraction of all accidents. Well-documented research on workplace accidents in North America indicates that for every serious workplace injury or fatality there are:

- 10 minor injuries.
- 30 property damage accidents or incidents.
- 600 near miss accidents or incidents with no visible damage or injury.

Taking these figures into consideration, serious accidents and minor injuries are only 6% of all mishaps occurring in the workplace.

This is an alarming figure and clearly indicates that there are many unreported, not talked about mishaps and near misses which occur each and every day. This also suggests that:

- The *severity* of an accident is largely a matter of chance. Accidents, which do not result in damage or injury, may, under slightly different circumstances, cause serious injury and/or loss.

- Several non-serious accidents may occur before a serious accident of the same type happens. Serious accidents represent only a small fraction of all accidents and are relatively rare in most workplaces. For each accident which results in injury, there are often many similar ones which do not. If the causes of the non-serious accidents can be identified, the serious accidents can be prevented.

*Note: Supervisors, members of occupational health and safety committees and safety personnel are encouraged to investigate any accident or incident which has caused, or has the potential to cause, injury or loss.*

## How Can Reporting Be Encouraged?

It is important that the organization develops a plan to encourage workers to report all accidents and incidents. Those which go unreported cannot be investigated and may happen again. The employer and the occupational health and safety committee can encourage accident and incident reporting by:

- Educating all employees. Employees should know why accidents and incidents must be reported and how the investigation information will be used.

- Showing employees that their information is positively received and acted on immediately.

- Ensuring that the information given is not used to discipline anyone.
- Demonstrating that the company is paying attention to safety in the workplace everyday.

## What Causes Should Be Looked For?

Accident and incident causes usually are broken down into:

- The direct cause.
- The indirect causes.
- The root cause.

***Direct Cause:*** The direct cause is the event which led directly to the accident or incident. Without the direct cause, the accident would not have occurred. To find out what the direct cause was, ask, "what was the last thing that happened before the accident."

*For example*, if a worker fell and was injured immediately after the ladder he was on collapsed, the direct cause of the accident would be the collapse of the ladder.

***Indirect Causes:*** Indirect causes occur before the direct cause and may produce the direct cause.

*Continuing with the ladder example:*

- The worker may have used a defective ladder.
- The worker may have set the ladder up at an incorrect angle.
- The ladder may not have been secured against movement.
- The worker may have been leaning too far out to one side.

***Root Cause:*** The root cause is what really caused the accident or incident. It is often a defect or deficiency in the safety program which created an unsafe condition or work area.

Had this defect or deficiency not been present, the substandard acts and conditions involved would not have arisen.

Root cause is found by analyzing the evidence collected during the investigation, drawing some conclusions, and pinpointing the real and true cause of the accident - the root cause.

*Continuing with the ladder example*, if the worker was using a defective ladder, it was because:

- No one reported the ladder was defective because there was no program in place for inspecting or reporting defective or damaged ladders.
- The supervisor was completely unaware that the ladder was defective because no one reported it.
- The ladder was not replaced because no one knew it was defective or damaged.
- There were no standards for ladders in the workplace.

- It was the only ladder around, the job had to get done, and the worker knew he had to complete the job, so he used a defective ladder to continue his work.

**Substandard Acts and Conditions**

A substandard act or condition means that a poor work procedure was used. To prevent substandard acts and conditions from occurring, consider the following points:

- Have safe work standards in place and communicate these to the workers.
- Encourage reporting of defective tools, equipment and machinery.
- Provide adequate training to workers to allow them to know which acts or conditions are substandard.
- Be prepared to enforce safe work practices. Do not allow substandard acts to occur or to be practiced.

*Note: The accident/incident investigation should determine what should have happened, based on the required safe work procedure, applicable policies and legislation, and what actually happened (substandard acts and conditions). Usually there will be a "gap" between what should have happened and what actually did happen. The investigation must determine why the gap exists.*

## Investigation Questions

When conducting accident/incident investigations it is important to be skilled at asking questions.

Questions will be directed to the victim(s), witnesses, co-workers and supervisory staff. The intention is to want to learn everything possible about the accident, such as:

---

**Questions about ability and experience:**

— Was the worker capable of doing the job?

— Did the worker clearly know what he was supposed to be doing?

— Who gave the instructions to the accident victim?

— Did the worker have any personal or medical related problems?

— Did the accident victim know what results were expected?

— Was the supervisor experienced in the work being performed?

— Was the worker oriented, trained and experienced to do the job?

— Who did the orientation or training?

— Where was the supervisor and everyone else during the time of the accident?

— When was the last time the worker received refresher training?

### Questions on Tools, Equipment, and Materials

— What equipment and tools were required?
— What equipment and tools were actually used or provided?
— Were there safer substitutes available?
— Was anything defective, contaminated, worn or abused?
— What safety guards and lockout devices were used?
— Were they present and used properly?
— Were the tools and equipment adequate for the job?
— Were the materials safe to work with?
— What precautions should have been taken with the materials used?

### Questions about the Workplace and the Job

— What were the hazards of the job?
— What controls should have been in place?
— What hazard controls were actually in place?
— What training and orientation were required for the job to be performed safely?
— What training and orientation was provided and when?
— What safe work procedure was to be used?
— What work procedure was used?

#### Questions about the Safety Program, Policies and Supervision

— What safety rules and policies were in place?
— Were safety rules and procedures followed?
— What procedures were in place to ensure safe work procedures were used?
— What changes, if any, were introduced before the accident?
— What support and supervision should have been provided?
— Did the supervisor know about, approve, and supervise the work practice used?

#### Questions about the Location

— What impact did the location and environment of the workplace have on the accident?
— Did the location interfere with normal work procedures?
— Did the workers use substandard work procedures because of the location or environment?
— What was different or unusual, if anything, at the time of the accident?
— Was the location suitable for the job?
— What were the weather conditions like at the time?
— What were the physical conditions at the time (lighting; moisture; chemical contaminants; dust; cold/hot; noise; smell; taste)?

| Questions about the Time |
|---|
| — What time did the accident occur? |
| — What time during the shift did the accident occur? |
| — Which shift was on at the time of the accident? |
| — Did the accident occur during a coffee or lunch break? |
| — Did the accident occur shortly after the start of the shift? |
| — Did the accident occur near the end of the shift? |
| — What else happened in the work area at the time of the accident? |
| — If something else did happen, what impact did it have on the accident? |
| — Were any changes introduced before the accident? |

— What happened immediately before the accident?

— What happened during the accident, event by event?

— What happened immediately after the accident?

— What ultimately led to the conditions which caused the accident?

— Why did each event in the accident happen?

*Note: To help determine what caused the accident, put "why" in front of the answers you receive to the questions you have asked up to now. Continue asking "why" until you are satisfied you have found all of the accident's indirect causes. Determine what root cause produced the indirect causes.*

## Conducting an Accident Investigation

To investigate an accident or incident:

- Gather evidence.
- Analyze the evidence.
- Make recommendations.

## Investigation Steps

*1. Take Control of the Situation.*

*2. Evacuate the Injured.*

*3. Secure the Area.*

*Contact Appropriate People* As the investigation is underway, notify the appropriate supervisors, managers, and local occupational health and safety inspectors and government officials. There should be people available at the accident scene to answer questions and respond to the press. At this stage of the investigation, the witnesses to the accident should be gathered and the process of interviews should begin.

Experience suggests that if witnesses talk together before being interviewed, the facts of the accident may become confused and misleading. As a result, the information from the interviews could be less effective.

Once contacted, the accident/incident investigation team should put their investigation procedures into operation:

- Gather the necessary investigation materials and equipment.
- Contact any specialists who should be involved.
- Prepare a tentative action plan.
- Begin the first steps of carrying out the investigation.
- Do not disturb the accident scene

The accident/incident scene area should be reviewed by the investigators. The following activities are recommended:

- Make notes, write descriptions of the scene.
- Take photographs.

- Make sketches, simple line drawings.
- Try to draw a "bird's eye" view of the accident scene and the work area, try to fit everything involved - tools, materials, equipment, conditions.
- Collect evidence specimens.

*Note: Photographs, illustrations, drawings and sketches are useful during the witness interviews, as they serve as powerful reminders.*

## How Should Witnesses Be Interviewed?

### 1. Qualify Each Witness

— Consider the expertise, background and credibility of each witness.
— Consider where the witness was when the accident happened.
— Think about the information each witness provides.

### 2. Interview Witnesses Shortly After the Accident

— If interviews are not done quickly, memories fade and information becomes distorted.
— Interview witnesses, including the victim, separately.
— Conduct "face-to-face" interviews if possible.
— If necessary, conduct more detailed interviews later as evidence becomes available.

### 3. Interview in an Appropriate Place

— The accident/incident site may be suitable.
— The site can help witnesses to remember and describe events.
— Consider that some witnesses may be upset if interviewed at the site.
— May have to provide a non-threatening, neutral, quiet site to conduct the interviews.

### 4. Interview Witnesses Separately

— Attempt to keep witnesses apart during the interviews.
— Interview each witness separately.
— Prevent witnesses from influencing each other's testimony.

### 5. Put Witnesses at Ease

— If the accident/incident was serious, witnesses may be upset.
— Take note of the each person's well being and emotional state and proceed accordingly.
— Use photos and illustrations to prompt the memory.
— Find out how each witness is feeling before beginning the interview.
— Explain that the purpose of the interview and the investigation is for accident prevention, not punishment.
— Be friendly and professional.

### 6. Use Open-ended Questions

— Begin slowly by asking "yes" and "no" questions to break the ice.
— Use open-ended questions to obtain each person's version of the events.
— Consider using a series of structured questions (same questions for all witnesses).
— Avoid using "leading" questions, such as "Didn't you think that _?".
— Use photos and illustrations to prompt the memory

Ask each person to describe what happened:
    — What did you see?
    — What did you hear?
    — What did you think?
    — Where were you at the time?
    — What did you do first, next?
    — What do you think really caused the accident?
    — What could be done to prevent the accident from happening again?

### 7. Use Control Questions

— Do not interrupt the witness, unless he or she gets too far off topic.
— Do not be too quick to judge or make statements which could provoke the witness.
— Do not say any uncalled for things like, "Boy, that sure was a stupid thing to do."

*Tip: To check the reliability of witnesses, consider asking a few questions you already know the answers to. You can also ask the same question in different forms during each interview. Compare the answers for consistency.*

### 8. Expect Conflicts

— It is normal to have conflicting statements from one witness to another.
— People see things differently and remember things differently.
— Each witness likely saw the accident from a slightly different angle.
— Opinions and perceptions will differ.
— Avoid accepting opinions as fact until you have all the evidence.
— Clear up any uncertainties.
— Summarize unclear statements and feed each back to check understanding.
— At the end of each interview, read the witness's statement back.
— When the witness is satisfied that the statement is correct, have them review it again and sign it.
— End each interview on a positive note by thanking each witness.
— Ask a witness to call if they think of anything else later.

*Note: If witnesses are under a great deal of stress, ask each witness to go into a separate room alone and write out their statements. If possible, attempt to interview the witness separately afterwards. Read each person's statement back and clear up uncertainties.*

### Investigation Notes, Sketches, Maps

— Collect notes, sketches and maps immediately.

— Note and map where each piece of evidence taken for study came from .

— Include a description of the conditions surrounding the evidence and the condition of each specimen.

— Don't worry about making drawings to scale.

— Note, measure and map the positions and conditions of:

> Injured workers.
> Tools, equipment, and materials involved.
> Safety devices and personal protective equipment.
> Machinery and equipment controls and operating mechanisms.
> The final position of casualties and debris.

### Investigation Photographs

— Take photographs or video recordings as soon as possible.

— Have witnesses direct photographers, note their comments.

— If still photos are used, use a camera that is either "automatic everything" or a Polaroid.

— For best photo results:

> Take photos from all sides and several angles. Start by photographing the general area, taking each shot from the same distance if possible.

> Then photograph the actual scene itself. Finally, take close-ups and isolation shots. Photograph anything which may be moved or destroyed/disturbed soon.

> Photograph smoke and flames to show fire intensity and characteristics. Photograph position of controls, instruments, gauges and other readings or measurements.

*Note: Create a photo log which includes reference to when and where the shot was taken from and by whom.*

## Collecting Investigation Evidence

| Collecting Investigation Evidence |
| --- |
| — Collect any tools, equipment or material samples which may require closer examination. |
| — Carefully package, wrap and label the samples collected. |
| — Note where each piece of evidence was collected from. |
| — Avoid destroying exhibits until after the examination and investigation is completed. |
| — Check records, such as:<br>    Equipment operator manuals.<br>    Procedure manuals.<br>    Instruction manuals.<br>    Maintenance manuals.<br>    Maintenance log books.<br>    Training manuals.<br>    Training records.<br>    Material Safety Data Sheets (MSDS). |

## Completing the Investigation

As the investigation is nearly over, it should become fairly clear how the accident happened and what the immediate causes were. This information can be used to determine why the accident occurred. If the evidence has been gathered properly, the "who, what, where, when and how's" technique should provide many of the "why's".

**(Who + What + Where + When + How = Why)**

| Completing the Investigation |
| --- |
| — Clear up any uncertainties. |
| — Conduct additional interviews and research if necessary. |
| — Analyze the evidence and reach some conclusions. |
| — Develop controls for all accident causes (direct and indirect). |
| — Look for causes until you run out of answers. |

## List of Accident Investigation Tools and Equipment

The company should have an investigation kit and an approved Accident/Investigation Form to be used by supervisors and members of the investigation team. Illustration #267 shows a typical Accident/Investigation Form.

| Investigation Kit |
|---|
| The kit will contain general investigation tools and equipment, such as: |
| — Flashlight or lantern |
| — Steel tape measure - 100 feet (30 metres) |
| — Scaled ruler |
| — Small mirror for viewing inside machinery or small spaces |
| — Roll of string |
| — Length of nylon rope - 150 feet (50 metres) |
| — Magnetic compass |

— Magnifying glass
— High visibility spray paint
— Heavy-duty duct tape
— Warning signs, tags and labels
— Traffic flares or reflectors
— Traffic cones
— Rolls of highly visible perimeter ribbon
— Highly visible vests or jackets
— Personal protective equipment
— Note paper, graph paper, pens, markers, tape
— Witness statement forms
— Large envelopes, file folders
— Clipboard
— Camera (Automatic or Polaroid)
— Spare film, spare batteries, flash unit and lenses
— Video equipment if desired
— Evidence/sample containers and labels or tags

| | |
|---|---|
| **Accident Report (Example)** | **OSHA/OCHS file number:** _____ |
| **Company:** _____ | **Location of Accident:** _____ Date _____ Time _____ am/pm |
| **Injury** ☐ Yes ☐ No | **Reported     OSHA/OCHS** ☐Yes ☐ No |
| Name of Injured: _____<br>Injury Cause: _____ | Age: _____ Experience: _____    Nature of injury: _____<br>Occupation: _____    Supervisor: _____ |
| Property Damage: _____ | Cost: $_____ |

Summary of the accident:

Describe the direct cause:

Describe the indirect causes:

**Illustration #267A - Accident/Investigation Form**

Describe the root cause:

Immediate corrective action to prevent reoccurrence:
(recommended action plan)

Target date for corrective action:

Long term solutions to correct management system defects:

Target date for completion of long term solutions:

**Illustration #267B - Accident/Investigation Form (continued)**

Sketch of the accident site:

Direction

Person responsible for taking corrective action: _____   Person(s) responsible for following up: _____

Name and position of witnesses interviewed: _____   Date interviewed: _____ By:

Additional comments:

Investigators: _____        Position: _____
              _____                   _____

Date reviewed by occupational health committee: _____
(signatures)
Employer co-chairperson: _____   Worker co-chairperson: _____   Date: _____

**Illustration #267C - Accident/Investigation Form (continued)**